American Georgics

American Georgics

Economy and Environment in Early American Literature

TIMOTHY SWEET

PENN

University of Pennsylvania Press

Philadelphia

Copyright © 2002 by University of Pennsylvania Press
All rights reserved
Printed in the United States of America on acid-free paper

10 9 8 7 6 5 4 3 2 1

Published by
University of Pennsylvania Press
Philadelphia, Pennsylvania 19104-4011

Library of Congress Cataloging-in-Publication Data
Sweet, Timothy, 1960–
American georgics : economy and environment in early American literature /
Timothy Sweet.
p. cm.
Includes bibliographical references (p.) and index.
ISBN 0-8122-3637-8 (acid-free paper)
1. American literature—History and criticism.   2. Environmental literature—History and
criticism.   3. Pastoral literature, American—History and criticism.   4. Didactic
literature, American—History and criticism.   5. Economics and literature—United
States—History.   6. Agriculture in literature.   7. Economics in literature.   8. Nature in
literature.   I. Title.
PS169.E25 S94   2001
810.9'355—dc21

2001037029

To the memory of my grandparents,
Minnesota farmers

Contents

Introduction

"The earth . . . has a certain magnetism in it, by which it attracts the salt, power, or virtue (call it either) which gives it life, and is the logic of all the labor and stir we keep about it, to sustain us."[1] So writes Henry David Thoreau in the "Bean-Field" chapter of *Walden*, quoting the seventeenth-century English agricultural writer John Evelyn. That logic—the magnetism that draws labor from us as we draw sustenance from the earth—is the subject of this book. It is, as Thoreau's experiment at Walden Pond indicated, at once simple and complex, according to one's field of vision.

To make his living, Thoreau labored in his bean field. But he did not eat the beans he grew; rather he exchanged them for rice, corn meal, rye meal, and other commodities. Whether, as he says, he wanted to follow the Pythagorean dietary maxim or whether he thought it "fit that [he] should live on rice, mainly, who loved so well the philosophy of India," in his simple acts of satisfying his ascetic taste he depended on the labor of others (61). The "$8[.]74, all told" that he confesses he ate during one eight-month period came to him already planted, cultivated, harvested, threshed, transported from distant environments, milled, and stored (59). All this labor and more remains largely invisible in *Walden*, reduced to the transactions recorded in Thoreau's ledger sheets. We might not notice its absence at all, but that the very terms of Thoreau's experiment call it forth. Seeing him work his beans—seeing too that he deliberately worked them badly, by his neighbors' standards—we think about the nature of labor.[2] Knowing that he exchanged the beans for the products of others' labor, we come to realize the ways in which acts of production and consumption can connect us to complex and far-reaching social, economic, and environmental networks.

Discerning the traces of these networks in *Walden*, we begin to reflect on the social and economic aspects of our own, often indirect, engagements with the physical environment. Yet because such reflections may seem incompatible with Thoreau's lived experience of self-sufficiency and his apparently pastoral relation to nature, they may trouble us. They had already troubled Thoreau's sometime mentor Ralph Waldo Emerson.

Although Emerson never lamented, as Thoreau did, that "trade curses every thing it handles" (70), he did register an even deeper alienation when he observed, in the conclusion to the "Spirit" chapter of *Nature*: "Yet this may show what discord is between man and nature, for you cannot freely admire a noble landscape, if laborers are digging in the field hard by." [3] For Emerson, such a "discord" exceeds the specificity of local economic arrangements to become a general indictment of humankind's relation to nature.

Let us consider a resolution of the Emersonian discord that depends not on excluding the laborers from the landscape, but rather on understanding how and why they are integral to it. A suggestive direction has recently been proposed, for example, by Brian Donahue. In *Reclaiming the Commons*, Donahue locates the cause of our environmental crisis in the fact that our economy does not have a sound ecological basis, and argues that environmental protection "will follow from a society that has at last worked out a healthy relation with its everyday landscape, with its productive forests and farmlands." [4] If we would save the environment for future generations, we must begin not with the part of it that is defined by its separation from us, the wilderness, but rather with that part in which we are already necessarily engaged, whether we realize it or not, as members of the human community.

In the chapters that follow, I trace the early history of such engagements in North America as they are registered in a particular mode of environmental writing, which I am provisionally calling the American georgic. Writings in this mode take as their primary topic the work of defining the basic terms of the human community's relationship to the natural environment. Since this problem, to the extent that it has been taken up in American literary studies, has generally been thought to lay within the domain of the *pastoral* tradition—and since georgic has been theoretically bound up with pastoral in a mutually defining relationship—I will begin by making some distinctions, if only to bring an enriched sense of georgic into pastoral broadly construed. [5]

The first of these distinctions goes back to a difference in environmental orientation already evident in the works of Virgil. Where in the *Eclogues* Virgil understands the natural world primarily as a site of leisure, in the *Georgics* he understands it primarily as a site of labor. Distinguishing the two modes, Renato Poggioli observes that in pastoral the individual is "the opposite of *homo oeconomicus* on both ethical and practical grounds." [6] While this distinction has become blurred since Virgil's time, I will suggest that it is worth reanimating. I will note here at the outset, however, that I am less attached to the particular term *georgic* than to the set of concerns I am using the term to indicate.

Such a distinction is implicit in Leo Marx's foundational study of the

American pastoral tradition. Marx identifies a "pastoral design" in texts that set up an ideal, rural landscape and then introduce a counterforce of some kind, a threat of "an alien world encroaching from without."[7] "Complex" as opposed to "sentimental" pastoral introduces this counterforce in such a way as to prohibit any simple affirmation of the rural scene (25). The key question of affirmation indicates that for Marx, two constitutive features of pastoral are the act of perceiving nature and the emotional response perception triggers. Marx's focus on attitude allows him, for example, to characterize Thomas Jefferson as a pastoralist rather than an agrarian: the "mythopoeic" power of the pastoral ideal compels Jefferson to ground his ideas of virtue in a particular configuration of landscape even as he "admits that an agricultural economy may be economically disadvantageous" for America (126, 127). Even in this difficult test case then, Marx retains the classical pastoral's sense that the individual subject is the opposite of *homo oeconomicus*. Indeed, Marx argues that where the counterforce to classical pastoral was history in general, the predominant counterforce to American pastoral has been history in the specific form of economics, figured in images of technological innovation.[8]

Paul Alpers's recent work *What Is Pastoral?* is less concerned with a structure of external threat than with internal qualities, shifting the focus from the perception of landscape to the conditions of human action. Alpers defines the mode in terms of its "representative anecdote": pastoral is a story of "herdsmen [or their equivalents in a given historical moment] and their lives, rather than landscape or idealized nature." The herdsman is a representative person, "figuring every or any man's strength relative to the world."[9] Even though Alpers is not much interested in American writers (he discusses only Sarah Orne Jewett, Robert Frost, and Wallace Stevens) and is committed to formal rather than historical analysis, nevertheless his emphasis on the contents of rural lives, as they reveal a realist sense of human qualities, provides an important guidepost.

Lawrence Buell's summative definition addresses both Marx's concern with perceptual attitude and Alpers's interest in the qualities of human lives. For Buell, "pastoral" refers "broadly to all literature that celebrates an ethos of rurality or nature or wilderness over against an ethos of metropolitanism. This domain includes . . . all degrees of rustication, temporary or longer term, from the greening of cities through metropolitan park projects to models of agrarianism and wilderness homesteading."[10] The inclusiveness of Buell's definition, which, he recognizes, blurs the distinction between pastoral and georgic, raises at least two important issues (439). One is the theoretical question of locating human agency with respect to the several domains of the rural, wilderness, or nature in general. Another is the historical question of identifying various ethoi specific to these domains, which are not coextensive and have each been sites of significant debates.

Taking up the first of these questions, we can observe the production of pastoral sites by means of human agency. Some of this production has been conceptual—as for example the development of the logic of possessive individualism as traced by Myra Jehlen, in which an "American" (that is to say, an Emersonian) self transcends its own mortal limits by taking imaginative possession of an infinite world.[11] Yet the most important aspects of this production have been material, even in cases where we are apparently facing pure nature. For example, we might consider the fact that the raw wilderness that Europeans *thought* they saw in their first New World encounters had already been actively shaped by Native Americans.[12] Or, to take a more contemporary example, we might consider the ways in which efforts at wilderness preservation and restoration today are, in themselves, practices that produce the material reality of "wilderness" for us; we might think, that is, about the labor and consumption involved in creating, maintaining, and experiencing a space nominally defined by the absence of labor and consumption.[13] In this sense, even wilderness is part of the Heideggerian category of the standing-reserve, nature as answerable to human need (the need here being the feeling of escape from economy). In the case of more quotidian natural spaces such as farms, woods, parks, and so on, the role of human labor is more clearly evident, but even here we sometimes forget about it, unless the laborers themselves are present to remind us as they did Emerson.

The complicated questions of human agency and social relations recall Raymond Williams's critique of pastoral as a form of false consciousness. Williams finds the pastoral design to proceed from an ideological division of leisure from labor: in pastoral, nature as an object of beauty or site of bounty is screened off from the human activities of creating and maintaining that beauty or producing that bounty. He develops this assessment of pastoral through an implicit appeal to its classical differentiation from georgic. Thus the modern georgic, as in the works of agriculturalist and social critic William Cobbett, for example, suggests for Williams the possibilities of a progressive ideology. Yet even here there are complications, particularly in two of georgic's key terms, *cultivation* and *improvement*. As Cobbett's observations are taken up by novelists such as Jane Austen or George Eliot, they are subjected to the screening process of pastoral: "The working improvement, which is not seen at all, is the means to [the] social improvement" desired by the novelists' characters.[14] Williams's critique of pastoral, then, stresses the importance of contextual analysis. Buell also stresses contextual analysis as he argues (against Williams) that pastoral topoi such as the "'retreat' to nature" are ideologically indeterminate of themselves but can, "depending on context," be "counterinstitutional" or "institutionally sponsored" (49, 50).

The question of ideological valence returns us to the second of the issues raised by Buell's definition, the specificity of the ethoi of "rurality or nature or wilderness" celebrated by pastoral. Attending to the function of human agency in its engagements with nature and to the historical variability of the ethoi according to which such engagements are assessed complicates any modal definition of pastoral, making provisional room for georgic, as I am using the term here, as a useful category. Georgic, in this sense, treats those aspects of pastoral, broadly construed, that concern not the retreat to nature or the separation of the country from the city, but our cultural engagement with the whole environment. As Buell argues, "the promise of pastoral aesthetics as a stimulus to ecocentrism can fulfill itself completely only when pastoral aesthetics overcomes its instinctive reluctance to face head-on the practical obstacles to the green utopia it seeks to realize. Only then can it mature as social critique" (307). Recovering the georgic tradition of environmental writing can help guide this maturation process. For example, this tradition bridges the gap between what Donald Worster has identified as the two major schools of environmental thought, the *arcadian* and *imperial* stances toward nature. According to Worster, proponents of the former stance, such as Gilbert White and Thoreau, advocate the "peaceful coexistence" of human beings with other organisms, while proponents of the latter, such as Francis Bacon or Linnaeus, advocate humankind's "dominion over nature."[15] In the classical distinction I have reprised here, it may seem that on Worster's terms, georgic would line up with the "imperial" stance. Yet I will argue that any such conceptual alignment breaks down when we think about the category of labor, for here "peaceful coexistence" cannot mean mere passivity. As even the arcadian Thoreau recognized, we must labor to produce our lives. We can do so in a variety of ways, and this is what the American georgic attempts to work out. And more than this: at its most sophisticated, the georgic addresses the fundamental questions underlying Worster's dichotomy: what is the relationship between humankind and the rest of nature? What ought it be?

There are, to return to Alpers, many anecdotes, more or less representative under different circumstances. There are many stories of American nature, proceeding from different assumptions about the environment and peoples' place in it. Tracing one kind of story in particular, this study assumes that a full understanding of the struggle to define the basic terms of the human relationship to the natural environment must include an understanding of the transformations of that environment which are necessary to produce human life and culture. From Sir Thomas More's account of Utopian colonization practices, through George Perkins Marsh's warning about the long-term effects of deforestation, to the current paradigm of steady-state or sustainable economics, this understanding has always been directed toward the future, and thus at least implicitly toward questions of environmental capacities and limits.

Although the term *agrarian* might suggest itself as encapsulating the social, political, and economic analysis of environmental engagement that I am advocating here, I would like to reserve the term *georgic* in light of agrarianism's identification with a specific ideology or program, for I am concerned precisely with debates over ideologies and programs. Of course agrarianism has featured prominently in these debates. In his now classic study of the topic, Henry Nash Smith took a mimetic approach to rural literature, arguing that prior to Hamlin Garland, American writers, overly committed to genteel romance or adventure story, could not find a literary form adequate to represent the agrarian ideal.[16] This ideal—a cultural symbology of a classless, democratic, fee-simple empire of yeomen farmers—Smith assumed (despite his critique of Frederick Jackson Turner) was embodied in the actual experience of the agricultural West. Earlier writers, however, had significantly different conceptions of the public good than did those later nineteenth-century agrarians. Moreover (to anticipate Chapters 5 and 6 of the present book) as something like Smith's conception of the agrarian ideal began to emerge in the late eighteenth century, it was fraught with conflict over the organization and disposition of rural labor. This conflict may, in fact, partly account for the failure of literary form that Smith traces prior to the inception of rural realism.

I do not claim to offer a comprehensive history of the American georgic's ideological contestations here, but only to visit several important moments and texts, tracing some significant lines in the development of American environmental consciousness. I begin by identifying the origin of the mode in the sixteenth-century English recognition of a general, systemic relationship between the human economy and the natural environment, a recognition that was significantly catalyzed by the European discovery of America. As William Spengemann demonstrates, this discovery required Europe not only to recognize the existence of something new in the world, but beyond that "to reconceive the fundamental idea of the world itself—its geographical form and symbolic meaning, and the role of human activity in the determination of these things."[17] For early promotional writers such as the elder and younger Richard Hakluyts, this reconceptualization meant theorizing economics anew in relation to environmental capacities. These writers began to define the English nation as an economy and to understand that nation-economy as a system. They argued that the well-being of the realm depended on opening this system to New World environments and, in some respects, closing it off from other Old World economic systems. Speculating on expansion, boundaries, and limits, they transformed the existing economic vocabulary of "commodity," "waste," and "vent" in relation to this newly recognized environmental context. Such considerations invite us to read early promotional literature's generic focus on the relation between economy and environment in terms of the recent interdisciplinary insights of sustainable economic theory.

Although, as I observe in the conclusion to Chapter 1, the trajectories of modern economic and environmental thought began to diverge soon after the sixteenth-century promoters' initial theoretical insights, fully to reconverge again only recently, these strands remained interwoven in the American georgic tradition. This tradition from its inception, following the promotional texts of the Hakluyts and their cohort, had the same ultimate goal as that of modern sustainable economics: to articulate a relationship between economy and environment that would foster the public good. Different contexts shaped different determinations of the public good, while local concerns sometimes submerged aspects of the systems-theory perspective articulated by the first promoters. Chapter 2 begins by observing that where the Hakluyts had divided the Old from New Worlds and had identified them respectively as the conceptual loci of economy and environment, with colonial trading posts as boundaries or *vents* mediating between the two, the first generation of Virginia colonists found that this theoretical division could not correspond neatly with any *spatial* division, even if the vast ocean separating America from England encouraged such a conceptualization. To colonize in search of new input and output capacities was to bring the English economy to America and thus to translate all concerns about capacities and boundaries to that ground. Thus the *True Declaration of the Estate of the Colonie in Virginia* (1610), for example, conceptualized the mediation between the two realms as on-site exchange and identified the medium of exchange as labor. In his *Generall Historie* (1624), John Smith accepted this position but gave a more considered discussion of how labor ought to be ordered, based on a more thorough environmental observation. Despite his current status in the literary canon as an originary spokesman for the American virtue of free enterprise, Smith was acutely aware of the difficulties of proper management posed by an emergent capitalist system, in which "the desire of present gaine (in many) is so violent, and the endevors of many undertakers so negligent, every one so regarding their private gaine, that it is hard to effect any publike good."[18] Some of his specific suggestions, such as the implementation of governmental price supports for grain crops, seem intriguingly modern. In general, Smith attempted to balance the concerns of centralized economic-environmental management and the individual production of wealth—a balance that we have not yet managed to strike.

Like the first-generation Virginians, first-generation New England colonists recognized that America could no longer be thought of in terms of the Hakluyts' imagination of the colonization project, as a mere boundary and transfer point between economy and environment. Rather, they understood colonial New England itself as an economic system requiring environmental inputs and producing of itself certain excesses. Chapter 3 considers Edward Johnson's and William Bradford's evaluations of land use in terms of the public good as representing, respectively, optimistic and pessimistic attitudes toward economic growth. The views of both, however, proceeded from the nostalgia at the heart of Puritan religious primitivism, a nostalgia that radiated outward to economic and environmental concerns. Johnson, unable fully to align the social and religious consequences of the Bay colony's rapid economic development with the primitivist ideals of Puritanism, finally advanced a millennialist historiography. Bradford, more fully able to recognize the conflict, drew up short of any such eschatological theorizing. Yet any resolution to the contradiction that troubled both of their histories—the conflict between the ideals (both still current today) of social cohesion and unlimited free-market growth through ever increasing engagement with environmental capacities—remained inconceivable within historical time and space.

A different sort of nostalgia inflects Robert Beverley's *History and Present State of Virginia*. Chapter 4 argues that Beverley, more willing than the Puritans to entertain the possibilities of a material environment's embodying a Golden Age, elaborated John Smith's critique of Virginia's tobacco monoculture, based on a comparison of economic-environmental relations before and after colonization. Beverley registered contemporary economic dissatisfactions by mapping a Native American culture's apparently harmonious relation to the environment, which had been disrupted by colonization, onto Golden Age mythography. Rather than mourning the loss of paradise, however, he turned to the classical georgic's calculus of compensation, according to which improvement could stand in for such loss. Virginia, he found, offered a double prospect for improvement: the environment would benefit familiar English cultivars, while cultivation would develop native species to yield useful products. Two factors, however, vitiated against any such program for improvement. The tobacco economy was structurally predisposed against diversification. Moreover, that economy, despite (or because of) its stagnation in the latter part of the seventeenth century, had enabled the consolidation of the gentry class, the primary audience for Beverley's program. This class was in the process of developing a pastoral orientation to the environment, traces of which begin to emerge in Beverley's text.

Although the pastoral moments in the *History* generally bear a georgic inflection that criticizes pastoral's lack of economic consciousness, the colonists' increasing dependence on unfree labor cut against any radical potential of Beverley's program for environmental-economic transformation.

Chapter 5 goes on to examine the ways in which the assessment of economic-environmental engagement that had preoccupied American georgic writers in various local contexts through the seventeenth and early eighteenth centuries coalesced in a discourse of national scope. America thought of itself as a nation of farmers. Yet even bracketing the question of slavery, Americans did not agree about the nature of agriculture itself. Farming was not a single, uniform activity, but rather included diverse and conflicting practices, complicated in both class structure and environmental orientation. Contemporary recognition of these complications led to an assessment of the merits of two general methods, characterized respectively by seminomadic or "backwoods," subsistence-oriented practices or by sedentary, intensive, market-oriented practices. Participants in this assessment included Hector St. John de Crèvecoeur, Thomas Jefferson, and Benjamin Rush, as well as authors of various agricultural treatises. To address conflicts over farming practices in the late eighteenth and early nineteenth centuries, the literature of agricultural improvement developed a discourse of rural virtue that linked economic-environmental intensification to national stability. This discourse excluded the "backwoods" voice, partly through the fact of its dissemination in print culture, to which those practitioners of nonintensive agriculture had little access. Although it was satirized by Charles Brockden Brown, it set the terms on which future debates over resource use would be conducted.

Chapter 6 examines one of the most volatile of these debates in the antebellum era, over the economic-environmental activity of America's indigenous peoples. In the dominant white American assessment, Native Americans were, on the one hand, characterized as savages whose land was not cultivated, not "improved," and thus could not ground American political virtue. On the other hand, the virtue of the rural was extended to them in arguments that they ought to be removed westward, where they and the land could simultaneously be cultivated. One indigenous nation, however, coopted the terms of the discourse of rural virtue to argue against removal from their homeland. Drawing on georgic topoi familiar to whites, but which had roots in their own agricultural tradition as well, Cherokees such as Elias Boudinot and David Brown developed a counternarrative of "improvement," recontextualizing and reorienting the georgic's concerns so as to critique both the white image of Indian "savagism" and the idealization of the rural, middle landscape as white property. The Cherokees invoked the radical potential of the American georgic, demonstrating that it was possible to develop an agrarian economy and sustain sociopolitical cohesion by defining their resource base as a national, rather than a set of individual possessions. Although it succeeded aesthetically, the Cherokee georgic failed politically. Its aesthetic success may even have been politically counterproductive, as white Georgians eyed greedily the beautiful, fertile agricultural environment that the Cherokees showed they had made. The struggle over rights to Cherokee lands thus clarified the American georgic mode's primary theoretical project and revealed its political limitations within the antebellum context.

While the Cherokees were arguing that their mode of economic engagement with the environment was good and just, even according to the dominant white terms of valuation, James Fenimore Cooper projected through the figure of the Indian a desire to escape from economy altogether. In *The Pioneers,* Cooper set before his American readership an environmental debate which both pitted wilderness values against settler culture and analyzed the complexities of economic-environmental engagement within the terms of that culture. The concluding chapter of this study follows that debate from Cooper to the later writings of Thoreau and George Perkins Marsh. Although Cooper could not resolve the larger conflict he posited between economy and its other, the wilderness, his study of the social ecology of the Templeton settlement stressed the importance of environmental knowledge. In this way, his local investigation anticipated Marsh's global investigations. Refusing the illusory escape from economy held out by Cooper, Marsh posited that labor is the one universal constant in humankind's engagement with the environment. Like the Hakluyts almost three centuries before, he promoted a systemic perspective, analyzing the economy's dependence on the environment and the environment's limits on carrying capacities. Beyond this, he recognized that the history of the georgic raised a closely related philosophical question, "whether man is of nature or above her."[19] In asking this question, Marsh made explicit the georgic tradition's conceptual separation of humankind from the rest of nature, clarifying the tradition's assumptions of moral obligation to both the environment itself and the future of humankind—the largest sense of the public good. Marsh's moral discourse thus confronted head-on the problem that all georgic writers up to this time had considered and that the Cherokee case had laid bare: the question of agency. Cooper had raised this issue only to let it drop. The Cherokees, whose political structure suggested the possibilities of national rather than individual agency, had been disempowered. Thoreau addressed the question locally in his late work on forest succession, which he recognized held significant implications for land management, as well as nationally in his remarks on wilderness preservation. In Marsh's analysis, it took on a global scope.

Marsh urged us to become "co-worker[s] with nature," to direct our economic engagements in accordance with natural processes (35). Yet the agency by which this cooperative georgic would be directed remained unsettled. Although Marsh held out modest hopes for government regulation, his fundamental assumptions regarding the capitalist structure of property relations led him to count primarily on the enlightened self-interest of individual landowners. The discourse of moral obligation that Marsh directed toward these landowners was not, however, necessarily coextensive in practice with their perception of self-interest. Thus the question of agency—of who would manage, and by means of what structures—remained open. It remains open today.

I began by distinguishing between georgic and pastoral based on their modal orientation to the world: labor versus leisure. Today, most Americans' experience of nature (if we think of having such experience at all) is pastoral rather than georgic. Yet if we do not participate in an explicitly georgic mode of life, we can at least use the insights of georgic literature to recognize the social and economic realities of our own, too often indirect environmental engagements. The georgic's reminders of the nature of these engagements can help reorient our understanding of the American literary tradition and, I hope, our place in the world.

Chapter 1

Economy and Environment in Sixteenth-Century Promotional Literature

We owe the first recorded moment of ecological insight in British North America to Stephen Parmenius, intended chronicler of Sir Humphrey Gilbert's ill-fated second voyage of 1583.[1] Gilbert, hoping to establish a colony in what is now New England, stopped off for provisions at St. John's harbor, Newfoundland, where an international fishing fleet had made its base. According to the terms of his patent, Gilbert took possession of the territory on which the fishermen had established drying stations and let these lands back to them as his tenants. Anxious to search for ores and other resources that could support a colony, Gilbert and company found it difficult to get inland. Parmenius reported, in a letter to the younger Richard Hakluyt, that the thick pine forest, clogged with trees "fallen by reason of their age, doth so hynder the sighte of the Lande, and stoppe the way of those that seeke to travell, that they can goe no whither."[2] To gain an unobstructed view and entry into the interior, Parmenius urged Gilbert to burn the woods near shore, but Gilbert refused, "for feare of great inconvenience that might thereof insue: for it was reported and confirmed by verie credible persons, that when the like happened by chance in another Port, the fish never came to the place about it, for the space of 7. whole yeere after, by reason of the waters made bytter by the turpentyne, and rosen of the trees, which ranne into the ryvers upon the fyring of them."[3] We can infer that it was not pine sap but soil erosion from the burned-off shore that polluted the estuary for seven years, until new growth stabilized the banks.[4] Gilbert and his crew, however, interpret this "verie credible" story of environmental interaction in a different way, seeing therein a relationship among the commodities of the New World. They imagine so much sap being released in a fire that it cannot burn off but instead renders enormous amounts of "turpentyne" and "rosen."[5] The superfluity of these commodities courses down the banks, turning the water "bytter" and obstructing the harvest of another commodity, fish.

Reading Parmenius's letter from Newfoundland, we imagine what

Gilbert imagined—a narrative of environmental change—but we understand its causal mechanism differently. This difference alerts us to Gilbert's interest in the economic dimension of environmental representation. Economy enters Gilbert's environmental understanding under the category of "commodity," which to him means both a specific good or resource and, more generally, due measure, fitness, or convenience. As the younger Hakluyt would argue in the "Discourse of Western Planting" (1584), the "manifolde comodyties that are like to growe to this Realme of Englande by the Westerne discoveries lately attempted" included economic recovery, full employment, trade with indigenous Americans, discovery of a northwest passage, geopolitical advantage relative to Spain and other European nations, the extension of Christendom, the glory of the Crown, and so on, as well as the particular natural resources that might be found there (O, 2:211). Promising new possibilities for commodity in the most general sense, then, the American environment invited the English to develop a new mode of political economy, one that theorized economics in terms of environmental capacity in a way that the then dominant mode, agrarianism, had not yet done.

Early promotional literature's fundamental linkage of economics and environment invites us to read the genre in terms of steady-state or sustainable economic theory.[6] Sustainable economics works in systemic terms, describing the economy as an open subsystem of the ecosystem: the economy "tak[es] in useful (low-entropy) raw material and energy" from the natural environment while "giving back waste (high-entropy) material and energy" for the natural environment to absorb and, to some extent, "reconstitute . . . into reusable raw materials."[7] Sixteenth-century promoters anticipated such concerns about inputs, outputs, and boundaries. Participating in the consolidation of economics as a distinct field during the latter part of the sixteenth century, the promoters began to define the English nation as an economy and to understand that nation-economy as a system.[8] In tracts promoting colonization, they argued that the well-being of the realm depended on opening this system to New World environments and, in certain respects, closing it off from other Old World economic systems.[9] Speculating on the expansion, boundaries, and limits of the economy, they redefined existing economic terms such as "commodity," "waste," and "vent" in relation to the capacities of this newly discovered environmental context. With respect to input, one of the primary concerns of sustainable economics, the early promoters argued that more resources—more oil, more timber, more wine and gold, and so on—had to be brought into the English economy, but now from New World environments rather than Old World trading partners. As for output, the early promoters were not in a position to theorize the accumulation of antiproductive waste, since early modern technologies did not stress the environment's absorptive capacity in the way that today's technologies do.[10] Even so, in both seeing the New World as an outlet for one kind of "waste," people, and speculating on the transformation of waste into productive resources, they pointed toward sustainable economics' understanding of output in relation to environmental absorption and transformation.

Where subsequent economic thought would separate the domain of economy from that of the environment in order to enable the analysis of economies as closed systems (as I will indicate in the conclusion to this chapter), early promotional texts theorize a systemic relationship between the two domains. Seen in this light, these texts compel the attention of anyone interested in ecocritical and environmental issues, even though they are not what we would call "green" texts.[11] They are not "ecocentric."[12] Nor are they antigrowth; on the contrary, in a proto-Lockean recognition that wealth derives from the human transformation of the environment, the sixteenth-century promoters articulated the paradigm of growth that has since become naturalized in political and economic discourse.[13] However, they did not promote economic growth as an end in itself, but always directed growth toward a larger social end, a public good such as relieving poverty, providing full employment, or maintaining sociopolitical stability. Since sustainable economics is primarily interested in determining the environmental limits on growth in a way that will promote the public good, it provides a useful apparatus for understanding the colonial promoters' own theorization of growth and Americans' subsequent economic engagements with the environment.

The early promoters describe the late sixteenth-century English economy as entropic, requiring new capacities for input and output. Sustainable economics defines potential inputs and outputs as ultimately finite, arguing that the economy cannot continue to grow indefinitely without detrimental results for the public good, but "may continue to develop qualitatively" without growing; defining the nature of this "qualitative" development poses the one of the discipline's central problematics.[14] Thus while one critique of reading these early texts in relation to sustainable economics is obvious—for it is not clear whether the promoters recognized absolute environmental limits as such—this point should not dissuade us from thinking through their originating insight. This insight, which became invisible to subsequent economists until sustainable economics brought it into view again, was to theorize the link between economic development and environmental capacities and to assess that link in terms of the public good.

Colonization Theory

England's first theoretical text on colonization, Sir Thomas More's *Utopia* (1516), found its inspiration in the Columbian discovery and located its idealized political economy in the New World but showed little interest in the material specificity of New World environments. In one respect anticipating the arguments of Thomas Jefferson and Frederick Jackson Turner, More developed a theory of the frontier as safety valve, describing colonization as the best solution to overpopulation and thus a means by which an ideal society could be maintained. When the population of More's Utopia exceeds a fixed quota, citizens colonize the "nexte lande where the inhabitauntes haue muche *waste and vnoccupied grounde.*"[15] The Utopian economic base, which resembles that of agrarian England in important respects, is replicated on this "waste" land. Such a view of colonization established an assumption that would become crucial in legitimating the appropriation of indigenous Americans' land: it is assumed the natives have not cultivated the land; they can either join with the Utopians, who will make the land abundantly productive, or they can resist colonization, in which case they are driven off by war. The Utopians consider it just to wage war to bring "voyde and vacaunt" land into cultivation, for "bye the lawe of nature" such land ought to "nowryshe" and "relieue" human life rather than being allowed to remain "to no good nor profitable vse" (*U*, 67). While it would be some time before the English prosecuted such a war of conquest in America, More's passage on colonization registers the important characterization of New World land as waste, even though inhabited, which was taken up by the late sixteenth-century promoters.

More's Utopians do not colonize to gain commodities for import or trade, since the realm produces abundant quantities of all goods which are free for the taking in the marketplaces. Nevertheless, complications introduced by their import of iron, gold, and silver suggest a conflict between two ideologies of national wealth in sixteenth-century England, the dominant agrarianism and emergent mercantilism.[16] Like the natives in More's source text, Vespucci's account of the New World, the Utopians are supposed to regard gold and silver as valueless within their own society.[17] They use these metals to fashion chamber pots and chains for slaves, storing them in these forms in case they should need them to pay tribute to avoid a war. Yet the paradox involved in their "ritual debasement" of these metals suggests, as numerous commentators have pointed out, the repression of a desire for their evidently innate value.[18] Thus while More advances the Utopian theory of colonization in the name of agrarianism—here an ideology of pure use value in which iron is valuable but gold and silver are not—the Utopians' import of precious metals hints, if only by way of prohibition, at an ideology in which trade is the primary source of wealth. Even on the surface, however, it is clear that they need to import gold and silver in order to conduct their foreign policy. These metals in fact acquire value in protecting the Utopians' national sovereignty, thus enabling them to maintain the stability of their agrarian political economy. Importing the iron necessary for agriculture and manufacturing seems less politically charged, but in one respect it is even more revealing; it indicates that their agrarian economy is fundamentally dependent on trade, though the Utopians do not fully realize this dependence.[19]

To pursue the analogues in contemporary England: colonization practice embodied agrarian theory during most of the sixteenth century in the effort to colonize Ireland, which the English represented as a waste region inhabited by an uncivilized people.[20] At the same time, mercantilism was beginning to describe the English economy's dependence on trade, but had not yet theorized colonialism as a means of securing new sources of inputs. The most important sixteenth-century mercantilist text, *A Discourse of the Commonweal* (written 1549, revised c. 1576, published 1581), identified a negative balance of trade in England. Yet even in the face of evidence that Spanish gold from the New World was a significant cause of the problem, this treatise proposed purely domestic means to correct the imbalance, "first, by staying of wares wrought beyond the sea which might be wrought within us from coming to be sold; secondly, by staying of our woolens, tins, and fells, and other commodities from passing over unwrought," and finally by instilling good order among the laboring classes.[21] Some commodities must always be imported, "since men will needs have silks, wine, and spice," but if England's manufactures were sufficiently developed, the overall balance of trade with other Old World nations would promote economic recovery.[22]

Input: "Commodity"

Beginning in the late 1570s, the elder and younger Hakluyts and their cohort grafted this emergent mercantilist ideology onto the existing agrarian theory of colonization in order to articulate, in the new literary genre of the promotional tract, a new practice that would redress the balance of trade and related problems. These writers shared a particular economic narrative regarding New World environments. England, they argued, was suffering from the decline of its textile industry. More raw wool and less finished cloth was being exported to uncertain and diminishing markets, while imports of other goods had remained steady or increased. Moreover, in the absence of disease and war, the population was increasing. The result was widespread unemployment and unrest, and the general impoverishment of the realm. Colonization would provide a solution to all of these interlinked problems: America's indigenous population could be induced to trade for finished cloth and/or a large enough colony of English settlers would provide such a New World market. In return for cloth, the New World promised to supply all the commodities that England was currently importing or hoping to import from their enemies or doubtful friends (Spain, Portugal, France, the Levant, Russia, etc.) and at cheaper rates. Some of the poor could be transported to the colonies, where they would find employment in commodity production, while those who remained in England would find employment in both a revitalized wool trade and new industries based on adding value to import commodities from New World environments.

The promoters' first and most obvious step was to identify specific new sources of input. Thus the memorandum that the elder Richard Hakluyt prepared in 1578 for Sir Humphrey Gilbert's first voyage advises prospective colonists to "discover al the naturall commodities" of the country and then proceeds to discuss means of production (*O*, 1:118). If, for example, "the soyle and clymate bee such as may yeelde you the Grape as good as that" in Portugal, Spain, or the Canaries, "then there resteth but a woorkeman to put in execution to make wines, and to dresse Resigns of the sunne" (*O*, 1:118).

Unlike More's Utopians, the Hakluyts and their cohort see colonizable environments as both empty and full. The Utopians replicated their agrarian political economy by colonizing the "waste," "voyde and vacaunt" land held by less civilized peoples. The promoters similarly propose colonizing what they called the "waste Contries" of the New World, but they emphasize not the vacancy but the fullness of these new environments (*O*, 2:319). They regard the indigenous inhabitants less as people to be conquered than as prospective trading partners. They value the physical environment for what it produces naturally as well as for what it could be made to produce. Following classical climatology, the promoters assume that latitude predicts weather and other environmental factors (*climata* being the classical geographic term for latitudinal bands of the globe), so that Old World environments could simply be mapped laterally onto New.[23] Surveying extant reports on climate in his compendious "Discourse of Western Planting," the younger Hakluyt argues "that this westerne voyadge will yelde unto us all the commodities of Europe, Affrica and Asia, as farr as we were wonte to travell" in previous trading (*O*, 2:222). He begins at 30 degrees, Florida, and continues systematically north to 63 degrees, Newfoundland, more or less correlating commodities to climate according to Old World patterns. The early promoters were also interested in what was unique to the New World, but they did not anticipate all subsequent developments. Hakluyt does describe sassafras at length, for example, but he does not yet mention tobacco, which would soon become far more important. "As for Tabacco," Captain John Smith would later recall, "wee never then dreamt of it."[24]

Many of the desired commodities were derived from Mediterranean cultivars. Emphasizing this category in the summary of his climatic survey, Hakluyt asserts that the North American soil in general is "apte to beare olyves for oile, all kindes of frutes as oranges, almondes, filberdes, figges, plomes, mulberies, raspis, pomi appij, melons, all kindes of odoriferous trees and date trees, Cipresses, Cedars, bayes" (*O*, 2:232–33). If the first item on Hakluyt's list strikes us as curious, in his time it was especially significant, serving as a synecdoche for the replacement of trade for Mediterranean commodities in general and reaching to the heart of England's most important industry, wool fabrication. The wool had to be cleaned with large quantities of soap made from sweet oil; soap made from animal products gave the finished cloth an unpleasant odor.[25] Domestic experimentation with vegetable oils, for example rapeseed, had not been successful; thus the elder Hakluyt noted in 1582 that oil was still the one thing that England could not supply to its own wool industry (*O*, 1:189–90). The Mediterranean was of course the greatest source of olive oil, but to trade with "Barbarye, Spayne, Portugale, [or] Italy" was, as Hakluyt remarked, to "inrytche our doubtfull frendes and infydelles as nowe by our ordynary trade we doe" (*O*, 2:341).

Promoters were reluctant to give up their goal of replicating Old World commodity environments, even as they gained more experience of America. Thomas Hariot's *Briefe and True Report of the New Found Land of Virginia* (1588) is a case in point. Having spent some time in Virginia, Hariot could attend more closely than the Hakluyts to the specificity of the environment. For example, he seems quite interested in tobacco, a plant indigenous to America. However, he does not treat tobacco in the section on "Merchantable commodities"; instead, he describes it in the section on "victuall and sustenance of mans life, usually fed upon by the naturall inhabitants; as also by us, during the time of our abode," along with beans, corn, pumpkins, and the like.[26] On the lookout for familiar commodities, Hariot begins his account with "Silke of grasse, or Grasse silke. There is a kind of grasse in the country, upon the blades whereof there groweth very good silke in forme of a thin glittering skin to be stript off." This promise is confirmed by the fact that "the like groweth in Persia, which is in the selfe same climate as Virginia, of which very many of the Silke works that come from thence into Europe are made." He describes the environmental transformation necessary to fulfill this promise: although "there is great store thereof in many places of the countrey growing naturally and wild," yet "if it be planted and ordered as in Persia, it cannot in reason be otherwise, but that there will rise in short time great profit to the dealers therein. . . . And by the meanes of sowing and planting it in good ground, it will be farre greater, better, and more plentifull then it is" (68). Hariot's desire for Old World commodities leads to some mistakes; what he took for silk grass may have been yucca.[27] Even so, his experience of Virginia and his skill as a naturalist temper his projections to some extent, uniquely among the early promoters. While he knows that a source of oils for various uses is especially important, he does not propose growing olives as other promoters do. Instead, he goes to great lengths to identify local substitutes, arguing that "a commodity . . . may be raised" of "Oke-akornes" or "two sorts of Walnuts, both holding oile," and reclassifying the "fatnesse" of bears, which "because it is so liquid, may well be termed oile, and hath many speciall uses" (70). The most environmentally sensitive of all early promoters of American colonization, Hariot nevertheless maintains their Old World frame of reference while enlarging their fundamentally economic characterization of New World environments.[28]

Output: "Waste"

While the hope of replacing Old World commodity sources defined the relationship between economy and environment in terms of input, the question of output was more complex. This complexity is evident in the elder Hakluyt's innovative use of the term "waste." In his "Inducements to the Liking of the Voyage intended towards Virginia," written for Sir Walter Ralegh in 1584, Hakluyt advises that "since great *waste* Woods be there, of Oake, Cedar, Pine, Wall-nuts, and sundry other sorts, many of our *waste* people may be imployed in making of Ships, Hoies, Busses and Boats; and in making of Rozen, Pitch and Tarre, the trees naturall for the same, being certeinly knowen to be neere Cape Briton and the Bay of Menan, and in many other places there about" (*O*, 2:331, emphases added). This passage encapsulates the English history of the term *waste* and participates in its conceptual transformation by applying it to both the potential of land as commodity environment and the potential of people as labor power. The passage thus rethinks waste in terms of productive capacity. The discovery of economic input in America's waste woods reminds us of the discovery of the untapped agricultural capacity of England's waste lands, as commons, forests, and fens were enclosed, cut, or drained during the era of agrarian improvement, especially beginning in the seventeenth century.[29] More than domestic projectors, however, Hakluyt values woods precisely in their waste state, for that state yields many of the commodities he seeks. The waste American forests are not here, as in England, merely a stage on the way to agrarian land use.

Hakluyt's reference to "waste people" in this passage is more innovative still. Invited by the New World context, his usage in 1584 antedates similar usages in domestically oriented texts. The *OED* identifies the first use of the term *waste* to characterize people as Thomas Nash's pamphlet, *Pierce Penilesse*, published eight years later. Like Hakluyt, Nash addresses an economic problem (albeit the much narrower one of providing better remuneration for professional authors like himself). He similarly identifies an excess of population in England, "a certaine waste of the people for whome there is no vse, but warre," and suggests staging more plays, "some light toyes to busie their heads withall," to prevent their becoming disruptive to the state.[30] In the seventeenth century, agrarian improvers such as Gervase Markham (in *The English Husbandman*, 1613) would follow Hakluyt in referring to "waste persons" as a source of labor.[31] The management of this labor power—the transformation of the poor into the working class—would become increasingly important in English economic analysis over the course of the century.[32]

A conjunction of circumstances and attitudes compelled Hakluyt to conceptualize the poor as waste. It was a commonplace that England was overpopulated. One explanation, given by Nash and numerous others, was that there had been no wars of late. Thus in a prefatory poem commending Sir George Peckham's 1583 promotional tract, John Hawkins cites a classical precedent for colonization.[33] When the Roman population "grewe so great, / As neither warres could waste, nor Rome suffice them for a seate," they were settled in "divers Colonies, unto the Romaine raigne."[34] Hakluyt's "waste people" were those who could be "wasted" by war, if necessary (a sense that continues in our vernacular usage of "waste" as a synonym for "kill"). The sense of waste as economic loss or lack of gain also contributed to Hakluyt's labeling of the unemployed poor as excess, "waste people." Christopher Carleill refers to "our poore sorte of people, whiche are verie many amongst us, livyng altogethere unprofitable, and often tymes to the great disquiet of the better sorte," and similar formulations appear in all contemporary promotional tracts.[35] The early promoters characterized this class of people as expendable, a waste, because they were consuming without producing. Yet in proposing colonization as a means of expelling this waste from the English economy, they conceptually transformed it into a productive resource.

Boundary: "Vent"

Some of the "waste people" might have found employment at home, the early promoters argued, but for the decline of England's primary industry, wool fabrication. It is telling that despite their assumption of the New World's potential to produce everything of the Old World, the promoters never suggest wool as a colonial product. Even Peckham, who (unlike most other early promoters) hoped to found a colony devoted not only to trade but to extensive agrarian settlement as well, does not mention good pasturage among his inducements to colonization.[36] True, the country was mostly wooded, but woods could sooner be converted to pasture than to olive groves, as Peckham and many others propose, or to fields of silk grass or woad, as the more moderate Hariot would suggest. However, the importance of wool production to the mercantile construction of England's national image determines its treatment in the promotional literature as a commodity in need of a New World "vent," rather than as a commodity to be produced in the New World.

The crisis in the wool industry became an important locus for the question of economic boundaries not only by providing a motive for creating cheap sources of commodity input (such as oils and dyestuffs), but also by impelling merchants to look for a new vent for the finished cloth. From the mid-fifteenth to the mid-sixteenth century, England's exports of wool cloth had doubled, most of it being sold through Antwerp. However, in the second half of the sixteenth century, financial and political crises resulting from Spanish control of the Netherlands made export difficult, and the cloth trade experienced a depression. Trade was developing with more distant markets, such as the Baltic region and Russia, but these were uncertain markets and involved distant or difficult routes.[37] Thus all of the 1580s promotional tracts speculate strongly on a New World wool trade. Fourth among the elder Hakluyt's "Inducements" for Ralegh's Virginia project (rhetorically subordinate only to the glory of God, the increase of Christians, and the honor of the Queen) is a vision of "an ample vent in time to come of the Woollen clothes of England, especially those of the coursest sorts, to the maintenance of our poore, that els sterve or become burdensome to the realme: and vent also of sundry our commodities upon the tract of that firme land, and possibly in other regions from the Northerne side of that maine" (*O*, 2:327). Hakluyt projects markets among both transplanted English laborers and indigenous peoples, but he remains rather vague about the nature and development of these markets. Peckham works out more closely the logistics of the projected wool trade. The indigenous Americans, he argues,

so soone as they shall begin but a little to taste of civillitie, will take mervailous delight in any garment be it never so simple. . . . The people in those partes, are easily reduced to civilitie bothe in manners and garments. Which beeing so, what vente for our English clothes will thereby ensue, and howe great benefit to all such persons and Artificers whose names are coated in the margent [sidenote: "Clothiers. Wolmen. Carders. Spinners. Weavers. Fullers. Sheremen. Diers. Drapers. Clothiers. Cappers Hatters. etc. And many decayed townes repayred."], I doo leave to the judgement of such as are discrete.[38]

An English trading colony would thus mark the boundary between the English economy and its outsides, other as yet undeveloped economies whose sources of input would be directly from New World nature. Input and output would be mediated through this boundary. Yet despite Hawkins's invocation of Roman precedent, Peckham does not promote an imperial vision. He thought that rather than encompassing the world, as the Roman economy had attempted to do, the English economy would develop within limits marked by trading outposts. This limitation thus marks a conflict within Peckham's text and beyond it, a conflict in ideas about the economics of colonization and the versions of nationalism implied by those ideas. For the merchants, colonization was a means of opening the economy, of creating permeable but distinct boundaries; for the agrarian gentry, colonization implied the extension of empire, the full subsumption of New World lands under English law and practice. Only in his address to the merchant class does Peckham concern himself with the logistics of "vent," for only there can he think in terms of a clearly defined inside and outside.

In late sixteenth-century promotional literature generally, the term *vent* brings together etymologies of sale (*vendere*) and outlet (*ventus*). To pursue these etymologies fully through the French to their Latin origins—a pursuit complicated by the fact that it is "ad*vent*urers" (to come, to chance, *venire*) who speculate on the "vent" of commodities—could involve us in a Nabokovian game of word golf. It is enough here to identify the ultimate convergence of *ventus* and *vendere*, which indicates both a boundary pierced by an opening and sales seen from the point of view of the seller—a logic of supply and outflow rather than demand and inflow. The other frequent term in this literature for the sale of commodities, "uttering" or "utteraunce" ("out"), carries similar connotations. Fully wrought commodities seem naturally to seek an outlet, an empty space into which they might be sent. In this respect, English goods wanting "vent" are like the English "waste people" whom the promoters identify as a colony's potential labor supply: both need an outlet, which could be provided by New World environments.

In this context, the elder Hakluyt uses the term *vent* to develop a conceptual linkage between excess people and commodities. In notes probably prepared for Ralegh in 1584, he envisions a "large and ample vente not only of our wolleyn Clothes of Englande but also of the labor of our poore people at home by sale of Hattes, Cappes, and a thousande kynde of other wrought ware that in tyme may be brought in use amounge the people of those Countryes to the great relief of the multitude of our pore people, and to the wounderfull inrytchinge of this Realme" (*O,* 2:343). He concludes with an appeal urging "not onlye the marchaunts and Clothiers but alsoe all other sortes and degrees of our nacion to seeke newe dyscovereyes of peopled regions for *vente* of our Idle people, other-wyse in shourte tyme many mischeifs maye ensue" (*O*, 2:343, emphasis added). While this use of "vente" refers explicitly to the transportation of the "idle" or "waste" poor to the colonies, it resonates with other contemporary uses of the term to refer both to the commodities to be wrought by the poor at home and to the labor that, as an abstract quality, would be embodied in those commodities. English products, English labor, and even the English people themselves are all poised to take advantage of the vent offered by New World environments, simultaneously supplying the English economy with goods and ridding it of its excesses.

Entropy and Nostalgia

Where the elder Hakluyt wrote his promotional texts primarily for the merchant adventurers themselves, his younger cousin had opportunity to reshape the genre for an audience specifically concerned with the question of national identity. Commissioned by Ralegh to organize information on North America and arguments for colonization into a form that would enlist the Crown's active support, the younger Hakluyt wrote "A particuler discourse conceringe the greate necessitie and manifolde comodyties that are like to growe to this Realme of Englande by the Westerne discoveries lately attempted," now generally known as the "Discourse of Western Planting" (1584). Perhaps it was the challenge of locating the merchant adventurers' concerns in relation to English national identity and policy that drew him, in a key moment, back to More's meditations on these issues. In the debate concerning England's social ills in Book 1 of *Utopia*, the company particularly address themselves to the increase in crime attendant on widespread unemployment and rising prices. They are drawn into this debate by the traveler Raphael's recollection of a topic that had emerged during the course of a dinner with the Archbishop. One of those at table had set forth a paradox of crime and punishment; he "began dyligently and busily to prayse that strayte and rygorous iustice, which at that tyme was there executed upon fellones, who, as he sayde, were for the moste part .xx. hanged together vpon one gallowes. And, seyng so fewe escapyd punyshement, he sayd he coulde not chewse but greatly wonder and maruell, howe and by what euill luck it should so cum to passe, that theues neuertheles were in euery place so ryffe and ranke" (*U*, 11–12). In reply, Raphael had argued the economic causes of crime, until the Archbishop rather tediously turned the conversation back to the more abstract question of justice. The present company, however, are more interested than the Archbishop had been in political economy, and so they ask Raphael to describe Utopia.

Hakluyt's consideration of England's social ills moves similarly from the animating topic of crime and punishment to larger concerns of political economy. Incorporating an economic explanation of crime that Raphael would have approved into a scene of multiple execution that alludes to More's text, Hakluyt points out that

wee are growen more populous than ever heretofore: . . . yea many thousandes of idle persons are w th in this Realme, w ch havinge no way to be sett on worke be either mutinous and seeke alteration in the state, or at leaste very burdensome to the common wealthe, and often fall to pilfering and thevinge and other lewdnes, whereby all the prisons of the lande are daily pestred and stuffed full of them, where either they pitifully pyne awaye, or els at lengthe are miserably hanged, even xx ti. at a clappe oute of some one Jayle. (*O*, 2:234)

Abundance of population and skill turn to excess, waste, and consumption: "So that nowe there are of every arte and science so many, that they can hardly lyve one by another, nay rather they are readie to eate upp one another" (*O*, 2:234). Hakluyt argues that there is not enough wealth in England's economy to support this unproductive, indeed subtractive behavior. In such an entropic situation, state-imposed deaths, a score at a time on one gallows, seem to provide the only regulation for a system that cannot regulate itself. More's Raphael had identified domestic solutions to the problems of poverty and crime, such as legislation against enclosure, before transporting the reader to a New World society in which political economy is organized so as to prevent the emergence of these problems. Just as More's Utopians established colonies to draw off their surplus population, Hakluyt argues that "yf this voyadge were put in execution, these pety theves mighte be condempned for certen yeres in the westerne partes" (*O*, 2:234). The crucial difference is that this population would work not so much to support itself as to produce numerous and varied commodities for English import, and it would also serve in turn as an export market for English goods. Thus Hakluyt reconfigures subtraction or consumption as outlet and links it to input, elaborating the conceptual transformation of waste envisioned by his elder cousin.

Citing the legal and penal context invited by his engagement with More, Hakluyt presents the nation with two alternatives: England will continue as a land of criminals, jails, and gallows, or it will become a land of full employment and ample wealth. In addressing the Crown, however, he needs an argument that does more than balance law against economy as competing forces. The argument he develops in the concluding section of the "Discourse" proposes a primarily economic-environmental understanding of English national identity in general. Here Hakluyt returns to another of More's topics, the importance of the wool industry for England's national well-being, giving it a quite different interpretation. In Book 1 of *Utopia*, Raphael forcefully describes the effects of enclosure, a practice necessary for the expansion of wool production: sheep have devoured the people and depopulated the countryside, turning formerly cultivated land into wilderness. As one shepherd replaced several plowmen on estate after estate, the resulting unemployment became a standard theme in the literature of agrarian complaint, of which More's passage is the most famous example.[39] Historical evidence complicates this theme. Some of the population forced off the land by enclosure found work in the cloth-producing districts that began to grow up in the late fifteenth century, as the wool industry expanded and found export markets on the continent.[40] Even so, the "nostalgic vision" of More's complaint—its implicit appeal to an idealized set of social relations disrupted by economic transformation—had great emotional power.[41]

It is therefore somewhat surprising that Hakluyt should represent the wool industry itself, the very emblem of negatively valued modernity in More's text, as an object of nostalgia in his concluding arguments. Yet this nostalgia looks back from a hypothetical future that England might avoid through colonization. In this way, Hakluyt taps the power of nostalgia while skirting any admission of present loss. England, he says, "nowe for certen hundreth yeres last passed" had by virtue of wool production "raised it selfe from meaner state to greater wealthe and moche higher hono^r, mighte and power then before" (*O*, 2:313). However, with the increase of the Spanish wool trade in the West Indies,

the wolles of England and the clothe made of the same, will become base, and every day more base then other, wch prudently weyed, yt behoveth this Realme yf it meane not to returne to former olde meanes [meanness] and basenes, but to stande in present and late former hono^r glorye and force, and not negligently and sleepingly to slyde into beggery, to foresee and to plante at Norumbega or some like place, were it not for anything els but for the hope of the vent of our woll indraped, the principall and in effecte the onely enrichinge contynueinge naturall commoditie of this Realme. (*O*, 2:314)

Making the wool industry a synecdoche for England's national identity, Hakluyt introduces temporal complications that enable multiple readings of that figure. He compares a "former olde" state to a preferable "late former" one, but he has already described the value of wool as "every day" becoming "more base." These complications identify the present moment as a systemic crisis point, a critical juncture from which England might or might not "negligently and sleepingly . . . slyde into beggery."

The growth of the wool industry during the fifteenth century, which Hakluyt views nostalgically from the hypothetical perspective of an entropic future, had required an economic and environmental transformation of the sort that Hakluyt is now inspired to propose on a larger scale for America. In the early to mid-fifteenth century, large landholders, responding to agricultural depression, had expanded sheep production; as the wool industry developed, population declined in areas previously devoted to tillage but increased in new cloth-producing districts. That is, the growth of the wool industry transformed land use from subsistence to market production. A center-periphery organization emerged, in which the countryside supplied wool to be worked in the towns. For traditional agrarians such as More, this reorganization was the target of nostalgic complaint. For Hakluyt it suggested a paradigm for revitalizing the "decayed townes" that were the objects of his own mercantile nostalgia (*O*, 2:235). If England was poised on the brink of irreversible, entropic decline, "ymmynent mischefe hanginge over our heades," the only hope of recovery was opening the English economy to the wastes of the New World, where a sparse population of native inhabitants still produced only at subsistence levels but where the environment's capacity for greater input and output held the promise of systemic balance for England's economy (*O*, 2:314).

Economy and Environment

The early promoters' New World speculations took place in a critical historical moment, after which modern economic and environmental discourses gradually diverged, to reconverge again only recently. The larger pattern of this divergence was to some extent anticipated by local responses to economic recovery and subsequent depression in the early seventeenth century. Analysts of the period, in thinking about the economy, looked only to the Old World and thought only of money. After the stagnation of the cloth industry during the 1590s (which Hakluyt had predicted), treaties with Spain and France opened up Mediterranean vents for the wool that Hakluyt would have directed toward the New World. (This is one reason why England was relatively slow to colonize America.) For these new markets, manufacturers began to produce lighter, less durable woolens, which provided greater employment than had the heavier, traditional goods because more labor was required per pound of wool. Soon, however, foreign competition in these manufactures increased, and the resulting decline of England's export trade ushered in the depression of the 1620s. In response, economic analysts formulated a monetarist approach, arguing that the readily observable outflow of the realm's treasure was caused by an unfavorable balance of trade, but failing to theorize the root causes of the imbalance. Concentrating instead on pricing, coinage, and currency valuation, the economists of the 1620s ignored environmental considerations, giving mercantilism its now familiar monetarist character.[42] For the first time, as Joyce Appleby puts it, "economic factors" were "abstracted . . . from their real context" of "social and political [and, we must add, environmental] entanglements."[43]

The larger historical divergence of economic and environmental discourses followed this local pattern. During the seventeenth century, questions of the production and distribution of commodities became detached from moral and social issues and an overall concern for the public good, and subjected to technical and rational analysis.[44] In the new economics, any social goal came to be formulated as merely the sum of private goals, until the very idea of an overarching social goal disappeared into Adam Smith's familiar figure of the invisible hand.

In thus closing itself off from the consideration of any larger social or moral purpose, the discourse of economics began to detach itself from environmental analysis. Traditional agrarianism had assumed a closed system in which wealth, understood as rights to land and its produce, was finite (although, as the sixteenth-century literature of agrarian complaint argued, this wealth was often unfairly distributed). The paradigm of growth suggested by the colonial promoters began to be realized in the 1630s, as New World commodities such as tobacco, timber, pelts, and fish provided a basis for the economic recovery in England that would develop fully after 1660. This paradigm was formalized in economic models developed by Adam Smith, David Ricardo, and the Physiocrats, who criticized the seventeenth-century monetarists and described growth as requiring increased inputs of environmental resources.[45] Yet in understanding resources primarily as agricultural land, the classical economists argued that resource-based growth would be subject to diminishing returns over greater inputs of labor and capital. Thus their followers soon turned their attention to manufacturing, which, since machines could be replicated and improved, promised constant or increasing growth. In classical analysis, resources came to be treated under the general head of "capital," ignoring the distinction between natural and human-made capital that sustainable economics insists is fundamental.[46] Neoclassical through Keynesian economic models, assuming the paradigm of growth, focused on exchange relations, analyzing the production-consumption cycle and surplus value in ways that closed off economic theory from any significant consideration of the environment.[47] Postmodern theorists of exchange, such as Jean-Joseph Goux, have since extended this logic to all aspects of the social without theorizing any relation between the social and what is outside it, in effect completing the neoclassical-Keynesian description of the economy as a system closed off from the material environment.[48]

Ironically, while economic theory increasingly excluded the environment from its domain of analysis, modern environmental science came to draw on economic models to work out eighteenth-century speculations that there might be an economy of nature itself, representing nature as an interrelated system of production, consumption, and exchange. But only with the full development of the concept of the ecosystem—the understanding of nature in terms of energy systems rather than traditional economic categories—could environmental science offer modern economics a significant paradigm in return.[49] According to this paradigm, the economy is a subsystem of the ecosystem, conceptually separable but materially dependent on the ecosystem's capacities to provide low-entropy input and absorb high-entropy output.[50] More recent ecological theories, which describe nature in terms of disequilibrium or chaos, have complicated the systems-theory model, making it more difficult to calculate the values of sustainable inputs and outputs than bioeconomists had previously assumed.[51]

The promotional writings of the Hakluyts and their cohort develop a suggestively similar position. That is, in certain respects they return us to our present crisis. They describe an economy threatened with entropic decay and see that the reversal of this trajectory must come from a direct engagement with the physical environment, an engagement that involves considerations of input, output, and boundary ("commodity," "waste," and "vent") even if the exact specification of those considerations remains uncertain in theory. They propose that the health of the economy depends only on the limits of nature, even if they cannot fully conceptualize those limits. Since we feel we are much closer to nature's limits (and have more science) than they, it is easy to criticize them for a failure of insight in this regard. I hope I have demonstrated that it is more interesting to try to understand them on their own terms, for those terms can prompt our own thinking about the relation of economy to environment.

Chapter 2

"God Sells Us All Things for Our Labour"
John Smith's Generall Historie

In 1588, Thomas Hariot claimed that Virginia naturally produced "Silke-wormes faire and great, as bigge as our ordinary Walnuts."[1] Following the program set out by Hakluyt's "Discourse of Western Planting" and other such promotional texts, he went on to assess the possibilities for commodity offered by these silkworms:

Although it hath not bene our hap to have found such plenty, as elsewhere to be in the countrey we have heard of, yet seeing that the countrey doth naturally breed and nourish them, there is no doubt that if arte be added in planting of Mulberie trees, and others, fit for them in commodious places, for their feeding and nourishing, and some of them carefully gathered & husbanded in that sort, as by men of skil is knowen to be necessary: there wil rise as great profit in time to the Virginians, as thereof doth now to the Persians, Turks, Italians and Spanyards. (68–69)

The source of Hariot's information about this "plenty" is not clear. If he heard it from indigenous Americans (for evidently he became competent in some Algonquin dialect), we must wonder whether they behaved as did the peoples Columbus encountered on his first voyage, always suggesting that the commodities he sought could be found elsewhere.[2] On the other hand, Hariot might have heard of the abundance of silkworms only from Hakluyt and other promoters. In either case, he couples such speculative reports (differently motivated, although he might not have realized it) with empirical observations about the environment's natural capacities, here the evident abundance of mulberries, to develop an aspect of the georgic projected by the Hakluyts. The particular program he had in mind here would never pay off, partly because the indigenous species of mulberry, red rather than white, was not well suited to sericulture no matter how artfully it was planted.[3]

Hariot's unwarranted projection of sericulture in Virginia and similar such instances raise questions that had remained implicit the Hakluyts' speculations: what precisely was the nature of the linkage between economy and environment in practice, and from that how ought labor to be ordered? The literature of first-generation colonists answered these questions in two conflicting modes. Sixteenth-century optimism about new economic capacities persisted, but was now often accompanied by criticisms that the environment was being mismanaged. The colonists, it seemed, were not always living up to the promise of the land. At first, this failure of the American promise was simply the colonists's failure to produce their own subsistence from an obviously fertile land. Soon, however, the critique of mismanagement took a more complicated turn. As the tobacco economy developed in Virginia, the problem was defined as one of simultaneous overproduction and underproduction: the colonists were misusing the environment's capacity, producing tobacco but not food for subsistence and other important commodities for trade, thereby developing land practices that worked against the public good. Thus while writings from colonial Virginia follow the Hakluyts in urging economic growth, they resonate with modern critiques of growth when they explore the specific ways in which economic activity depends on local environmental capacity and when they assess that capacity in order to propose the regulation or management of economic activity. Like much of modern green writing, that is, they argue that there is something fundamentally wrong with Americans' relation to the land and sometimes offer tentative solutions to the problems they identify. In their criticisms of the tobacco economy in particular, these texts also run up against economic resistance to such solutions—and in this respect as well will sound somewhat familiar to modern environmentalists.

In specifying the role of human labor, first-generation colonial writings such as *A True Declaration of the Estate of the Colonie in Virginia* (1610) problematized the distinct separation that had provided the Hakluyts and their cohort with the starting point for their promotional efforts. The latter had differentiated the Old from the New Worlds and had identified those domains respectively as the conceptual loci of economy and environment, with colonial trading posts as boundaries or vents mediating between the two sites. Yet in practice, the theoretical division could not correspond neatly with any spatial division, as the sixteenth-century promotional texts had seemed to imply, even if the vast ocean separating America from England encouraged such a conceptualization. To colonize in search of new capacities was to bring the English economy to America and thus to translate all concerns about inputs, outputs, and boundaries to that ground. The *Declaration* conceptualized the mediation between the two realms as on-site exchange and identified the medium of exchange as labor. This recognition and simultaneous complication of the first promoters' division between economy and environment defined a central problematic of the American georgic tradition.

While Captain John Smith shared the sixteenth-century promoters' enthusiasm for the New World's potential productivity, in the *Generall Historie* he developed a more refined sense of environmental capacities. Comparing his early experience of Virginia with the subsequent rapid growth of the tobacco economy there, Smith criticizes the colonists for not living up to the promise of the land that he had begun to map.[4] Bermuda, in contrast to Virginia, he characterizes as an uncertain environment, a land of extremes, a site of remarkable preservations and providences but not a place in which labor would unfailingly be rewarded as it would be, if rightly ordered, on the mainland. In the *Generall Historie,* Book V on Bermuda thus serves as a meditative interlude. As Smith came to shift the focus of his promotional efforts from Virginia to New England, his text enacted this shift.[5] Returning here to the entopic scenario of Hakluyt's "Discourse of Western Planting," Smith observed that New England represented great untapped capacities, "her treasures having yet never beene opened, nor her originals wasted, consumed, nor abused."[6] While this figure's implications for gender and power are quite clear to us, Smith is not merely conceptualizing the land to embody, as Annette Kolodny puts it, "the total female principle of gratification."[7] The figure indicates a recognition of the finitude and vulnerability of the New World's resources, suggesting that Smith had begun to think about environmental limits on economic activity.[8] The overall structure of the *Generall Historie,* then, presents an unresolved conflict between human mismanagement and uncertainty and environmental potential, between experience and possibility—a conflict that remains unresolved to this day.

Virginia

Reports from the new colony on the James river continued Hariot's Roanoke project of integrating firsthand observation with classical climatology and other Old World discourses that had so influenced the late sixteenth-century promoters, to theorize the relation between economy and environment in the New World. The *True Declaration of Virginia,* for example, weighed present failure against future promise, asking the Virginia Company investors not to give up, but to take a considered view of the colony's prospects: "If any man shall accuse these reports of partiall falshood, supposing them to be but Vtopian, and legendarie fables, because he cannot conceiue, that plentie and famine, a temperate climate, and distempered bodies, felicities, and miseries can be reconciled together, let him now reade with judgement, but let him not judge before he hath read" (14). As it had been for key sections of Hakluyt's "Discourse of Western Planting," the touchstone for the *Declaration*'s plea here is More's *Utopia.* More had simply assumed colonizable environments to have carrying capacities identical to those of the Utopians' homeland.

Hakluyt had theorized the relationship between the economy (England) and the physical environment (the New World) in terms of inputs and outputs vented through a permeable boundary, imagining not only the export of surplus population, as More had done, but beyond that the intensification of production and consumption in the home economy developed from specific kinds of resources not available in England. Where European economic theory, as we have seen, successively closed itself off from environmental considerations, the American georgic tradition began to investigate the theoretical opening that the early promoters first identified. So it was that the *Declaration*, in the face of pervasive mismanagement, desertion, and disease, criticized the colonists' misrecognition of a natural source of economic intensification: in Virginia, "all things committed to the earth, do multiply with an incredible vsurie" (12). The paradox of the land's great promise and the colony's failure so far, of "plentie and famine . . . together," begged for explanation (14).

In this context, the *Declaration* characterizes the colonists as participants in a particular kind of exchange: "*Dij* [*sic*] *laboribus omnia vendunt,* God sels vs all things for our labour" (15). This exchange of labor was not merely a matter of the production of goods but encompassed commodity in the largest sense: the entire human relationship to the environment, including basic survival and the maintenance of bodily health. For example, answering criticisms that Jamestown had been planted too near "fennes and marshes," so that "100. sickned, and halfe the number died" from the "vnwholsome & contagious vapour" there, the *Declaration* argues that environmental factors cannot take the whole blame, for "the Wilds and Hundreds of Kent and Essex" at home are equally marshy. Rather, he cites as counterevidence "Sir Thomas Gates his experiment" with his shipwrecked crew in Bermuda, wherein Gates "recovered the health of most of them by moderat labour, whose sicknesse was bred in them by intemperate idlenes" (14). Labor would similarly produce health at Jamestown, the argument went. Certainly it was in a colonial manager's interest to praise the salubrious effects of labor, for how else could commodities be extracted and returned home for the company's profit and the manager's honor? Yet as specified by the *Declaration*, the labor required by Gates was moderate, as was that recently ordered by Lord De La Warr, who arrived at Jamestown just in time to rescue the colony from mismanagement and decreed that all colonists should work "from six of clocke in the morning vntill ten, and from two of the clocke in the afternoone till foure" during the summer, and less in the winter (20). A six-hour workday was considerably shorter than the minimum of ten hours prescribed by English law, and was seemingly irrational in a starving colony.[9]

Yet the colonists were concerned for the results of their exchange of even a small amount of labor, "as though the sappe of their bodies should be spent for other mens profite" (20). So in practice it was clear that their labor had to be induced and regulated. Men would not enter needlessly into that exchange with God defined by the *Declaration.* The specialized artisans among the colonists thought that they had no work to do (smelters, for example, could not refine gold if no ore had been mined) while a gentleman's very self-definition consisted in doing nothing. No husbandmen or yeomen, whose proper business it was to grow food, came to the colony until the resupply of 1611, a year later, and then only a few.[10] Meanwhile, the colonists lived as they could, or would, the *Declaration* reported: "some of them eat their fish raw, rather than they would go a stones cast to fetch wood and dresse it" (15). Captain John Smith had had some success in trading for corn with the Indians, but their interest in English goods soon waned. As the *Declaration* put it, "that copper which before would haue prouided a bushell, would not now obtaine so much as a pottle" (17).[11] Such observations on the basic problem of getting food in the new colony no doubt encouraged the *Declaration* to develop the formulation of labor as an exchange with God mediated through the environment: labor could be thought of as a constant value. Not subject to the apparently arbitrary fluctuations of a metal such as copper (or gold), labor provided a solid medium of exchange.

The environment, divinely ordered, would even pay interest on the labor exchanged: the *Declaration* claimed that crops "multipl[ied] with an incredible vsurie" (12). Hariot for example had remarked particularly on the wonderful "increase" of Indian corn in Virginia:

that countrey corne is there to be preferred before ours: besides, the manifold wayes in applying it to victual, the increase is so much, that small labor & paines is needful in respect of that which must be used for ours. For this I can assure you that according to the rate we have made proofe of, one man may prepare and husband so much ground (having once borne corne before) with lesse then foure and twenty houres labour, as shall yeeld him victual in a large proportion for a twelvemoneth . . . the sayd ground being also but of five and twenty yards square. (74)

Although Hariot's estimates of labor and land were in reality far too small —two acres per person was probably the appropriate figure for land— maize does yield an increase that the colonists must have found marvelous in comparison to the yield of wheat and other English grains.[12] Yet this amazement at specifically New World productions easily led to unrealistic expectations about labor, as Hariot's undue optimism here suggests. Such expectations would soon be satirized by Captain Smith, who worked tirelessly to dispel the Virginia Company's belief that "all the world was Oatmeale there" (3:271). For example, voyaging up the Chesapeake, Smith and his crew found "in divers places" an "aboundance of fish, lying so thicke with their heads above the water, as for want of nets (our barge driving amongst them) we attempted to catch them with a frying pan: but we found it a bad instrument to catch fish with: neither better fish, more plenty, nor more variety for smal fish, had any of us ever seene in any place so swimming in the water, but they are not to be caught with frying pans" (2:168). Smith's characteristic wit makes his central argument: no matter how naturally productive an environment, there is a point at which human labor and technology must interact with it in order to sustain life and create wealth, and the point could easily be misjudged, particularly by those unfamiliar with the environment.

Still, for all Smith's emphasis on labor, one begins to suspect that the very fertility of the land vitiates against human industry—a theme that would be taken up at greater length by later Virginia writers such as Robert Beverley and William Byrd, II. In his account of how the Indians get their living, Smith foreshadows his subsequent criticism of the English colonists' lack of industry and management in Virginia, from which in turn he develops his proposals for proper management in the promotion of New England. Notwithstanding that the Indians' corn had kept the colonists from starving during the first years, Smith's brief account of their agriculture concludes that "when all their fruits be gathered, little els they plant, and this is done by the women and children; neither doth this long suffice them, for neare three parts of the yeare, they onely observe times and seasons, and live of what the Country naturally afordeth from hand to mouth, etc." (2:113). What had been an abstraction to the early promoters who remained in England became, for Smith, a practical question: given the supposed (and readily observable) great natural productivity of the environment and low population density, he must have wondered at times why the Indians seemed to have a comparatively low standard of living. The combination of great potential in theory and poverty in practice could be explained only by Indians' (and later, the colonists') improvidence. The Indians did labor, but they did not thereby order the land in their best interest.

Smith's first description of the Virginia environment, in *A Map of Virginia* (1612), later reprinted in reprinted in Book II of the *Generall Historie* (1624), opens with this theme: "Virginia doth afford many excellent vegetables, and living Creatures, yet grasse there is little or none, but what groweth in low Marishes: for all the Countrey is overgrowne with trees, whose droppings continually turneth their grasse to weeds, by reason of the rancknes of the ground, which would soon be amended by good husbandry" (2:108). One instance of the land's potential (and of the Indians' lack of cultivation) is the natural state of the grapevines. We recall that the sixteenth-century promoters, in seeking for commodity environments to replace the Mediterranean trade, had been quite interested in grapes, as well as olives, citrus, and the like. Thus Smith reports, "Of vines great abundance in many partes that climbe the toppes of the highest trees in some places, but these beare but few grapes. Except by the rivers and savage habitations, where they are not overshadowed from the sunne, they are covered with fruit, though never pruined nor manured. Of those hedge grapes we made neere twentie gallons of wine, which was like our French Brittish wine [i.e., wine from Brittany], but certainely they would prove good were they well manured" (2:108–9). Not the very best wine, that is, but a species and an environment promising better, under proper management. We know that the indigenous people did manage the land to create such edge environments, burning and clearing woods, thus encouraging the vines, but Smith does not recognize their management.[13] Elsewhere, however, Smith does find a hint in their practices of the sort of foresight that ought to characterize the English response to the environment. Noting that in general they "live of what the Country naturally afordeth from hand to mouth, etc.," he remarks that "it is strange to see how their bodies alter with their dyet, even as the deere and wilde beasts they seem fat and leane, strong and weake" (2:113, 116–17). Yet "Powhatan their great King, and some others that are provident, rost their fish and flesh upon hurdles . . . and keepe it till scarce times" (2:117). Indeed, without means of storing surplus, especially of corn (the method for which Smith never describes), they could not have been so generous in providing the English with food during the early years (for example, 2:143). The irony did not escape Smith that, as late as 1621, the year before the infamous massacre at Jamestown, the English were still "depending continually to be supplied by the Salvages" (2:284).

Although it seems that Smith would rather go out to discover mines, rivers, and peoples than stay at Jamestown to manage crops and manufactures, he argues strongly, in a letter to the treasurer of the Virginia Company in 1608, that the colony needed to make sure of its own subsistence, rather than being forced to live "from one Supply to another" (2:190). This letter is particularly interesting because it gives what is perhaps Smith's clearest assessment of the potential of the Virginia environment. Sent back to England along with the "tryals of Pitch, Tarre, Glasse, Frankincense, Sope ashes; with that Clapboord and Waynscot that could be provided" as directed by the Company, the letter discourages hope for the production of most of these commodities (2:187). Of timber products and naval stores (pitch, tar, masts, planking, and the like) in particular, Smith argues,

if you rightly consider, what an infinite toyle it is in Russia and Swethland, where the woods are proper for naught els, and though there be the helpe of both man and beast in those ancient Common-wealths, which many an hundred years have used it, yet thousands of those poore people can scarce get necessaries to live, but from hand to mouth. And though your Factors there can buy as much in a week as will fraught you a ship, or as much as you please; you must not expect from us any such matter, which are but a many of ignorant miserable soules, that are scarce able to get wherewith to live, and defend our selves against the inconstant Salvages: finding but here and there a tree fit for the purpose. (2:188–89)

Here Smith begins to dismantle the sixteenth-century promoters' hopes of finding replacement commodity environments for all of the Old World. Virginia, he says, will not produce all things. Timber products and naval stores in particular, even were there trees fit for the purpose, require so much labor over and above subsistence that the workers would have to live "from hand to mouth" (Smith's characteristic phrase for the Indians' improvidence) at best, unless others would supply them; thus "it were better to give five hundred pound a tun for those grosse Commodities in Denmark, then send for them hither, till more necessary things be provided." He also cautions against "send[ing] into Germany or Pole-land for glass-men" for the colony (2:190). Of the results of his "tryals" of glass he says little, although we can surmise that his discovery of "a great Rocky mountaine like Antimony," a mineral useful in glass production, "proved of no value" for the time being (2:187, 167, 168). Smith is cautiously optimistic about only one kind of resource, the "two barrels of stones, and such as I take to be good Iron ore at the least; so devided, as by their notes you may see in what places I found them." Even so, "as yet you must not looke for any profitable returnes" until the colony is better supplied (2:189, 190).

Although Smith was right about those barrels of stones (Virginia would produce some iron, and some glass as well, in the seventeenth century) the most "profitable returnes" soon came in the form of tobacco. The resulting questions of economic-environmental management would preoccupy Virginia's georgic writers for the next two centuries. Before tobacco cultivation was introduced, the colonists, with the benefit of the "three hundred men, and one hundred Kine and other Cattell, with munition and all other manner of provision that could be thought needfull" which arrived in August 1611, had begun to transform the landscape of Virginia into an ordered agricultural space (2:241). Land was mapped and "laid out . . . in severall hundreds" (administrative divisions characteristic of agrarian England) or ordered into other towns (2:242). At the new town of Henrico, for example, "a good quantitie of Corne-ground" was "impailed, sufficiently secured to maintaine more than I suppose will come over this three yeeres," while at Rochedale Hundred "our Hogs and Cattell have twentie miles circuit to graze in securely"; everywhere "are many faire houses already built, besides particular mens houses" (2:241, 242). A further ordering of the landscape the following year is evident in a reorganization of labor similar to that described by Governor Bradford at Plymouth (see Chapter 3). Deputy Governor Thomas Dale "allotted every man three Acres of cleare ground, in the nature of Farmes" (excepting the hundreds, which were administered on a more feudal model), from which each farmer had to contribute "two barrels and a halfe of Corne" to the common store and one month of labor per year (2:247). However, the introduction of tobacco "as the most present commodity they could devise for a present gaine" had by 1616 disrupted that ordering of labor in the landscape (2:256).

The turn to tobacco marks the point at which entrepreneurial individualism conflicts with the order of the commonwealth and becomes the primary force in shaping the colonists' relation to the land. The allotment of individual three-acre plots under Deputy Governor Dale's direction had resulted in increased productivity (as it would do for the Plymouth colonists). Smith reports that under the prior communal organization of labor, "the most honest among them would hardly take so much true paines in a weeke, as now for themselves they will doe in a day . . . so that wee reaped not so much Corne from the labours of thirtie, as now three or four doe provide for themselves" (2:247). However, tobacco cultivation encouraged the individual taking of land well beyond those original three-acre corn plots and enabled the pursuit of private "gaine" to the detriment of social organization: "every man betooke himselfe to the best place he could for the purpose" of growing tobacco, regardless of other considerations (2:256). In 1617, the newly arrived Governor Argall viewed the dismal results of privatization: "In James towne he found but five or six houses, the Church downe, the Palizado's broken, the Bridge in pieces, the Well of fresh water spoiled; the Store-house they used for the Church, the market-place, and streets, and all other spare places planted with Tobacco, the Salvages as frequent in their houses as themselves, . . . the Colonie dispersed all about, planting Tobacco" (2:262). Here, within a decade of the Virginia Colony's founding, we find a negative feature of tobacco culture that would persist well into the eighteenth century: dispersed settlement patterns that worked against the establishment of good social order. Soon there is just a hint as well of the second major complaint that would be laid against tobacco, that it exhausts the soil. As yet soil exhaustion was not a problem—and need not have been even in the long run, if tobacco farming were properly managed and conducted on a small scale—but the colonists are already becoming alert to the possibility.[14] By 1619 they have learned that "an industrious man not other waies imploied, may well tend foure akers of Corne, and 1000. plants of Tobacco, and where they say an aker will yeeld but three or foure barrels, we have ordinarily foure or five, but of new ground six, seven, and eight" (2:267). Yet even slightly declining yields on older ground may have led to overplanting and diminishing returns, for as Smith remarks, "many are so covetous to have much, they make little good," while even those who did not overplant would soon need to take new land (2:267).

Tobacco culture posed two more immediate problems, however. It distracted the colonists from better uses of the land and their labor, and it made for problematic relations with the Indians, which resulted in the massacre of 1622 (and would erupt again in Bacon's Rebellion). Smith approves the Virginia Company's orders for 1621 calling for "the suppressing of planting Tobacco, and planting of Corne, not depending continually to be supplied by the Salvages, but in case of necessity to trade with them, whom long ere this, it hath been promised and expected should have beene fed and relieved by the English, not the English by them." The colonists needed also, according to the 1621 orders, "by all dilligence [to] seeke to send something home to satisfie the Adventurers, that all this time had only lived upon hopes" (2:284). While such orders hoped to deter the colonists from "rooting in the ground about Tobacco like Swine"—an image that suggests the destructiveness of tobacco culture not only for the colonists but for the land itself—"as yet from Virginia" there were "little returnes but private mens Tobacco" along with only "faire promises of plentie of Iron, Silke, Wine, and many other good and rich commodities" (2:285, 292). Smith goes on to argue that greed for tobacco wealth blinded the colonists to the Indian conspiracy that would result in the massacre of 1622: "such was the conceit of this conceited peace, as there was seldome or never a sword, and seldomer a peece, except for a Deer or Fowle, by which assurances the most plantations were placed straglingly and scatteringly, as a choice veine of rich ground invited them, and further from neighbours the better" (2:293). This dispersal from each other and proximity to the Indians had left them vulnerable to attack. Yet in the end, Smith remarks, the 1622 massacre may prove "good for the Plantation" because now the colonists have "just cause to destroy [the Indians] by all meanes possible" (although Smith argues it ought to have been done "long agoe"): if the Indians were eliminated, "we may take their owne plaine fields and Habitations, which are the pleasantest places in the Countrey," rather than being so much "troubled in cleering the ground of great Timber" (2:298).

There were some, in England at least, who dissented from such a program of eradication. Among them was John Donne, who in a sermon for the Virginia Company preached in November 1622 (the massacre had taken place in March) argues rather for the propagation of the Gospel among the Indians, hoping that the colonists "could once bring a *Catechisme* to bee as good ware amongst them as a bugle, as a knife, as a hatchet."[15] As he proposes that mission work become the equivalent of trade, Donne conceptualizes the colonization project primarily in terms

of the logistics of vent, rather than the subsumption of land. The report
of the massacre on which Smith particularly draws, by Edward Waterhouse, had argued that "we, who hitherto haue had possession of no
more ground than their waste, . . . may now by right of Warre, and law
of Nations, inuade the Country, and destroy them who sought to destroy
vs: whereby we shall enjoy their cultiuated places, turning the labouri-
ous Mattocke into the victorious Sword (wherein there is more both ease,
benefit, and glory) and possessing the fruits of others labours."[16] Donne
will not go so far, not even admitting as much as More had concerning the doctrine of *vacuum domicilium.* Donne argues that "Law of *Nature*
and *Nations*" may authorize plantations only in cases where the land was
"never inhabited" or if the present inhabitants "doe not in some measure
fill the Land, so as the Land may bring foorth her increase for the use
of men," but he does not extend this doctrine to justify a war over occupation (274, emphases in original). Even by Waterhouse's own account,
the Indians did in some measure fill the land, for he draws a distinction
between "their cultiuated places" and their "waste," the latter being all
the English have inhabited so far. Where Waterhouse sees a prospect for
usurping the "fruits" of the Indians' "labours" by moving off their waste
and onto improved ground, Donne recalls the arguments made, beginning with the Hakluyts, for colonization projects as means of drawing off
England's waste and in the process turning New World waste into productive resources.

Donne then imagines that transformative process as exchange or vent.
"Bee you not discouraged," he urges the Virginia Company investors, "if
the Promises which you have made to your selves, or to others, be not so
soone discharg'd; though you see not your money, though you see not
your men, though a *Flood*, a *Flood* of *bloud* have broken upon them, be not
discouraged" (271, emphases in original). The Virginia environment will
itself replenish that blood:

It shall redeeme many a wretch from the Jawes of death, from the hands of the
Executioner. . . . It shall sweep your streets, and wash your dores, from idle persons, and the children of idle persons, and imploy them: and truely, if the whole
Countrey were but such a *Bridewell*, to force idle persons to work, it had a good
use. But it is already, not onely a *Spleene*, to draine the ill humors of the body,
but a *Liver*, to breed good bloud; already, the imployment breeds Marriners; already, the place gives essayes, nay Fraytes of Marchantable commodities. (272,
emphases in original)

Donne emphasizes the restorative and transformative power of the New
World environment even more extensively than the Hakluyts had done.
Like them, he emphasizes a systemic relation between economy and en-
vironment: the New World environment drains off the Old World econ-

omy's wastes and gives it new life and wealth. Yet in developing his conceit of Virginia as the primary organs of England's circulatory system, Donne minimizes the place of labor. That is, in his scheme labor is only a solution to unemployment; it is not a problem to be theorized in itself, remaining as mysterious as the inner workings of the liver. He is not interested in how those "Fraytes" of commodities get produced (although perhaps neither were Donne's audience, the members of the Virginia Company in England, so long as they could be assured of a profitable return in time on investment). In fact, he argues that the Company should "*Post-pose* [*sic*] the consideration of temporall gaine" (274, emphasis in original). Waterhouse, and to some degree Smith as well, also bypass this problem, in seeing in the eradication of the Indians a means to substitute "ease" for "labour." The immediate opening up of great new capacities promised by the removal of Indians from so much fertile land made the question of labor seem temporarily irrelevant.

The immediate result of the Jamestown massacre was not retaliation against the Indians and a great opening up of resources, but consolidation and an uneasy truce. In the face of continued threat on the frontier, the Company reined in the straggling, smaller plantations. Smith recognized that this sort of concentration might lead to decreasing returns on tobacco cultivation, and thus to renewed attention to the question of how labor could be differently ordered in the colony. If England would not send a force to subdue the Indians, Smith suggests impaling the peninsula between the James and York rivers, a tract of land "much bigger then the Summer Iles, invironed with the broadest parts of those two maine Rivers, which for plenty of such things as Virginia affords is not to be exceeded, and were it well manured, more then sufficient for ten thousand men" (2:303). By a very rough estimate, this fortified territory would be about 500 square miles; at 10,000 persons, the population density would be twenty per square mile, or one person for every thirty-two acres, including nonarable land.[17] This was ample room by English standards, but not enough to sustain tobacco culture.[18]

The Crown's investigations into the management of the Virginia Company following the massacre, which were proceeding as Smith assembled the *Generall Historie*, prompted him again to offer his thoughts on the Virginia economy.[19] Of particular interest here is his explanation as to why, "though the Country be good, there comes nothing but Tobacco" from the colony: the "oft altering of Governours it seemes causes every man to make use of his time, and because Corne was stinted at two shillings six pence the bushell, and Tobacco at three shillings the pound, and they value a mans labour a yeere worth fifty or threescore pound, but in Corne not worth ten pound, presuming Tobacco will furnish them with all things" (2:327). Thus observing that a combination of market forces and the Company's regulations had determined the colonists' use of the land, Smith proposes to alter land practices by adjusting the market: "now make a mans labour in Corne worth threescore pound, and Tobacco but ten pound a man [per year], then shall they have Corne sufficient to entertaine all commers, and keepe their people in health to doe any thing, but till then, there will be little or nothing to any purpose" (2:327).

Although its goal differed from that of modern parity pricing mechanisms, this was the first American proposal for agricultural price supports. Smith observes that grain prices remain artificially low despite drastic underproduction while tobacco prices, on the other hand, have been driven up by unregulated demand. He argues for governmental intervention to correct individual farmers' crop selection. The Crown, which would take over the management of the colony after the dissolution of the Virginia Company, was in a position to provide price supports if it chose to do so, but Smith's idea would not be instituted. When the United States government first established agricultural price supports, during the decline in prices following the crash of 1929, the goal was to maintain the production of long established commodities (eventually including, of course, tobacco).[20] Smith had a different goal: he wanted to promote diversification. He did not propose a pricing system that would encourage the colonists to grow corn exclusively, but rather one that would discourage any sort of monoculture. He would make a man's labor in corn worth £30 per year, which would leave about half the man's labor (the remaining £20 to £30 per year) to be devoted to other endeavors: production of iron, potash, silk, glass, wine, and so on, or (if he must) a small amount of tobacco. Such endeavors could support a greater population density than could tobacco culture and would thus discourage the dispersed settlement patterns that had resulted in a weak social order and vulnerability to Indian attack.

Smith's program for diversification was complicated by the fact that the crop he wanted to regulate was becoming, in effect, the means by which any regulation would have to be accomplished. Smith measures a man's labor in pounds sterling, but in Virginia, tobacco itself "passes there as current Silver, and by the oft turning and winding it, some grow rich, but many poore" (2:314). Fortunes are made in the "turning and winding," that is, in exchanging tobacco for all other goods and services, which would benefit the large planters (with whom the small planters consigned their crop) and ultimately the merchants, for "there are so many sofisticating Tobacco-mungers in England, were it never so bad, they would sell it for Verinas [a luxury tobacco grown in Venezuela], and the trash that remaineth should be Virginia, such devilish bad mindes we know some of our owne Country-men doe beare" (2:267). Although corn was formally valued in shillings and pence, in practice it was valued as so many pounds of tobacco. Labor and initial capital investment on a given acre of land for corn and for tobacco were thus directly comparable not in terms of an abstract general equivalent (specie) but in terms of a local economic-environmental standard, the capacity of land and labor to produce a certain amount of tobacco. It might have seemed more profitable to grow tobacco for sale and to buy even corn for food than simply to grow one's own food and hope to exchange the surplus, at impossible rates, for clothing and other necessities. Soon, however, overproduction of tobacco would lead to declining prices and economic hardship. Over the next century and a half, Virginia would see various attempts to limit tobacco production in response to declining prices (see Chapter 4), but it would not see any successful means of promoting some other crop or industry to replace tobacco until a European market for grain opened up in the late eighteenth century.

Bermuda

The immediate problems of tobacco culture notwithstanding, Smith represents the Virginia environment overall as stable, capable of being productively ordered, and predictably rewarding industry, given proper management to encourage diversification. He is less certain that such would be the case in Bermuda, to which he turns next in Book V of the *Generall Historie.* Here we find numerous unusual occurrences. One William Millington goes fishing and is "drawne into the Sea by a fish, but never after seene" (2:357). Many are "suddenly surprized" by a strange, deadly "disease called the Feauges" (2:357). The whole colony is "neere devoured with rats" (2:366). The colonists try every means to eradicate them, but in the end the rats mysteriously just disappear. Some say that wild dogs and cats ate them while others say that an unusually cold winter killed them, but neither seems a satisfactory explanation. Smith thus reports that "as God doth sometimes effect his will without subordinate and secondary causes, so wee need not doubt" that here, in the absence of observable environmental reasons, the sudden disappearance of the plague of rats indicates "a secret worke of God" (2:367–68). The secret of such works would have been even harder to discover in the strange cases of a chicken that "had two heads" and of a cock that "did so frequently tread [a] Pigge as if it had beene one of his Hens, that the Pigge languished and died within a while after," whereat the cock resorted to a sow "in the very same manner" (2:387).

While the Virginians evidently did not witness such bizarre occurrences, other aspects of the Bermuda colonists' relation to the land are familiar from Smith's account of Virginia. Yet there are some twists that suggest uncertainty about the nature of the environment and its capacity to reward labor according to the predictable logic of exchange identified by the *Declaration*. Like the Virginians, the Bermuda colonists fail to plant enough corn, "endeavour[ing] so much for the planting Tobacco for present gaine, that they neglected many things that might have prevailed for their good, which caused amongst them much weaknesse and mortality" (2:367). By the Company's instruction they enact laws regulating the quality and quantity of tobacco that may be grown and "compell[ing] the setting of a due quantity of corne for every family" (2:380). However, those who do set enough corn are not necessarily rewarded even with their own sustenance. Those "good husbands" who "with much labour" husk and hang their corn to dry immediately after harvest find the crop ruined by a massive infestation of "Weavels," but those "that never cared but from hand to mouth," like the improvident Virginia Indians, simply throw their corn into a great heap to find that "not a graine of theirs had been touched nor hurt" by the insects. From this the planters conclude that there was "no better way to preserve it then by letting it lie in its huske, and spare an infinite labour" (2:386). Environmental factors also make tobacco production less certain in Bermuda than in Virginia, for "they are still much troubled with a great short worme that devours their Plants in the night, but all day they lie hid in the ground, and though early in the morning they kill so many, they would thinke there were no more, yet the next morning you shall find as many. The Caterpillers to their fruits are also as pernicious" (2:390). Trying to find an alternative crop, the Bermuda Company instructs the colonists to plant sugar cane, "for which," Smith remarks, "the Iland being rockie and dry, is so unproper, that few as yet have beene seene to prosper: yet there are others hold the contrary opinion, that there is raine so ordinarily, the Iles are so moist, as produceth all their plants in such infinit abundance: there is no great reason to suspect this, were it rightly used, more then the rest" (2:381). The meaning of this last clause remains unclear, adding to the sense of uncertainty. Adaptation to this unfamiliar environment seems to occur by chance, questioning English assumptions about the rewards of labor.

Summarizing the history of Bermuda to 1623, Smith finds that, considering the "accidents [that] there hapned," the colonists have been "set upon the highest Pinnacles of content, and presently throwne downe to the lowest degree of extremitie . . . the which to overcome, as it is an incomparable honour, so it can be no dishonour if a man doe miscarry by unfortunate accidents in such honourable actions." At present there are "complaints betwixt the Planters and the Company," at which point Smith "leave[s] them all to their good fortune and successe, till we heare further of their fortunate proceedings" (2:391). The Bermuda Company came through the Crown's investigations of 1623 more successfully than did the Virginia Company and continued to direct colonial activity until 1684.[21] This may account for Smith's emphatic repetition of "fortune" in his conclusion to Book V. Yet his equal stress on "accident" makes the issue of "fortune" uncertain. In contrast to Virginia, to prosper or even to get a living in this environment takes not so much industry as luck. The possibility of environmental management requires predictability, and it is not clear to Smith that such conditions obtain in Bermuda.

Smith's uncertainty would soon be reaffirmed by Edmund Waller, whose rather odd poem, "The Battle of the Summer Islands" (1638), takes its setting from Smith's account in the *Generall Historie*.[22] Waller begins by describing the productivity of the island, which enjoys the perpetual spring and various natural bounties noted by Smith. The report that "many a pound . . . of ambergris is found" on Bermuda's shores gives Waller a transition to his main subject, whaling.[23] (No doubt he recalled that in Smith's account a quarrel over ambergris had marked the beginning of the island's political economy.) Two whales are temporarily trapped in a tidal pool. The colonists in their greed

> Behold with glad eyes . . . a certain prey;
> Dispose already of the untaken spoil,
> And, as the purchase of their future toil,
> These share the bones, and they divide the oil. (100)

Yet that apparent "certain[ty]" is frustrated. As the colonists drive lances, pikes, and swords into the larger whale, "Blood flows in rivers from her wounded side," but they cannot kill her. The whale fights back, capsizing the boat—in mock-heroic conceit, "unhorsed," they "fall drenchèd in the moat" (101)—and a great battle ensues. The hunters at last think to aim cannon from the fort at the whales, but to what effect

> Great Neptune will not have us know, who sends
> A tide so high that it relieves his friends.
> And thus they parted with exchange of harms;
> Much blood the monsters lost, and they their arms. (103)

Samuel Johnson judged "the beginning" of this poem "too splendid for jest, and the conclusion too light for seriousness."[24] Yet precisely because of the modal confusion noted by Dr. Johnson, the jarring shift from praise of nature's bounty to mock-heroic economics, the poem is perhaps more interesting than Andrew Marvell's "Bermudas" (also indebted to Smith), to which it is sometimes compared. In Waller's poem, the colonists try to exploit the whales for profit; they fail, and in so doing evidently kill one or both of the whales. That is, they destroy what they would use. Waller does not envision the possible extinction of whales as a result of hunting (Herman Melville, two centuries later, would still deny this possibility), but he does describe the event as a misguided seeking after profit that ends in a waste of resources. This is a more complex understanding of the environmental situation than that given by Marvell, who merely represents the island's "eternal Spring" with all its bounty as a gift from God, who "makes the Figs our mouths to meet." God

> . . . hangs in shades the Orange bright,
> Like golden Lamps in a green Night.
> .   .   .   .
> With Cedars, chosen by his hand,
> From *Lebanon*, he stores the Land.[25]

Whether or not Marvell knew it, by the time he was writing this poem (c. 1653–54), proclamations had been issued to try to preserve the very cedars he mentions, which were being depleted at an alarming rate as land was cleared for orange or tobacco plantations. There was also some concern that the island's palmettos would soon be exhausted as the colonists cut them down to produce liquor and that other native fruits were being overharvested.[26] Waller's earlier poem had been written before such concerns were registered, yet evidently Waller saw in Smith's *Historie* a misuse of resources that prevented him from imagining a simple paean to nature's or God's beneficence. He did not write a lament for the demise of whales, of course, nor did he write a georgic on whale hunting (as Melville would do). This instance of destruction, and of the failure of labor and profit, contrasted with the environment's initial promise evidently left him puzzled. This is how Smith leaves Bermuda as well.

New England

In turning to New England, where his promotional interests lay as he compiled the *Generall Historie*, Smith finds neither the uncertainty of the Bermuda environment nor the mismanagement that had characterized Virginia's history to date. The report of the first colonial expedition in 1608, which represented New England "as a cold, barren, mountainous, rocky Desart," had been corrected by subsequent observation (2:399). Drawing on his own accounts in the *Description of New England* (1616) and *New Englands Trials* (1622) as well as other recent reports, Smith returns to the rhetoric of sixteenth-century promotional texts with proof of their environmental assessments.[27] Like those first promoters, Smith appeals to the authority of classical climatology (2:410–12). Yet he is not led into such dubious claims as the *True Declaration of Virginia* had made, that for

example "the Orenges which haue been planted, did prosper in the winter" at Jamestown (22). Smith only hints at the "gold and silver Mines"
that such climatology would predict while spending a great deal of time
describing the trade in fish, "which howbeit may seeme a meane and a
base Commoditie; yet who will but truly take the paines and consider
the sequell, I thinke will allow it well worth the labour" (2:410, 409).
This "sequell" is a story of how the Dutch trade Newfoundland fish to the
"Easterlings" for timber products and naval stores, and so on, and then
trade these in turn to the French, Spanish, and English "for what they
want"; the Dutch "are made so mighty, strong, and rich" by that trade
(2:409). As the first promoters looked to the New World for replacement
commodity environments, Smith claims that New England can supply
many things for which the Dutch have traded, going beyond the first promoters, however, in grounding these claims on firsthand observation: "I
dare boldly say, because I have seene naturally growing or breeding in
those parts, the same materials as all these are made of, they may as well
be had here" (2:412).

Smith thus projects replacing the circulation of certain commodities in
the increasingly complex European economy with labor invested in New
England sources of the raw materials for all these commodities. English
labor will replace European trade as the means of providing the value that
England consumes, for "labour is all [that is] required to take these necessaries without any other tax" (2:415). That is, Smith, like the first promoters, envisions bringing England's economy into direct engagement
with new environmental sources of wealth. He thereby emphasizes the
importance of the environmental-economic nexus at a time when English economists (as we saw in the conclusion to Chapter 1) were focusing
primarily on matters of trade, pricing, and currency valuation. It is true
that such a direct engagement had gone awry in Virginia, where the land
was used to produce only tobacco wealth, to the detriment of both the
colony's sociopolitical organization and, Smith thought, England's economy, which wanted not tobacco but iron, glass, timber, naval stores, wine,
flax, and so on. New England, however, promises to supply those sources
of material input that Virginia has failed to provide, and Smith catalogs
them at length at various points in Book VI. He would continue his criticism of Virginia's mistaken choices in the *Advertisements for the Unexperi-
enced Planters of New-England* (1631), by which time tobacco prices were
beginning to fall as a result of overproduction: "Now having glutted the
world with their too much overabounding Tobacco: Reason, or necessity,
or both, will cause [the Virginians], I hope, learne in time better to fortifie
themselves, and make better use of the trials of their grosse commodities
that I have propounded, and at the first sent over" (3:274). Meanwhile,

he turns his attention in Book VI of the *Generall Historie* precisely to such "grosse commodities" as timber, iron, and fish.

Smith follows earlier promoters in another respect as well, in considering New England as an outlet for England's idle, excess population. He frames this discussion, a standard topos of colonization literature as we have seen, with an essay on "covetousnesse." In this way he brings up what is repressed in More's *Utopia* (through the debasement of gold) and only implicit in earlier mercantilist arguments. The desire for wealth is a sort of *pharmakon*, both poison and cure. "Private covetousnesse," Smith argues, caused the falls of both Rome and Constantinople, and may do so for England, where now too many live "in borrowing where thou never meanest to pay," and by other such "shifts" and "tricks" (2:422, 421). All this subtractive activity, consumption without production, might be prevented if the gentry were to invest their fortunes, which their sons are now wasting, in colonization: "although you would wish them any where to escape the Gallowes and ease your cares, though they spend you here one, two or three hundred pound a yeere, you would grudge to give halfe so much in adventure with them to obtaine an estate, which in a small time, but with a little assistance of your providence, mighte bee better then your owne." The fathers themselves would "gaine more thereby" than they now possess in the estates that are being spent down (2:422). Thus while arguing against covetousness and its ill effects, Smith simultaneously appeals to covetousness in the promise of return on investment based on faith in economic growth.

Limits

Beneath Smith's warning is the assumption of England's growing population and finite resources. As in the writings of More, the younger Hakluyt, and Donne, the shadow of the gallows looms across the scene. Again, the alternative to this entropic scenario is to open the English economy to America's environmental capacities, "for our pleasure here is still gaines, in England charges and losse" (2:423). Yet Smith is the first promotional writer to show some caution in this regard, the first to think about limits. Having observed the depletion of resources in England, he brings this observation to bear on New England. For example, "of woods, seeing there is such plenty of all sorts" here, "if those that build ships and boats, buy wood at so great a price" in Europe, "what hazard will be here but to doe much better, and what commodity in Europe doth more decay then wood?" (2:415). The *Declaration* had remarked that in England, "our mils of Iron, and excesse of building, haue already turned our greatest woods into pasture and champion, within these few yeares; neither the scattered Forrests of England, nor the diminished Groues of Ireland, will supply the defect of our Nauy" (25). Not until 1662 would the English improver John Evelyn advocate planting the country's waste lands to trees as a domestic solution to this problem. Meanwhile, the American forests could supply England's "defect." Yet Smith worried that even New England's great plenty of trees could be mismanaged. Noting in the *Advertisements* that "the trees are commonly lower" than in Virginia, but of "much thicker and firmer wood, and more proper for shipping," he still cautions that the colonists not "carelesly or ignorantly cut downe all before you," as they have done in Virginia, "and then after better consideration make ditches, pales, plant young trees with an excessive charge and labour, seeing you may have so many great and small growing trees" (3:289). Woods needed to be cleared for farming of course— and in fact Smith goes on to describe the quickest way "to spoile the woods" for "pasture and corne fields," by girdling the trees—yet large trees, "ready growne to your hands," will protect fields, orchards, vineyards, and houses "from ill weather, which in a champion you could not in many ages" by planting new trees (3:291, 289).

Similarly, the fishing industry, which Smith argues will make no small part of New England's fortunes, is another instance in which the production of wealth would need to be balanced against the preservation of resources. Smith observes that the Newfoundland banks had "beene so long, so much over-laid with Fishers, as the fishing decaieth, so that many oft times are constrained to returne with a small fraught" (2:412). The implications for the future of New England's fishery are clear although Smith does not spell them out. Nor did others notice. William Wood, for example, who may have consulted Smith on this point when writing *New England's Prospect* (1634), does not mention the possibility of overfishing, even though he does wonder about the impact of colonization on another natural resource, asking whether "to much shooting will fright away the fowls" there.[28]

We should, of course, be wary of overreading Smith's environmental sensitivity. Smith represents New England as a land of such great plenty— "her treasures having yet never beene opened, nor her originals wasted, consumed, nor abused" (2:411)—that one could conclude he remains largely unconcerned about preservation. On the other hand, he is aware that environmental inputs to the economy entail the consumption of resources, and he registers the effects of consumption and waste in certain observable instances. His claim that New England's "originals" have never been "wasted" or "abused" distinctly implies the possibility that they could be. He contextualizes the issue of use in terms of ongoing natural cycles of production: "all these and divers other good things doe here for want of use still increase and decrease with little diminution"

(2:420). However, he has not yet seen an increase of economic inputs or outputs on a scale that significantly interfered with those natural cycles of "increase and decrease" he has observed so as to make him question the limits on use. If the fishing in Newfoundland "decaieth," that in New England provides a replacement. Forests, if rightly managed, continue to offer shipping and other material supports for agrarian and mercantile culture. Agrarian and mercantile culture, if rightly managed and not distracted by poor choices of resource use such as tobacco production, promise moderate wealth and security for all colonists. For Smith, even more than for the Hakluyts and their cohort, *not* to use the environment to increase the standard of living for England's poor, provide employment for the idle and debauched sons of the gentry, and generally undergird sociopolitical stability, would be a moral failing.

Smith thus agrees with the author of the *Declaration* that "God sels vs al things for our labour" but gives a more considered discussion of how to order that exchange. He becomes acutely aware as well of the difficulties of proper management in an emergent capitalist system, in which "the desire of present gaine (in many) is so violent, and the endevours of many undertakers so negligent, every one so regarding their private gaine, that it is hard to effect any publike good" (2:464). This question of the relationship among economy, environment, and the public good would continue to preoccupy thoughtful New Englanders and Virginians in different ways. In subsequent chapters we will turn first to New England, where Edward Johnson tested the theological surety of the *Declaration*'s economic analysis, and then to Virginia, where Robert Beverley imagined grounding the public good in the order of nature itself.

Chapter 3
"Wonder-Working Providence"
of the Market

In *New England's Prospect* (1635), William Wood makes a curious, nostalgic claim about the English environment. Evaluating the "Suitableness" of New England's climate for "English Bodies," he argues that "both summer and winter is more commended of the English there than the summer-winters, and winter-summers of England. And who is there that could not wish that England's climate were as it hath been in quondam times: colder in winter and hotter in summer? Or who will condemn that which is as England hath been?"[1] Over the course of this climatic change, English bodies have evidently remained the same, so that they will naturally respond positively to the extremes of the New England climate while retaining their essential Englishness, thereby refuting classical ideas of environmental determinism that could bear against colonization.[2] To move to New England, Wood suggests, would be to return to an earlier, better moment, before the seasons got mixed up as they are now, a moment more agreeable to the English. But what could have accounted for the change in climate to which he refers? We know that during the Little Ice Age, circa 1400 to 1700, England experienced especially cool periods, one of which was from 1590 to 1610.[3] Wood may have recalled the older generation's tales of those cold years, but since he probably would not have heard of warmer summers during the same period, it is quite possible that he thinks of "quondam times" as dating back to an even earlier era. Further complicating Wood's assessment was the effect of latitude. Because New England is "nearer the equinoctial than England," as Wood points out, its summer days are "two hours shorter and likewise in winter two hours longer than in England" (31). This fact might on the face of it predict that winters would be warmer in New England. Wood, however, remarks that New England winters are characterized by an "extremity" of "cold weather," which could be rendered "less tedious" by "build[ing] warm houses and mak[ing] good fires" (28). In any case, an argument from latitude could not explain England's climatic change.

Some force, then, has evidently been strong enough to overcome the effect of latitude.[4] Wood refers to another history that might be correlative. Comparing New England's soils with those of England, he concludes that "as there is no ground so purely good as the long forced and improved grounds of England, so is there none so extremely bad as in many places of England that as yet have not been manured and improved. . . . Wherefore it is neither impossible, nor much improbable, that upon improvements the soil may be as good in time as England" (35). England's soils had been made more productive during the era of agrarian improvement that began in the sixteenth century.[5] Given the same regime of improvement, New England's soils would some day be as good or better, following the historical trajectory of England. Yet correlating these two narratives of environmental change, we see that they run counter to each other according to Wood's purposes. If New England were to improve its soils through cultivation and manuring, as Wood recommends, it might experience England's climatic change. In fact Wood cites preliminary evidence of such change: "In former times the rain came seldom but very violently. . . . But of late the seasons be much altered, the rain coming oftener but more moderately, with lesser thunder and lightnings and sudden gusts of wind" (31). If this recent moderation of the weather is any indication, it seems that New England will eventually come to resemble contemporary England in terms of physical environment, with good soils but mixed-up climate. In that case, however, New England would no longer be the desirable environment that "England hath been" in "quondam times."

From the perspective of New England, Wood's countervailing environmental narratives embody conflicting forms of nostalgia: on the one hand, a desire for an earlier, purer era; on the other, a desire for England as the colonists knew it. Puritanism put additional pressure on this double nostalgia.[6] This pressure is especially evident in Edward Johnson's *Wonder-Working Providence of Sion's Saviour in New England* (1651), in which the project of recovering the ancient purity of church government and ordinances of worship intersects with the literal nostalgia (a longing for home) evident in the colonists' strenuous efforts to reproduce the economic-environmental context they had left behind.[7] As Johnson's first reader, the unidentified "T. H." of the preface, remarked, the colonists

forsooke a fruitfull Land, stately Buildings, goodly Gardens, Orchards, yea, deare Friends, and neere relations, to goe to a desart Wildernesse, . . . [where] the onely encouragements were the laborious breaking up of bushy ground, with the continued toyl of erecting houses, for themselves and cattell, in this howling desart; all which they underwent, with much cheerfulnesse, that they might enjoy Christ and his Ordinances in their primitive purity.[8]

Their nostalgia for the familiar English agrarian environment is here displaced onto another form of nostalgia, religious primitivism, after which point the emotional register of the passage shifts from loss to "cheerfule-nesse" and "enjoy[ment]."

While Johnson invokes the primitivist religious nostalgia that we may associate more closely with William Bradford, he is especially interested in describing the material recovery of the environment the Puritans had lost in their coming over. His account of "a civil engineering project in the wilds," as Cecelia Tichi characterizes it, is motivated by both the creation of the "new earth" promised in Isaiah 65:17 and Revelation 21:1 and the re-creation of the familiar English agrarian-commercial economy.[9] Thus he proclaims that the originally "rocky, barren" New England "wilder-ness" had by 1650 "becom a second England for fertilness," the colo-nists having evidently accomplished Wood's program of soil improve-ment (210). He reports that many New Englanders believed, as Wood had predicted in 1635, that "cutting down the woods, and breaking up the Land" through cultivation had "change[ed] the very nature of the seasons, moderating the Winters cold of late very much," creating a fur-ther resemblance (84).[10] New England was now the Puritan ideal of En-gland: a fertile, cultivated environment, "a mart for Merchants" and "a well-ordered Commonwealth, and all to serve his Churches" (247, 248). Bradford, in contrast, worries that such economic growth and concomi-tant geographical expansion would mean "the ruin of New England, at least of the churches of God there, and will provoke the Lord's displea-sure against them."[11]

Although Johnson and Bradford draw opposing conclusions from their observation of economic growth, they agree on the grounds of evalua-tion: both assess engagement with the land in terms of its implications for community.[12] For all that the Puritans valorized individualism (accord-ing to the Weberian understanding of Puritan culture), they also pro-fessed that economic activity ought, as John Cotton put it, to "tend to the publique good."[13] In proclaiming that New England had become "a well-ordered Commonwealth," Johnson assumed the systemic economic theory developed by the Hakluyts, but translated its understanding of the public good to the Puritan community. That is, New England was no longer the colonization project as the sixteenth-century promoters had imagined it, a mere boundary and transfer point between economy and environment. Rather, Johnson understood New England itself as a grow-ing economic system that required new environmental inputs and pro-duced certain outputs, including excesses. One excess evident early on was doctrinal liberty and its associated social disruptions: Johnson de-scribes the Antinomians for example as "daily venting their deceivable Doctrines," using the double meaning of "vent" we have seen in the Hak-luyts' writings (125). This excess was, they thought for a time, exported with Anne Hutchinson's banishment.[14] In general, Johnson sees New England much as the Hakluyts had described England, as a bounded but open system, and describes the exchanges of that system with its outsides. He notes trade with European economies but is especially interested in the exchanges between economy and environment evident in the expansion of New England's growing population onto "barren" lands and the conversion of these wastes to "fertilness." The individual enactment of such exchanges, however, threatens to exceed the colony's control. Near the end of his narrative, Johnson criticizes both outlying farmers and Boston merchants, those who are expanding the boundaries of the New England economy, as detrimental to the public good.

While in certain respects Johnson's critique anticipates later jeremiads that address economic concerns, such as William Hubbard's excoriation of land greed in his election-day sermon, *The Happiness of a People* (1676), it assumes a different understanding of boundaries. Where the typical second-generation jeremiad would construct consensus by accusing all New Englanders of sin and declension, Johnson's warning, like Bradford's lament, constructs church and political community by means of abjection, even as it assumes a universalizing economic ideology according to which all New England participated in the economic growth enabled by increasing inputs of land. The only possible limit Johnson identifies to such growth is the end of the world. Yet this limit remains untheorized in relation to the history's overall economic-environmental analysis. Johnson's late millennialism was, as at least one reader has recognized, a "supplement" to his "original purpose."[15]

A Relation of the First Planting

In addressing the linkages among economic, sociopolitical, and religious purposes, Johnson concerns himself extensively with agriculture, which sustained the Bay colony in its early years (as it did for Plymouth as well) and formed the basis of subsequent market relations.[16] From the arrival of John Winthrop and company in 1630 up to the depression of 1640–42, a substantial portion of the New England economy was oriented toward the production of agricultural surplus that could be sold to new immigrants. When the end of the Great Migration eliminated this source of demand, New England recovered from the resulting depression by finding new markets in the West Indies trade and the provisioning of ships (taking opportunities that Virginia passed by) without a major alteration of the pre-depression economic base, which remained largely agrarian through the 1640s.[17]

It proved ideologically significant that New England's agricultural production was oriented, theoretically at first and soon practically as well, toward livestock. Livestock production at once pointed forward, to economic growth and geographical expansion, and backward, toward God's original economic plan for his people. As John Winthrop put it, England "growes weary" with the burden of more population than it can support, but "the whole earth is the lords Garden & he hath given it to the sonnes of men, wth a generall Condition, Gen:1.28. Increase & multiply, replenish the earth & subdue it."[18] This ancient doctrine was now particularly applicable to America, for "god hath given to the sonnes of men a double right to the earth, there is a naturall right & a Civill right. . . . And for the Natives in New England they inclose noe land neither have any setled habitation nor any tame cattle to improve the land by, & soe have noe other but a naturall right to those countries Soe as if wee leave them sufficient for their use wee may lawfully take the rest, there being more then enough for them & us."[19] Livestock production, the most significant difference between English and indigenous farming methods, formed the foundation of Winthrop's theory of land tenure, for he argued that Christian society had progressed from a stage of primitive horticulture only, "when men held the earth in common every man soweing, and feeding where he pleased," to the state of agriculture now familiar to the English: "then as men and cattle increased they appropriated certaine parcells of ground by enclosing, and peculier manurance, and this in tyme gave them a Civill right" to the land they occupied.[20] William Wood adduced further environmental evidence of this right, noting the way in which cattle altered the land for their own benefit: "in such places where the cattle use to graze, the ground is much improved in the woods, growing more grassy and less weedy," thus better for pasture and able to support more cattle (34). Close grazing did in fact favor the growth of imported grasses over indigenous species, which were not adapted to coexist with cattle.[21]

Such changes had an environmental limit, however. Livestock not only provided a theoretical justification for taking more land, but soon materially required it. As William Cronon has demonstrated, livestock production was "a major reason for the dispersal of colonial settlements," because "market demand" coupled with "ecological pressures brought on by overgrazing . . . impelled colonial movement onto new land."[22] Agriculture-driven geographical expansion caused most of the English colonies' conflicts with the indigenous peoples.[23] It also brought the potential for internal social division and disruption, in the founding of new churches and local governments, in the colonies' competitions with each other to obtain Indians' lands, and, as the market developed, in the emergence of farmers as a distinct group with particular, although not necessarily always unified, interests, which threatened to fragment any coherent understanding of New England's public good.

William Bradford's familiar account of the individualization of agricultural production and its concomitant social effects provides a useful point of comparison for analyzing Johnson's larger account of the development of market relations. Bradford organizes Book II of *Of Plymouth Plantation* (from 1620 on) as a chronicle. At first, a regular feature of his annual accounts is a comment on the seasonal rhythms of spring planting and fall harvest, rhythms that gave shape to the lives of all Plymouth colonists.[24] These comments begin with the concern for subsistence and the now familiar story of Squanto teaching the colonists how to grow Indian corn. By the fall of 1623 there is a little extra and in the spring of 1626, "the Planters finding their corn (what they could spare from their necessities) to be a commodity (for they sold it at 6s a bushel) used great diligence in planting the same" (181). Significantly, this is Bradford's last mention of the agricultural seasons. In his entry for the following year, he describes the creation of the freehold—the individual allotment of land, accompanied by the first division of livestock as individual property (187–88)—but he does not describe spring planting as he had done for previous years. Bradford turns away from the agricultural seasons at the point when the freehold is created, rather than at the point of an earlier agreement, in 1623, that the Plymouth planters "should set corn every man for his own particular" (120). The 1623 reorganization resulted in increased crop production at a time when the colony was duly concerned for the stability of its food supply. By contrast, the creation of the freehold in 1627 was a solution to the ongoing economic problems posed by the colony's relation to the London Adventurers. Plymouth had both to furnish its own subsistence and to discharge a debt to its financiers, and so concerned itself with surplus production. The freehold structure differed from the previous, communitarian organization not merely in its individualization of labor (as in the 1623 reorganization), but more importantly in its individualization of capital: the means of production, both cattle and land, were for the first time allotted as private property. Farmers became independent producers engaging individually in market relations. Meadows remained in common for a time, but by the early 1630s, a time of rapid economic growth, even these were in private hands.[25] Thus the passage from 1627 more significantly registers the end of a communitarian and the beginning of a bourgeois mode of life at Plymouth.[26] The first absence of the agricultural seasons from Bradford's text at precisely this point marks a conceptual shift from a cyclical to a linear sense of time as the agricultural market develops—a shift from the annual renewal inherent in both farm life and the church calendar to a more teleological orientation that, in the end, Bradford's narrative could not sustain.

Bradford's concern over the threat posed to community by the development of market relations is particularly evident in the entry for 1632. With the beginnings of the Great Migration, corn and cattle rose to a great price, by which many were much enriched and commodities grew plentiful. And yet in other regards this benefit turned to their hurt, and this accession of strength to their weakness. For now as their stocks increased and the increase vendible, there was no longer any holding them together, but now they must of necessity go to their great lots. They could not otherwise keep their cattle, and having oxen grown they must have land for plowing and tillage. And no man now thought he could live except he had cattle and a great deal of ground to keep them, all striving to increase their stocks. By which means they were scattered all over the Bay quickly. (253)

Bradford feared that this would mean "the ruin of New England" (254). The particular occasion of his lament is the founding of a new church at Duxbury, a direct result of the new growth of the agricultural market. Although the Plymouth colonists had for some time been trading some corn to the Abnakis in exchange for furs and were using grain as a medium of exchange among themselves, the recent arrival of the Massachusetts Bay colonists created a great demand for agricultural surplus. Production, as Bradford notes here, now became heavily oriented toward cattle, which were a commodity in themselves and were also used to improve the land for cropping by giving manure and pulling plows. In the resulting geographical expansion, families moved to distant allotments with more extensive meadows; some at Duxbury "sued to be dismissed and become a body of themselves" (253). Yet Plymouth continued the privatization and hierarchization that had begun with the 1627 allotments, as Bradford notes: "to prevent any further scattering from this place and weakening of the same, it was thought best to give out some good farms [on previously unallotted land at Marshfield] to special persons that would promise to live at Plymouth, and likely to be helpful to the church or commonwealth, and so to tie the lands to Plymouth as farms for the same; and there they might keep their cattle and tillage by some servants there and retain their dwellings here" (253). The eventual result, as "this remedy proved worse than the disease," was a reversal of the plan's intent: some landowners rented out their town lots and removed to the new lots while others left for new lands entirely (254). More churches were founded after Duxbury, first at Marshfield and then at Eastham. As desires for market embeddedness and church community seemed to be moving in opposing directions, Bradford's summary comment evokes nostalgia for an earlier time of unity, figuring the original church as "an ancient mother grown old and forsaken of her children" (334). This figure, however, implicitly naturalizes geographical expansion, for children would, as they reached adulthood, need farms of their own.

Others viewed this growth positively on purely economic grounds. William Wood, for example, argued that it checked soil exhaustion as well as generating wealth. For him, geographical expansion was as a logical source of new environmental inputs: "Whereas some gather the ground to be naught, and soon out of heart, because Plymouth men remove from their old habitations," Wood argues that "they do no more remove from their habitation than the citizen which hath one house in the city and another in the country for his pleasure, health, and profit." This profit is enabled by expansion with a view to crop rotation and fallow cycles which might increase yields. Thus he asks, "what if they do not plant on [their old lots] every year? I hope it is no ill husbandry to rest the land, nor is always that [land] the worst that lies sometimes fallow" (35).

Johnson, like Bradford, begins with the question of subsistence, but works toward a larger consideration of the market than does Wood, linking this consideration to the geographical principle that shapes his text much in the way that the agricultural seasons had, for a time, shaped Bradford's. In general, the organizing structure of *Wonder-Working Providence* consists of accounts of the founding of towns punctuated by moments of crisis and memorable events.[27] Johnson begins his story, however, prior to the voyage over, by having Christ's herald address the prospective colonists' concern for subsistence: "assuredly (although it may now seeme strange) you shall be fed in this Wildernesse, whither you are to goe, with the flower of Wheate, and Wine shall be plentifull among you (but be sure you abuse it not)" (26). While specifying these two Biblical foods (as if to leave the basic diet of maize a surprise for the colonists), the herald does not mention livestock, which are prominently featured in both the Bible and contemporary justifications for colonization. These are, indeed, the barest conditions of subsistence, especially in contrast to the market orientation of later cattle production. However, horticulture allows for Johnson's subsequent metaphor, which herding would not. Alluding to John Winthrop's "Modell of Christian Charity" (which he probably heard aboard the *Arbella*),[28] Johnson follows his assurance of subsistence with a warning: "seeing you are to be set as lights upon a Hill more obvious than the highest Mountaine in the World, keepe close to Christ that you may shine full of his glory, who imployes you, and grub not continually in the Earth, like blind Moles" (29). For all his later glorification of the fact that the New England environment has become "a second England for fertilnes" (210), in this originary moment Johnson valorizes simple subsistence and shares Bradford's concern about the effects of an intensive concentration on farming, grubbing too much in the earth. The binaries inherent in the text's figures (high/low, light/dark) introduce a potential for various forms of social division.

Johnson manages such divisions by turning toward a larger perspective on the landscape. In this turn, he deals with two competing conceptions of the New England community: "the cohesive and the expansive."[29]

On the one hand, the colonists valued the organic society defined most famously by Winthrop's "Modell," with its images of the colony as a city on a hill and its inhabitants as a single body united in Christ. On the other hand, the Biblical rationale for colonization—God's command to Adam, "againe renewed to Noah," to "increase & multiply, replenish the earth & subdue it," which the colonists interpreted as a mandate to settle what they considered to be unimproved lands—led to geographical dispersal.[30] However, the seeds of expansion were sown even in Winthrop's sermon on social cohesion, when he proposed the first settlement as a prospective model of colonization, so "that men shall say of succeeding plantacions: the lord make it like that of New England."[31] Johnson again seems to take Winthrop as his inspiration in the accounts of the planting of towns over inland Massachusetts and the Connecticut valley that comprise the bulk of his narrative. The generic structure of these accounts— a topographical description of the town site, a report on the gathering of the church, an encomium on the minister, and an assessment of the town's economy circa 1650—offered a paradigm for the potentially infinite reproducibility of communities. But was there anything beyond their formal homology, produced in Johnson's historical representations (although perhaps only there), that could guarantee both the internal cohesion of each town and the cohesion of all towns into a common-wealth?

The founding of Salem at Naumkeag prior to the arrival of Winthrop and company gives Johnson his first historiographical challenge of this sort. Salem's first colonists were "a mixed lot" including Anglicans, Puritans, and the Separatists whom Roger Williams would come to find congenial.[32] They would soon see a conflict between Winthrop and their first governor, John Endecott. Those who emigrated with Endecott, according to Johnson, passed their first winter with "but little corn, and the poore Indians so far from relieving them, that they were forced to lengthen out their owne food with Acorns." The hardship of bare subsistence produced a sort of social cohesion, although not the sort that Johnson approves, since "they made shift to rub out the Winters cold by the Fire-side . . . turning down many a drop of the Bottell, and burning Tobacco with all the ease they could, discoursing betweene one while and another, of the great progresse they would make" come spring (45). Instead of drinking and smoking they ought to have been "building the Temple for Gods worship" (46). Two clergymen did begin to cut stones for a meeting house but soon left off: one "betooke him to the Seas againe, and the other to till the Land, retaining no simbole of his former profession, but a Canonicall Coate" (46). The choice of the latter, William Blackstone, to farm independently (he eventually moved to Rhode Island) rather than to preach, reactivates the potential for social division evident beneath Johnson's first comments on agricultural subsistence, a division that will recur later in his narrative.[33]

Of Succeeding Plantations

As Johnson goes on to describe the colony's geographical expansion, he links the social structure of the towns with the agricultural economy. The typical mode of colonial settlement in New England was the nucleated farming community, with land generally allotted according to the prospective owner's estate—that is, according to his capital, especially in the form of cattle, and his capacity to mobilize labor power.[34] This is the practice Johnson describes in the case of Woburn, where the Massachusetts General Court granted the seven founders, one of whom was Johnson himself, "such an ample portion, both of Medow and Upland, as their present and future stock of cattel and hands were like to improve" (213). There was also an ideological check on allotment. At Plymouth, for example, Bradford says that original freeholds went only to those shareholders who were "able to govern themselves with meet discretion, and their affairs, so as to be helpful in the commonwealth" (186–87). Dedham would similarly exclude the "contrarye minded."[35] Johnson too notes that at Woburn, "such as were exorbitant, and of a turbulent spirit, unfit for a civil society . . . came not to enjoy any freehold" (213). Even so, wealth and social position were equally or in some cases more important than church membership; at Boston, for example, some of the second group of freeholders admitted in 1631 were not church members.[36]

Land patterns thus played a major role in establishing a community's social structure, which could be more or less hierarchical, and more or less harmonious, depending on the comparative estates of the original settlers. Witness the contrast between Springfield and Dedham. Springfield, in its early decades, was characterized by a market-oriented economy, the prevalence of tenancy (as opposed to owner-operation of farms), and a highly stratified social structure.[37] In Dedham during the same period, a high level of land ownership and a subsistence-oriented economy produced what Kenneth Lockridge has argued was a society of "one class, one interest, one mind."[38] Although this seems an overstatement, it is clear that different economies produced different social relations in the two towns. Stephen Innes has demonstrated that "Springfield did not enjoy the strong communitarianism of Dedham"; in the former, "conflict, not communalism, was the rule."[39]

However, it suits Johnson's historiographic purpose to identify less market development in fractious Springfield than in socially cohesive Dedham. Dedham, according to Johnson, "abound[s] with Garden fruits fitly to supply the Markets of the most populous Towne [Boston, ten miles away], whose coyne and commodities allures [*sic*] the Inhabitants of this Towne to make many a long walk" (179). It is a godly town, its piety evidently reflected in its agricultural success: the inhabitants "have continued in much love and unity from their [Church's] first foundation, hitherto translating the close, clouded woods into goodly corn-fields" (180). In Springfield, the inhabitants also "live upon husbandry," but there the similarity ends. Although Johnson does note that they have "the benefit of transporting their goods by water," he gives no account of present commerce, remarking only on the demise of the fur trade some years earlier (a falsification, since the fur trade remained very active up to King Philip's War).[40] Instead, he hurries to report that "more then one or two" in that town have been "greatly suspected of witchcraft." In an accompanying poem, he also exhorts the minster there, George Moxon, to combat the "errors" that "crowd close to thy self and friends" (237).[41]

Johnson implicitly forms an alignment between a town's piety and social cohesiveness and its degree of participation in the market, manipulating his economic data accordingly. In forming this alignment, he elides the complicated history of Springfield's first decade—a history that would have demonstrated the sophistication of the town's market economy. By 1641, all but two of Springfield's original freeholders had left, driven off by a poor harvest in 1637, the depression of 1640, or the difficulty of coexisting with the town's most powerful citizen, William Pynchon. In their place, Pynchon recruited indentured servants and tenant farmers, who became both his employees and his customers. The Pynchon family soon owned most of the productive farm land. Also in 1641, Pynchon arranged the town's secession from Connecticut and admission to Massachusetts, in the process bringing his own legal and political authority over the town into line with his economic power. All of this indicates the highly capitalized nature of Springfield's economy even in its first decade.[42] However, telling such a story would distract Johnson from his strategy of demonstrating an alignment between market relations and social cohesion.

Johnson usually comments favorably on the emphasis on cattle production that led to the founding of new towns. One key instance of ambivalence, however, concerns "the beginning of the Churches of Christ, to be planted at Canectico," at Hartford (105). Here, Johnson's faith in the market seems to waver at least momentarily. In 1635, the residents of Cambridge,

seeing that Tillage went but little on, Resolved to remove, and breed up a store of Cattell, which were then at eight and twenty pound a Cow, or neare upon, but assuredly the Lord intended far greater matters than man purposes, but God disposes. These men, having their hearts gone from the Lord (Land),[43] on which they were seated, soone tooke dislike at every little matter; the Plowable plains were too dry and sandy for them, and the Rocky places, although more fruitfull, yet to eate their bread with toile of hand and how (hoe) they deemed it unsupportable; And therefore they onely waited now for a people of stronger Faith then themselves were to purchase their Houses and Land, which in conceipt they could no longer live upon. (106)

The farmers' interest in shifting to cattle production here evidently indicates their desire to increase their participation in the market, yet Johnson questions their motivation.[44] He does not express concern over the logistics of getting cattle to market, and in fact many inland towns were founded expressly for the purpose of specializing in cattle.[45] Rather, the issue concerns the farmers' attitude toward the land and the resulting religious and social structure.

Another perspective on the Hartford migration is provided by Winthrop's journal. Reporting on the debate of the General Court, Winthrop summarizes the Cambridge farmers' "principal reasons for . . . removal," giving the matter somewhat less economic emphasis than does Johnson:

1. Their want of accommodation for their cattle, so as they were not able to maintain their ministers, nor could receive any more of their friends to help them; and here it was alleged by Mr. Hooker, as a fundamental error, that the towns were set so near to each other.
2. The fruitfulness and commodiousness of Connecticut, and the dangers of having it possessed by others, Dutch or English.
3. The strong bent of their spirits to remove thither.[46]

Unlike Johnson, Winthrop's interpretation of agriculturally motivated dispersal does not identify a deliberate shift from grain to cattle production but rather assumes that the Cambridge economy was from the beginning oriented toward cattle. He further links economic choices to a concern over the "maintenance" of the religious and social structure— the payment of the clergy—rather than identifying a desire for greater market embeddedness as its own self-sufficient motive. Winthrop's comparative minimization of economic motives here is noteworthy because he disapproved of the proposed migration and presumably could have adduced such motives as criticisms.[47]

According to Johnson, the Cambridge farmers are wanting in "Faith"— in the land, in their labor and that of their servants, even perhaps in the Lord. Yet as it turns out, he does not need to find a historiographic resolution at this point to any conflicts generated by expansion and by what he perceives to be a desire for increased market embeddedness. The Cambridge migrants' motivations for settlement in Connecticut are subsumed in the larger divine plan soon to be enacted: "the Lord intended far greater matters than man purposes, but God disposes." This "greater matter" is the Pequot War, the causes of which Johnson discerns not as the colonists' usurpation of lands, such as Hartford, in the Connecticut River valley but rather as the "great insolency" of the Pequots, who were "big, swollen with pride" and directed by the devil, the "Serpent, who was the grand signor of this war" (147, 148). If Johnson realized that territorial expansion caused the war, this in itself would not have greatly troubled him; Winthrop and others had sufficiently justified the theory of *vacuum domicilium*.[48] Even so, the war was a crisis, a historical rupture, and Johnson textually marks it as such. Discussed at the opening of Book II of *Wonder-Working Providence*, the war seems to indicate a new beginning for Johnson, allowing him to resolve any residual tension from Book I that dispersal and fragmentation, or competition among the colonies for Indians' lands (also noted by Winthrop), might have created by narrating the Pequot War as a great, unifying event, in which the colonists come together as one body.[49]

That This Wilderness Should Turn a Mart

The next material crisis facing New England, the depression of 1640–42, resulted, like the Pequot War, from the overextended growth of the agricultural economy. Bradford reports in his entry for 1641 that "now that cattle and other things began greatly to fall from their former rates and persons began to fall into more straits, and many already being gone from them . . . it did greatly weaken the place. And by reason of the straitness and barrenness of the place, it set the thoughts of many upon removal" (314–15). Reading this passage in relation to his earlier lament over the Duxbury division we can see that in Bradford's view, it is not the particular state of the economy, but rather the very existence of the market with its evidently inevitable fluctuations, that works against the public good. Conditions of prosperity and depression alike compel people to leave the original social nucleus: both require the input of new land resources.

Winthrop's analysis of the depression begins by noting the decline of the immigration that had driven expansion through the 1630s. Hope for the success of the Puritan revolution

caused all men to stay in England in expectation of a new world, so as few coming to us, all foreign commodities grew scarce, and our own of no price. Corn would buy nothing: a cow which cost last year *L*20 might now be bought for 4 or *L*5, &c. and many gone out of the country, so as no man could pay his debts, nor the merchants make return into England for their commodities, which occasioned many there to speak evil of us. These straits set our people on work to provide fish, clapboards, plank, &c. and to sow hemp and flax (which prospered very well) and to look out to the West Indies for a trade for cotton. The general court also made orders about the payment of debts, setting corn at the wonted price, and payable for all debts which should arise after a time prefixed.[50]

The West Indies would prove to be a good market for agricultural produce and other commodities in the 1640s, as Winthrop anticipates here; this market would help New England to recover from the depression.[51]

Johnson's account of the depression ignores the issue of government intervention raised by Winthrop, minimizes the issue of outmigration noted by both Winthrop and Bradford, and delays any mention of the West Indies trade until much later in the narrative, in order to use the depression as an occasion to review the colony's accomplishments to date. He opens his chapter by reporting that

this Spring Cowes and Cattle of that kind (having continued at an excessive price so long as any came over with estates to purchase them) fell of a suddain in one week from 22 *l.* the Cow, to 6. 7. or 8. *l.* the Cow at most, insomuch that it made all men admire how it came to pass, it being the common practice of those that had any store of Cattel, to sell every year a Cow or two, which cloath'd their backs, fil'd their bellies with more varieties then the Country of itself afforded, and put gold and silver in their purses beside. (209)

However, rather than inquiring into the causes at which he hints—the fall of the prices, indicating overproduction relative to market demand—Johnson immediately draws back to ask "the Reader . . . to take notice of the wonderful providence of the most high God toward these his new-planted Churches," such that

this remote, rocky, barren, bushy, wild-woody wilderness, a receptacle for Lions, Wolves, Bears, Foxes, Rockoones, Bags, Bevers, Otters, and all kinds of wild creatures, a place that never afforded the Natives better then the flesh of a few wild creatures and parch't Indian corn incht out with Chesnuts and bitter Acorns, now through the mercy of Christ becom a second England for fertilness in so short a space, that it is indeed the wonder of the world. (209, 210)

Johnson thus makes the depression into an occasion for celebration. Especially since the market was beginning to recover by 1642 (the date of this entry), to read the effects of the depression as deprivation would be to deny the market's ultimate beneficence and its guidance by a hand that is not invisible but rather, at times, much in evidence to those who will see it. Elsewhere, for example, he notes that "the Lord hath of late altered the very course of the Heavens in the season of the weather, that all kind of graine growes much better than heretofore," attributing to divine intervention the climatic change that William Wood had thought resulted from increased tillage (154).

Johnson represents the depression not as a case of overproduction, which would cast God's providence in a negative light, but as a case of undercirculation, which raises the issue of the human understanding of that providence. One ought to respond to a depression not by cutting back, he argues, but rather by increasing consumption, which in turn will drive production. Emphasizing how well the colonists have fared in such a short time, in food, clothing, and housing, Johnson goes on to suggest that any depression-era privations were self-imposed, as with those who "hoard up in a wretched and miserable manner, pinch themselves and their children with food, and will not tast of the good creatures God has given for that end, but cut Church and Commonwealth short also. Let not such think to escape the Lords hand with as little a stroke, as the like do in other places" (211). The commonwealth suffered because commodities were not circulated; this resulted from the human error of not adjusting consumption to production. Much of the passage is thus devoted to the terms of economic recovery, the increase of trade, a point that Winthrop had also noted. For example, considering the abundance of wool, flax, and hemp, Johnson reports that, "for cloth, here is and would be materials enough to make it; but the Farmers deem it better for their profit to put away their cattel and corn for profit, then to set upon making cloth; if the Merchants trade be not kept on foot, they fear greatly their corne and cattel will lye in their hands" (211). There is a hint here that the increase of trade threatens the stability of the class structure, for the recent "plenty of [imported] clothing hath caused much excess of late in those persons, who have clambered with excess in wages for their work." However, Johnson sets aside this concern to be treated later—"the theam of our next discourse, after the birds are setled" (see below)—in order to continue his overview of providential development (211). Reviewing livestock holdings, land in tillage, orchards, and so on, Johnson concludes with the suggestion that individual economic status is, ultimately, divinely mandated: "thus hath the Lord incouraged his people with the encrease of the general, although many particulars are outed, hundreds of pounds, and some thousands, yet there are many hundreds of labouring men, who had not enough to bring them over, yet now worth scores, and some hundreds of pounds; to be sure the Lord takes notice of all his talents, and will call to accompt in time" (211–12).

When Johnson gives his final overview of the New England economy, in effect a calling to account, we find a state of diversified production, intensified market relations, and significant environmental transformation. The sign that "the Lord [has] been pleased to turn one of the most hideous, boundless, and unknown Wildernesses in the world in an instant, as 'twere (in comparison of other work) to a well-ordered Commonwealth, and all to serve his Churches" is the diversification that was evidently lacking during the depression (248). In his account of the depression only two occupations had been mentioned, farmer and merchant; now there are many:

Carpenters, Joyners, Glaziers, Painters, follow their trades only; Gun-smiths, Lock-smiths, Black-smiths, Naylers, Cutlers, have left the husbandmen to follow the Plow and Cart, and they their trades; Weavers, Brewers, Bakers, Costermongers, Feltmakers, Braziers, Pewterers, and Tinkers, Ropemakers, Masons, Lime, Brick, and Tilemakers, Cardmakers to work, and not to play, Turners, Pumpmakers, and Wheelers, Glovers, Fellmungers, and Furriers are orderly turn'd to their trades, besides divers sorts of Shopkeepers, and some who have a mystery beyond others, as have the Vintners. (248)

Agricultural expansion had provided the base for all this diversified production, but where once all "follow[ed] the Plow and Cart," now farmers are represented as being one group among many. Such a change would have been especially remarkable to first-generation New English and English readers alike, since extensive by-employment among farmers was the norm at this time in England.[52] Johnson, in contrast, describes non-agricultural occupations not as by-employments but as prospering trades in their own right. With the emergence of the division between agricultural producers and consumers indicated in Johnson's song for occupations, the yield of the land has undergone a conceptual transformation into trade commodities. It was "for a long time the great fear of many, and those that were endued with grace from above also, that [New England] would be no place of continued habitation, for want of a staple-commodity" (246). But these fears were allayed, for "in a very little space, every thing in the country proved a staple-commodity, wheat, rye, oats, peas, barley, beef, pork, fish, butter, cheese, timber, mast, tar, sope, plank-board, frames of houses, clabbord, and pipestaves, iron and lead is like to be also" (246–47). The existence of staple commodities implies the existence of a staple, that is, a place where such commodities are traded: a bounded economy in itself.[53]

Again, though, there is a hint of disruption in connection with market relations, as there had been in the passage on recovery from the depression. Again, Johnson defers a full account: "of late the Lord hath given a check to our traffique, but the reason may be rendered hereafter" (247). Since his narrative is rapidly approaching the present of 1650, however, this deferral cannot be indefinite.

Minded of the End of Their Coming Over

In tracing Johnson's rhetorical management of the disruptions accompanying agrarian development, it will be helpful to return to another originary moment. Johnson's early account "of the laborious worke

Christ's people have in planting this wildernesse, set forth in the building the Towne of Concord, being the first in-land Towne" refers back to the opening commission of Christ's herald (discussed above) and provides a practical illustration of the premarket conditions represented there (111). At Concord, little at first serves to distinguish the colonists' farming practices from those of the people whose fields they usurped. The settlers live in "poore Wigwames" and suffer other deprivations: "the want of English graine, Wheat, Barly and Rie, proved a sore affliction to some stomacks, who could not live upon Indian Bread and water, yet they were compelled to it till Cattle increased, and the Plowes could but goe" (114, 115).[54] Cattle production, as we have seen, provided significant theoretical and material distinctions between English and indigenous agricultural methods and proved central to the development of the economy in general. Prior to the increase of cattle, when production was oriented toward subsistence, even the primary social division between clergy and farmers had been temporarily erased: "the toile of a new Plantation being like the labours of Hercules never at an end, yet are none so barbarously bent (under the Mattacusets especially) but with a new Plantation they ordinarily gather into Church-fellowship, so that Pastors and people suffer the inconveniences together" (114). This passage marks a state that is, if anything, more primitive than that envisioned by the colonists' original commission from Christ's herald, which specified that "you are not to put upon [the ministers and teachers] anxious Cares for their daily Bread" (26). Class as well as occupational distinctions are temporarily erased: "in this Wildernesse-worke men of Estates speed no better than others" since what few cattle there are die for want of winter fodder (114). Such leveling is only remarkable of course because a hierarchical class structure is the norm which the community will soon attain. Except in this passage, describing a time when all alike are "forced to cut their bread very thin for a long season" (114), Johnson takes the stratification of wealth as a given, and he simply ignores the contribution of landless laborers (often a numerous group, as in the case of Springfield) unless they prove disruptive, such as those who "clamber with excess in wages" (211). He does, however, become interested in the social divisions that emerge when towns such as Concord have come into market-level agricultural production, that is, when a clear division emerges between producers and consumers.

The division between clergy and farmers, for example, temporarily blurred in the initial work of forest colonization such as the first planting of Concord, returns as the market develops, and now the ministers do have "anxious Cares"—cares about how to perpetuate themselves as a class. In his account of the establishment of Harvard College, Johnson rails against the difficulty of the "promotion of learning" in an agrarian economy (198). "Many people in this age," he laments, "are out of conceit with learning, and . . . although they were not among a people who counted ignorance the mother of devotion, yet were the greater part of the people wholly devoted to the Plow . . . but *how to have both go on together, as yet they know not*" (200, emphasis added). The college being founded by a private grant, the "Commissioners of the four united Colonies" now look for public support, but it is "very much neglected" (201). "Verily it's a great pity," Johnson goes on to lament, that "such ripe heads as many of them be, should want means to further them in learning" (204–5). In order to produce those "ripe heads" of ministers, "this Colledg hath brought forth, and nurst up very hopeful plants" (201). Johnson closes with a "rustical rime" in which the current president, Henry Dunster, is metaphorically characterized as a cultivator, come from England as actual farmers had done, to labor in and improve New England's fields:[55]

> Industrious Dunster, providence provides,
>> Our friends supply, and yet our selves no lack:
> With restless labour thou dost delve and dung,
>> Surculus[56] set in garden duly tended,
> That in Christ's Orchard they, with fruit full hung,
>> May bless the Lord, thy toil gone, them expended,
> Thy constant course proves retrograde in this,
>> From West to East thy toil returns again,
> Thy husbandry by Christ so honored is,
>> That all the world partaketh of thy pains. (205)

Describing the ministerial class in terms of agricultural metaphors throughout this passage, Johnson deals with the farmers' resistance to funding the college by rhetorically forcing an analogy of interests.

The tension that surfaces in the passage on Harvard often remains submerged within the structure of the chapters on town-founding, which report on both the clergy and the state of the agricultural economy usually without describing conflict between the two. In certain cases however, such as Salem and Springfield, a conflict was clearly evident, and another instance would surface in the case of Braintree, where some landowners refused incorporation. Their motivations evidently concern taxation, for Johnson remarks, "how it comes to pass I know not, their officers have somewhat short allowance. They are well stored with cattel and corn, and as a people receives, so should they give" (197–98). However, the landowners who resisted incorporation and taxation were not actually residents of Braintree, but absentee landlords, wealthy farmers of Boston (of course already paying taxes there) who were granted additional lands in the mid 1630s.[57] Many of the residents of Braintree at this time were servants and tenants who operated the Bostonians' farms and thus would have no say on the issue of incorporation. These residents, Johnson says, include many "Erronists" who "countenance all sorts of sinful opinions, as occasions serves [*sic*], both in Church and Commonwealth, under the pretence of Liberty of Conscience" (197). Conflating the categories of residency and ownership, Johnson seems reluctant to provide a full explanation for the social and religious disruption accompanying agricultural expansion at Braintree. Instead, he draws back to issue a general warning, reminding the "Reader . . . of the admirable providence of Christ for his people in this, where they have been in a low condition, by their liberality they have been raised to much in a very little time: And again, in withdrawing their hands have had their plenty blasted" (198).

As Johnson begins to close his narrative, such a prophecy seems to have been fulfilled. In Chapter VIII of Book III, brief hagiographic mentions of founding elders soon give way to nostalgic critiques of certain merchants and farmers. If this tonal shift seems strange after the praise the latter groups have garnered so far, it suggests a growing uneasiness on Johnson's part about the social and religious effects of the development of New England's agrarian economy. God corrects the merchants, by means of two shipwrecks, because "they would willingly have had the Commonwealth tolerate divers kinds of sinful opinions to intice men to come and sit down with us, that their purses might be filled with coyn, the civil Government with contention, and the Churches of our Lord Christ with errors" (254). These merchants are a source of excess. The additions they enable—sinful opinions, contention, errors—detract from the colony's original purity of purpose. Curiously, Johnson does not mention the case of Richard Keayne, who was indicted for selling nails at greater than a just price.[58] He may have thought that Keayne's price gouging affected only the internal workings of the local economy, not New England's larger exchanges with its outsides, Europe or the wilderness, which defined its identity.

Johnson spends more time on the correction of farmers, for in their subsumption of more and more land (necessary for New England's continued economic growth) they threatened the community's control over economic inputs and outputs at least as much as did the merchants. "The Lord," reports Johnson, "was pleased to awaken us with an Army of caterpillars, that had he not suddainly rebuked them, they had surely destroyed the husbandmans hope." The particularity of this warning is emphasized, in both scope and direction. The caterpillars stripped some fields bare, left others verdant, and "in some fields they devoured the leaves of their pease, and left the straw with the full crop, so tender was the Lord in his correction" (253). Others remarked this event as well. The table of "memorable occurrences" in Samuel Danforth's almanac for 1648 similarly describes the caterpillars' particularity in fully stripping some fields, leaving others intact, and in others eating only the leaves but not the seed. His account in the 1649 almanac may have suggested the direction taken by Johnson: "the Lord sent multitudes of caterpillars amongst us, which marched thorow our fields, like armed men, and spoyled much corn."[59]

Where Danforth left the application of this providence implicit, Johnson argued that it was meant to remind all New Englanders "of the end of their coming over, but chiefly the husbandman," who is in special need of correction because he is a particular source of social and religious disruption. The farmers'

over eager pursuit of the fruits of the earth made some of them many times run out so far in this Wilderness, even out of the sweet sound of the silver Trumpets blown by the laborious Ministers of Christ, forsaking the assembly of the Lords people, to celebrate their Sabbaths in the chimney-corner, horse, kine, sheep, goats, and swine being their most indeared companions, to travel with them to the end of their pilgrimage, or otherwise to gather together some of their neerest neighbours, and make a preachment one unto another, till they had learn'd so much, that they could away with none other teaching. (253)

Bradford had noted a similar instance of divine correction, an earthquake that occurred in 1638 "at the same time divers of the chief of this town were met together at one house, conferring with some of their friends that were upon their removal from this place, as if the Lord would hereby show the signs of His displeasure, in their shaking a-pieces and removals from one another" (302). His qualification ("as if") may suggest that he is less certain than Johnson, even though he sees God's punishment (if it is that) for social disruption as enduring longer. For "divers years" afterward, he observes, summers were cold and harvests consequently poor, "but whether [the earthquake] was any cause," he "leave[s] it to naturalists to judge" (303).

The farmers Johnson criticizes may have chosen to take new land either to seek greater participation in the developing capitalist market or to escape the market's oppressive effects and so perpetuate an accustomed mode of living.[60] Either motivation could be characterized as an "over eager pursuit of the fruits of the earth." In either case the farmers should be understood as responding to the effects of an economy deliberately oriented toward growth, but in one interpretation they embrace the market and in another they resist it. If they are seen to embrace it, as Bradford suggests, they become harbingers of a spiritual decline accompanying material prosperity, the scenario of second-generation declension so familiar to scholars of the Puritan era. If, on the other hand, they are seen deliberately to refuse or minimize market embeddedness, for Johnson they demonstrate by counterexample the positive spiritual effects of the market. Yet by the latter characterization, the outlying farmers who preach only unto their "neerest neighbors" might also be thought of as having at least the primitive warrant of Christ's words in Matthew 18:20: "For where two or three are gathered together in my name, there am I in the midst of them." Such ambiguity suggests that, while farmers were increasingly identifiable as a distinct occupational group, this group did not constitute a class, that is, a group perceiving themselves to have a common set of interests, goals, and endowments.[61] Although farmers were potentially at odds with other social structures such as local governments, the clergy, or the mercantile establishment, they would not necessarily act predictably or in unison in aligning themselves with or against these structures, partly but not entirely because of their own disparate economic situations as large landlord, small freeholder, tenant, laborer, or servant. By the late eighteenth century, as we will see in Chapter 5, this sort of ambiguity and disparity, now on a national scale, would trouble the likes of Hector St. John de Crèvecoeur, Thomas Jefferson, Benjamin Rush, and Charles Brockden Brown. If, in New England's first generation, agricultural history had already become too complex to be subsumed under a paradigm that promised social cohesion, nevertheless the force of nostalgia, an appeal to an original unity of purpose, remained rhetorically powerful.

The Happiness of a People

Wonder-Working Providence and *Of Plymouth Plantation* were written for an elite readership and necessarily enjoyed limited circulation.[62] However, sermons on the topics they addressed would soon be heard by ordinary people—not the farmers whom Johnson criticizes for "celebrat[ing] their Sabbaths in the chimney-corner," but those who did attend meeting (253). In 1657, the Dorchester congregation heard Richard Mather warn that

the condition of many amongst you . . . is such as necessarily puts you on to have much imployment about the things of this life, and to labour with cares & paines taking in the workes of husbandry, and other worldly business . . . & experience shews that it is an easy thing in the middest of worldly business to lose the life and power of Religion, that nothing thereof should be left but only the external form, as it were the carcass or shell, worldliness having eaten out the kernell, and having consumed the very soul & life of godliness.[63]

William Hubbard would phrase the point more strongly. His sermon *The Happiness of a People*, preached on election day 1676 in Boston, exemplifies a later transformation of Johnson's and Bradford's nostalgic critiques concerning ideological disunity and disruption among farmers.

King Philip's War, like the Pequot War, had resulted from agriculture-driven environmental expansion. Hubbard observes that in afflicting the colonists with that war, "God our great Land-lord, layes his arrest upon our tillage."[64] He discerns "the spirit of covetousness" as one of the two chief sins provoking God's "chastisements in letting loose the rage of the Heathen [a]gainst us" at this time (the other sin, of course, is pride) (58, 59). In illustrating of the prevalence of "covetousness," he gives a brief history of the agricultural economy:

They that first came over hither for the Gospel could not well tell what to doe with more Land then a small number of acres yet now men more easily swallow downe so many hundreds and are not satisfied. If they be but never so little streight-ened, they must remove where they have room enough, that can part with a good neighbourhood, and the beautifull heritage of Church communion, or Gospel Worship, to pitch with Lot in the Confines of Sodom. . . . Is it a wonder then that we find war in our gates. God is knocking the hands of New-England people off from the world, and from new Plantations, till they get them new hearts, resolved to reform this great evill. (58–59)

Conveniently forgetting that Bradford, whose history he read in manu-script, had lamented this will to expansion during the first generation, Hubbard now holds that generation up as a model of proper economic-environmental behavior. While our usual understanding of the jeremiad as a ritual of consensus formation fits this instance in many respects, Hubbard's critique of the economy does not point toward an ideological func-tion of giving "free enterprise the halo of grace," but rather the contrary.[65] Hubbard represents all men of the second generation as facing the same temptations and having the same motive. The previous generation are also retrospectively portrayed as having a single, pure motive, to advance "the Gospel." Now that "the hands of New-England people" are being "knock[ed] off from the world, and from new Plantations," the common-wealth is unified under a different aegis, everyone's common participa-tion in the sin of coveting land. Even so, the very form and performance of Hubbard's sermon reenacts the division noted by Johnson between clerical and agricultural interests, for Hubbard is a minister excoriating the sins of farmers.

Where Johnson saw only "some of" the farmers dispersing beyond the reach of authority, a particularity emblemized in the particularity of the caterpillars' destruction, Hubbard in contrast generalizes to all New En-gland, as he needed to do when responding to the all-encompassing dis-aster of King Philip's War and the pervasive fear that the colonial charter would be revoked. Beyond this, Hubbard stresses the farmers' desire to accumulate capital, to "swallow down so many hundreds" of acres and so increase their worldly estates, inducing an increasing spiral of economic growth and geographical expansion as the consumption of new resources fuels that growth. Johnson, by contrast, identifies as the primary evil not the acquisition of land itself, but a single-minded focus on the activity of farming, the "over eager pursuit of the fruits of the earth." That is, where Johnson sees a sometimes misdirected desire for productivity, Hubbard finds the obverse of productivity, figuring accumulation as the consumption of resources. Unlike Johnson, who had emphasized greater circulation as the logical economic response to any increase in production, Hubbard registers the negative consequences of farmers' increasing market embeddedness, even if he thinks that they should acquiesce to being "a little streightened." In this sense, Johnson more clearly anticipates the strain of Puritan rhetoric that served to legitimate American capitalism than does Hubbard, who remains critical—even though it is Hubbard and not Johnson who preaches during the "decisive moment" in which we generally assume the jeremiad took on its modern ideological form.[66] On the other hand, Hubbard uses jeremiadic rhetoric to construct a national consensus, making all New Englanders into farmers, all of whom act the same way, whereas Johnson deploys a structure of abjection, the othering of those subsistence farmers whose material practices may indicate an "alternative" ideology—one that, as Raymond Williams defines it, "the dominant culture is unable in any real terms to recognize."[67]

*   *   *

Although Johnson wanted to believe in the beneficence of the market, I have suggested that he did not fully understand (or did not want to understand) the effects of market forces or religious beliefs on some farmers' material decisions. Even as he describes and evaluates what amount to individual economic choices regarding available resources and practices, he represents the market as operating according to its own logic—a logic that he hoped was God's. He so emphasizes the macroscopic view in his composite picture of New England's economy circa 1650 that he provides no economic plan or vision for the future. The structure of his history prevents it, for subsequent wilderness colonization and town-founding would simply be more of the same, as envisioned by the sermon that Winthrop had preached before the Bay colonists had yet landed on American ground. Economic growth would drive expansion onto new resource bases and expansion would in turn drive more growth. Thus pushing capitalist theory to the limit of ideological and environmental containment in the course of his narrative, Johnson reaches the end of history (some three and a half centuries earlier than did Francis Fukuyama). Unable fully to align the social and religious consequences of the Bay colony's rapid economic development with the primitivist ideals of Puritanism—unable, probably, even to understand the nature of this conflict as Bradford was clearly able to do—Johnson can finally advance either a millennialist historiography or none at all. In his day, as in ours, the only resolution to contradictions posed by an ideology promising both the public good and unlimited free-market growth through ever increasing environmental inputs must take place outside of historical time and physical space. But then, the price of cattle, grain, and land would not much matter in "the time of the fall of Antichrist" (268).

Chapter 4

"Admirable Oeconomy"
Robert Beverley's Calculus of Compensation

Near the end of *The History and Present State of Virginia* (1705), Robert Beverley pauses to remark that

> the admirable Oeconomy of the Beavers, deserves to be particularly remember'd. They cohabit in one House, are incorporated in a regular Form of Government, something like Monarchy, and have over them a Superintendent, which the *Indians* call *Pericu*. He leads them out to their several Imployments, which consist in Felling of Trees, biting off the Branches, and cutting them into certain lengths, suitable to the business they design them for, all which they perform with their Teeth. When this is done, the Governor orders several of his Subjects to joyn together, and take up one of those Logs, which they must carry to their House or Damm, as occasion requires. He walks in State by them all the while, and sees that everyone bear his equal share of the burden; while he bites with his Teeth, and lashes with his Tail, those that lag behind, and do not lend all their Strength. They commonly build their Houses in Swamps, and then to raise the Water to a convenient height, they make a Damm with Logs, and a binding sort of Clay, so firm, that though the Water runs continually over, it cannot wash it away.[1]

Fascinating for their humanlike culture as well as valuable for their pelts, beavers were discussed frequently in colonization literature. Their apparent industry and cooperative behavior were often held up as models for imitation.[2] Beverley's access to this topos came by way of John Banister's natural history manuscripts, on which he often drew in writing the *History and Present State*.[3] Banister, misinterpreting various aspects of beavers' behavior, describes their labor as being directed by an "Overseer walking with them, & biting or lashing forward with his tail those that keep not up & bear their equal weight."[4] Beverley deletes the word "overseer" from Banister's text, probably in an effort to generalize the analogy beyond slave labor. He adds a discussion of the beavers' "Government," thereby transforming Banister's observations into a hopeful allegory of colonization. A monarch rules supreme. Particular works are directed by a "Governor" who "walks in State" superintending his "subjects." Beyond the governmental direction of labor, Beverley is interested in the ends of that labor, the beavers' success in shaping their environment. The beavers, that is, show not only industry but also foresight and perseverance: faced with the dismal prospect of living in a swamp, they build a house as many as "three Stories high," design a dam to turn the swamp into a lake thus making their residence "convenient," and repair the dam as necessary when it is broken, "mak[ing] it perfectly whole again" (312).

Apparently, beavers can accomplish almost everything that the Virginians could not during the first century of colonization. Unlike the colonists, who "have not one Place of Cohabitation among them, that may reasonably bear the Name of a Town," the beavers "cohabit" in a way that encourages cooperative projects (58). Despite the tendency of a few to "lag behind" in their labors, they follow the direction of their governors. Their governors in turn show wisdom in their choice of projects, directing engagements with the environment so as to suit the needs of their society and foster the public good. In this way, Beverley's allegory of the beavers takes up a primary theme of the American georgic. From the *True Declaration of Virginia* and John Smith's *Generall Historie* through Thomas Jefferson's *Notes on the State of Virginia* and beyond, the environmental literature of Virginia often criticizes the settler culture's economy while proposing that proper management would sustain a well-ordered commonwealth.[5]

Motivating but at the same time complicating Beverley's critique was his apparent fascination with the image of America as a new Eden, an image that represented the possibility of a certain kind of human harmony with the environment.[6] He remarks, for example, that the Indians "seem'd to have escaped, or rather not to have been concern'd in the first Curse, *Of getting their Bread by the sweat of their Brows*" (17, emphasis in original). The "State of Nature" embodied by the Indians contrasts markedly with the industrious, regulated, yet sometimes violent society of the (one would assume at least equally natural) beavers (233). Both models are brought to bear as Beverley turns his attention directly to the Virginia colonists themselves, who exhibit neither the Indians' happiness nor the beavers' industry. Rather, they

depend altogether on the Liberality of Nature, without endeavoring to improve its Gifts, by Art or Industry. They spunge upon the Blessings of a warm Sun, and a fruitful Soil, and almost grutch [grudge] the pains of gathering in the Boun-ties of the Earth. I should be ashamed to publish this slothful Indolence of my Countrymen, but that I hope it will rouse them out of their Lethargy, and excite them to make the most of all those happy Advantages which Nature hath given them. (319)

The Indians' ease and "Pleasures"—for their "bare planting a little Corn, and Melons" evidently "took up only a few Days in the Summer" (156)— have become the colonists' "Lethargy" and unhappiness. These shifts elicit the questions that are at the heart of the *History*. How could the

"Liberality of Nature" call forth the sense of lack that so disturbs Beverley here? Why the Virginians' grudging attitude toward the manifest "Bounties of the Earth"? What need—indeed what possibility—of improvement in paradise?

We can seek the answers to these questions by reading the *History* referentially, mapping the metaphorics of paradise onto contemporary economic reality. The paradox of simultaneous abundance and lack that animates the passage quoted above was a fact of tobacco culture. This was not quite the paradox of "plentie and famine . . . together" that had been identified by the *True Declaration of Virginia*, but it did derive from a similarly overdetermining focus on a single commodity.[7] In 1610 it was gold, but soon tobacco replaced gold as the object of the colonists' economic obsession. Precisely because tobacco was so abundant in early eighteenth-century Virginia, there was not enough of it, and the colonists often "grutch[ed] the pains of gathering" it.

Beverley's critique of the tobacco monoculture thus evokes the entropic scenario of the first promoters' motivations for colonization. The Hakluyts and their cohort, we recall, proposed that an economic lack caused by the overproduction of one commodity (wool) and the underproduction of others could be remedied by opening up England's economy to new environmental inputs and outputs in America. Unlike the Hakluyts, however, Beverley does not propose a westering colonization. Rather, he suggests that the economy should be opened to new capacities within the already patented lands of Virginia itself by means of a shift toward diversified production.[8] His projections were no doubt influenced by the contemporary "georgic revolution" in England, which developed in the seventeenth century with the rise of Baconian science and its influence on agrarian improvement.[9] The English improvers maintained the Hakluyts' assumptions regarding the economy as a national system and linked disciplined labor to the successful creation of both individual and national wealth. From England's perspective, Virginia may have been, as Beverley describes it, the "most profitable Colony, depending on the Crown" (5). Yet England's profit was Virginia's deficit, for tobacco planters were burdened by low prices, debt, taxes, and labor costs, and were thus unable to capitalize new projects.[10] Because the tobacco economy was structurally predisposed against diversification, it seemed that Virginia could not fully participate in England's georgic spirit.

Arguing that the tobacco monoculture had in effect reached an economic limit, Beverley exhorted the colonists to engage more fully with what he identified as the Virginia environment's double prospect for improvement, by bringing their modes of production into line with the environment's diverse natural capacities. Recognizing however that nearly a century of tobacco culture had already wrought changes in the land, so as to render some of its precolonial "Native Pleasures more scarce, by an inordinate and unseasonable Use of them," he argued that increased attention to environmental management could, potentially, compensate for such losses (156). Thus returning to the calculus of compensation first described in Virgil's *Georgics*, Beverley in certain respects anticipated the approach taken by later georgics such as George Perkins Marsh's *Man and Nature*. As Marsh would argue (*pace* Emerson), we can enjoy no original relation to the universe. Rather, we can work only from our own location in economic-environmental history, even as a retrospective imagination of the environment's supposed original state, often figured as a bountiful paradise, provides a guide against which to measure our engagements.

The pastoral moments in the *History*—Beverley's adversions to myths of Eden or the Golden Age—thus serve to register dissatisfaction with the colonists' present economic engagements. Even these passages, however, often bear a georgic inflection, as if to question the pastoral's modal lack of economic consciousness. And yet rare moments of pure, uninflected pleasure remain, in which pastoral would seem to shear itself off from its dependence on georgic and attach itself directly to nature. Indicating the solidification of Virginia's class structure and the incipient codification of gentry class values in environmental representation, these moments predict the difficulty that direct imitators of Virgil's *Georgics* would subsequently face during the eighteenth century as they attempted to accommodate the realities of slave labor to the georgic's program of improvement. The pastoral strain of Beverley's text thus ultimately cut against the transformative potential of his environmental vision.

Monoculture and Diversification

Beverley begins by casting doubt on the metaphorics of Eden in the very first page of his *History*. He notes that the captains of the Roanoke expedition of 1584, "being over-pleased" with the profits gained by trading with the indigenous inhabitants, "gave a very advantageous Account of Matters," representing Virginia as "so delightful," "so agreeable, that Paradice it self *seem'd* to be there, in its first Native Lustre" (15–16, emphasis added). Such mistaken perceptions of environmental capacity continue through the present moment, exemplified by the intemperance of sailors who stop to refresh themselves after loading tobacco from plantation wharves: "they greedily devour all the green Fruit, and unripe Trash they can meet with, and so fall into Fluxes, Fevers, and the Belly-Ach; and then, to spare their own Indiscretion, they in their Tarpawlin Language, cry God D—— the Country" (297–98). Precisely in this intemperate use, we see the image of paradise dissolve, for we do not imagine fluxes and fevers in that happy state. Beverley sees that the Englishmen who overindulge in Virginia's fruits do not adjust their behavior to environmental requisites. They cannot simply eat and drink freely of nature's ever ripe bounty. Rather, as the georgic instructs, they need to observe nature to learn how to use it wisely.

Although, from the first settlement of Jamestown on, neither the Virginia Company nor the Crown did much to foster wise use, Beverley finds the colonists themselves much to blame for their exclusive concentration on tobacco production. Under the Company, "the chief Design of all Parties concern'd was to fetch away the Treasure from thence, aiming more at sudden Gain, than to form any regular Colony, or establish a Settlement in such a Manner, as to make it a lasting Happiness to the Country" (55). "Making so much Tobacco, as to overstock the Market," the colonists soon see the dissolution of the Virginia Company and the Crown's first attempt to govern their economy by setting production limits and "advis[ing] them rather to turn their spare Time towards providing Corn and Stock, and towards the Making of Potash, or other Manufactures" (49–50). Yet they ignore this advice, for the easy availability of land and

the Ambition each Man had of being Lord of a vast, tho' unimprov'd Territory, together with the Advantage of the many Rivers, which afforded a commodious Road for Shipping at every Man's Door, has made the Country fall into such an unhappy Settlement and Course of Trade; that to this Day they have not one Place of Cohabitation among them, that may reasonably bear the Name of a Town. (57–58)

Nor did Virginia fare better under the Protectorate. Beverley notes that Cromwell's Parliament passed the first of the Navigation Acts, which forbade the Virginians to trade "with other nations [i.e., the Dutch], at a time when *England* it self was in Distraction" and could not "take off above half the Tobacco they made" (64–65, emphasis in original). With the restoration of Charles II, the colony was subjected to an even "severer Restraint," the Navigation Act of 1660, which prohibited the import of any goods that had not been shipped from England. This "Misfortune," observes Beverley, "cut with a double Edge; For, First it reduced their Staple Tobacco to a very low Price; and, Secondly, it raised the Value of *European* Goods, to what the Merchants pleased to put upon them" (70, emphasis in original).

In this context, Governor William Berkeley devised a substantial plan for economic diversification. He was requested to prepare a report on the Virginia economy by the recently formed Council for Foreign Plantations, which was subsequently published as *A Discourse and View of Virginia* (1663).[11] The Council was primarily interested in increasing the Crown's revenues by any means and in solidifying England's claims to empire. Its first effort in this regard had been to devise the Navigation Act of 1660. Yet tobacco revenues would not increase substantially unless prices increased as well. The Crown was thus at least nominally willing to entertain any kind of proposal for the increase of revenues. Berkeley proposed a shorter shipping season, which would increase competition among merchants, and a one-year stint (a limit on tobacco production), both of which would theoretically drive up prices. The capital generated thereby could be used to bolster the Virginia economy by developing new commodities, which Berkeley hoped would be "more lasting and necessary" than monocultural staples like tobacco. He had seen that in the West Indies, staples such as "Sugar or Indico," "like flowers . . . were quickly at their full growth and perfection, and a *Nil ultra* is fixt on them."[12] Such staples had quickly reached their limit; the islands were planted to capacity and no additional increase of revenues was to be had from them. Virginia would soon be in the same straits.

Berkeley thus anticipates Beverley in arguing against a monocultural approach to environmental use. He opens his pamphlet by giving "a short description of the Scituation" of Virginia "as to the *Climate*," thereby reminding the Council of what promoters since the Hakluyts had repeatedly emphasized: not only fertility but great variety (1, emphasis in original). Thomas Hariot's natural history of Virginia, for example, had expanded the Hakluyts' catalogs into prescriptions for the production and use of numerous commodities. Alluding to the climatological orientation of such texts, Berkeley observes that Virginia "lyeth within the Degrees of 37. and 42. (*Mariland* included) which by all is confess'd to be a scituation capable of the diversities of all Northern and Southern commodities, some Drugs and Spices excepted, which *Florida*, on whose borders we are newly seated, may also probably produce" (1, emphases in original). With greater warrant than the Hakluyts and their cohort, Berkeley moves from a classical climatology modified by American experience to a familiar reiteration of their catalogs of diverse commodity inputs:

Now for those things which are naturally in [Virginia], they are these, Iron, Lead, Pitch, Tar, Masts, Timber for Ships of the greatest magnitude, and Wood for Potashes.

Those other Commodities, which are produced by industry, are Flax, Hemp, Silk, Wheat, Barley, Oats, Rice, Cotton, all sorts of Pulse and Fruits, the last of which in that perfection, that if the taste were the onely judge, we would not think they were of the same *species* with those from which they are derived to us in England. The vicious ruinous plant of Tobacco I would not name, but that it brings more money to the Crown, then all the Islands in *America* besides. (2, emphases in original)

Although this natural diversity had been turned to a "vicious ruinous" monoculture, Virginia would produce all things if the colonists "had but a mean price to quicken their industry" (3). Thus implicitly returning to Captain Smith's first proposals for agricultural price supports, Berkeley suggests that an additional tobacco tax of one penny per pound be levied to finance the "publick charges of the Countrey," providing the necessary capital to turn the colonists away from tobacco and toward numerous other occupations (8). During the 1650s, the Crown had experimented with tobacco stints and with bounties for the successful cultivation of silk, wine, and other products. These had benefitted a very few of the wealthier planters but had not drawn the Virginians away from tobacco.[13] The stint that Berkeley proposed in 1663 would probably not have had the effect he intended (none of the others did) even if Maryland had agreed to join Virginia in imposing limits on production.

Despite Berkeley's *Discourse* and the example of his experiments in the production of potash, flax, hemp, and so on, which Beverley characterizes as quite promising, the colonists did not diversify. Virginia continued to be afflicted by "the Disease of planting Tobacco" (71). One symptom of this disease was the "intestine Commotion" of Bacon's Rebellion, which erupted from "the extream low Price of Tobacco, and the ill Usage of the Planters in the Exchange of Goods for it," as well as high taxes and the restrictions imposed by the Navigation Acts (74–75). Underlying all these were conflicts over land use.[14] By the early 1670s, the colony's western frontier was the fall line, the area in which rivers flowing down through the Piedmont entered the coastal plain. According to a treaty that Governor Berkeley had negotiated in 1646 after subduing the Paumunkeys and their tributaries, the Indians were not to come within most areas below the fall line without his permission. In practice, this treaty meant that Berkeley controlled the fur trade, a control that Nathaniel Bacon argued was "illegall and not grantable by any power here present as being a monopoly."[15] Although the Berkeleyites had every interest in restraining English settlement from encroaching beyond the fall line, tobacco culture required a great deal of land because of the necessary fallow cycle. An individual could cultivate three or four acres of tobacco per year. On good ground, tobacco could be grown for three years, after which a field was sometimes planted to corn for another couple of years but then in any case allowed to go fallow. The appearance of maturing pine woods on a fallow tract, after about twenty years, signaled that the fertility was sufficiently restored for another crop cycle.[16] Including corn land, pasture, and woodlot (a source of timber for tobacco hogsheads as well as fuel, fencing, and building material), at least fifty acres were needed per working hand.[17]

Supposedly to ease the mounting pressure for land, the Virginia Burgesses set up an agency nominally to buy out large proprietary grants, freeing them for settlement, and authorized an extra tax to fund the buy-out. However, no tax was really necessary for the purpose, since James, Duke of York had already ordered the vacation of the proprietary grants without cost to the colony. In fact, these revenues were appropriated instead by Governor Berkeley and his coterie for their personal gain. Facing a tax burden that was now one-quarter to one-half of the average planter's income, many became disaffected. Yet land could have been freed up through an adjustment in the basic tax structure. Taxes were levied based on polls, or heads (every free adult male over sixteen). Small planters argued that land taxes, rather than poll taxes, would prevent the elite from engrossing large tracts.[18] Thus when raids along the frontier gave Bacon an excuse to question Berkeley's Indian policy and lead a punitive expedition, many land-hungry planters were willing to join him. Willing too were slaves, indentured servants, tenants, and others of the lower classes who saw in a conquest of the Indians hopes for land of their own.[19] When Berkeley refused to authorize a military commission for Bacon in this expedition, Bacon easily turned his men against the seat of government, using their complaints about oppressive taxes and hopes for land as his rallying cries.

As Stephen Webb has argued, Bacon's Rebellion marked a turning point in the colonial relation.[20] This turning point had environmental implications. Prior to the Rebellion, the Crown had at least nominally encouraged economic diversification in Virginia. It had (ineffectually) imposed limits on tobacco production by various means and had offered bounties for significant production of some especially desirable commodities. After the Rebellion, the Crown ceased to encourage diversification but rather concentrated solely on increasing tobacco production and enhancing tobacco revenues. Any alteration to Virginia's tobacco culture would now have to come from the impetus of the colonists themselves.[21]

Despite England's discouragement of diversification, Beverley thought the moment ripe for intervention. He may have sensed that the turn of the century marked a transitional era in tobacco culture.[22] Chesapeake tobacco prices had dropped steadily from 1620 to 1680, while exports had steadily increased. For a while, gains in productivity had offset declining prices so that tobacco planting had remained profitable, but as demand and prices leveled off after 1680, many planters found that they could barely cover their costs even if they produced at maximum capacity. In any case, the planters were perpetually in debt, mortgaging next year's crop against this year's purchases of import goods. At the same time, the character of the labor supply in Virginia was beginning to change. Virginia had drawn settlers in as England—in a scenario envisioned by More and the Hakluyts—pushed laborers out. The rate of immigration continued to increase through the 1650s as the labor supply in England continued to exceed demand.[23] From the 1670s on, however, a decreasing labor supply in England and drastically reduced opportunities in Virginia for servants who lived out their indentures combined to discourage immigration and drive up labor costs. As indentured servants became less available, planters reluctantly began to use African slaves. Since the slave population did not begin to reproduce itself until the 1720s or 1730s (most slaves imported until then were male), planters had to devote a substantial portion of their capital to maintaining their labor supply if they bought slaves. All of these factors coalesced into a sorting process. As the tobacco economy stagnated, from the 1680s through the 1710s, many marginal producers—smaller planters, those who produced lower quality tobacco, or those who had poorer land—got out of the business. Many sold up and emigrated to frontier areas such as Southside Virginia or North Carolina, often shifting their production to grain, meat, timber, or naval stores. Some small planters remained, but during these "thirty years of hard times," large planters gained social and economic dominance in the Chesapeake region.[24]

During this transitional era, land management decisions in Virginia's coastal plain came increasingly to reside with the gentry, the class that might be expected to read Beverley's advice and put it into practice— if they were not stung too sharply by his criticisms. Beverley attempts to manage the latter point in Book I by focusing those criticisms on the unpopular Governor Francis Nicholson as he brings his history up to the present. As lieutenant governor, Nicholson had shown some promise, being instrumental in passing "Acts for Encouragement of the Linnen Manufacture, and to promote the Leather Trade, by Tanning, Currying, and Shooe-making," and so on (100). On being named governor in 1698, however, Nicholson reversed his position on diversification:

He talk'd then no more of improving of Manufactures, Towns, and Trade. Neither was he pleased to make the Acts of Assembly the Rule of his Judgements, as formerly: But his own All-sufficient Will and Pleasure. Instead of encouraging the Manufactures, he sent over inhuman Memorials against them, which were so opposite to all Reason, that they refuted themselves. In one of these, he remonstrates, *That the Tobacco of that Country often bears so low a Price, that it will not yield Cloaths to the People that make it*; and yet presently after, in the same Memorial, he recommends it to the Parliament, *to pass an Act, forbidding the Plantations to make their own Cloathing*; which, in other Words, *is desiring a charitable Law, that the Planters shall go naked*. (104, emphases in original)

So far from forming a well-ordered commonwealth, the planters under Nicholson's governance are not even able to provide for their basic human needs. Nicholson, who was as unpopular as Beverley makes him out to be, was recalled soon after the *History* was published. When Beverley revised the *History* for a second edition in 1722, he muted some criticisms, such as a charge of religious hypocrisy, but retained this passage concerning Nicholson's misdirection of Virginia's economy.[25]

Virginia's Prospect

Having brought his history up to date, Beverley undertakes to educate his fellow colonists and prospective immigrants on the Virginia environment's potential for diversification, in effect elaborating on earlier proposals such as Berkeley's *Discourse*. Although Book II purports to describe "the Natural *Product and Conveniencies* of Virginia; in its Unimprov'd State, before the *English* went thither," Beverley in fact treats natural history as the social history of both the colonists' and the Indians' interactions with the environment (115, emphases in original). From Pliny's natural history on, the genre conventionally emphasized use. The work of contemporary natural historians was in theory moving away from the question of use and toward the environmental decontextualization of Linnaean taxonomic biology. Yet in practice, even the Linnaeans would preserve at least some of the social dimension of nature that had characterized earlier studies, a full description typically encompassing a plant's "whole history," including "its names, its structure, its external assemblage, its nature, and its *use*."[26] Where taxonomy and related operations such as the visual illustration of organismic structures focused on the specimen in itself, disassociating it from its surroundings, considerations of use returned the specimen to an environmental context by way of human interaction.

In drafting Book II of the *History*, Beverley relied on John Banister's natural history manuscript "Some Observations on Beasts, Birds, Fishes, Insects &c. Naturall to this Country" for accounts of the spring run of herring, characteristics of Indian corn and other vegetables, and a great deal of other such information.[27] This manuscript contains minimal taxonomic description but rather emphasizes production and use. Banister's catalogs of flora and fauna, on the other hand, are primarily taxonomic with a minimum of other information. Even here, however, considerations of use appear when they are least expected. Take for example his entry on a familiar plant: "Hedera trifolia erecta foliis glabris. It is the Poysonweed, and is alsoe called arbor Virginiana tinctoria, from the qualitie of its juice, which on linnen turnes black & will not loose its colour in the wash, with it our Negroes mark their shirts."[28] The species name itself gives particular traits of this variety of poison ivy (three leaflets, upright habit, smooth leaves). The catalog entry goes on to report to an

English audience that even such a noxious weed contributes to Virginia's economy, providing a readily available source of dye for slaves' clothing. Sometimes, of course, considerations of use are merely implicit, as in Banister's entry for grapes, which gives only the season of harvest: "Vitis. Fox grapes Black & White. and many other kinds sweet and sowre, or as we call them Summer and Winter grapes."[29] In general, Banister was interested in such information as "what quantity of that kind of Cotton they have begun to send [to England] will be produced on half an acre of ground with such quantity of seeds in a hill, & the hills at such distance," as well as in less use-oriented information.[30] Working in the tradition of Francis Bacon, he does not imagine a theoretical split between pure and applied science. The appreciation of nature for its own sake and for its capacity to sustain human life and culture are one and the same. Beverley, who wanted to align the human economy with nature, thus found in Banister's manuscripts an approach congenial to his purpose. Most of Book II emphasizes the environment's productive or regenerative capacities, especially with regard to human use.

In his assessment of these capacities, Beverley finds the Virginia environment to offer a double prospect for improvement. On the one hand, certain native species can be improved through cultivation to yield useful products; on the other hand, the Virginia environment can improve familiar English cultivars. On the use of native species, Beverley follows earlier promoters in mistakenly projecting the development of sericulture, observing that "the Mulberry-Tree, whose Leaf is the proper food of the Silk-Worm, grows there like a Weed" (295).[31] He is particularly interested in viticulture and so is much more observant than Banister on the topic of grapes. Having made some "tolerably good" wine from one variety of wild grape that grew "shaded by the Woods, from the Sun," he argues that such wine "would be much better, if produc'd of the same Grape cultivated in a regular Vineyard" (134).[32] Such cultivation would need to study the natural conditions favoring the vines. Beginning this study himself, Beverley develops significant observations on plant interaction, forest regeneration, and soil type:

The Pine-Tree and the Fir are naturally very noxious to the Vine; and the Vine is observed never to thrive, where it is in any ways influenced by them. Now, all the lower Parts of these Rivers naturally produce these Trees; insomuch, that if a Man clear the Land there, of the Wood, he will certainly find that the Pine is the first Tree that will grow up again, tho' perhaps there was not a Pine in that Spot of Ground before. Again; the Vine thrives best on the Sides of Hills, Gravelly Ground, and in the Neigbourhood of fresh Streams. But the Experiments that have been made of Vineyards, both in *Virginia* and *Carolina*, have not only been near the malignant Influence of the Salt-Water, but also upon the low Lands, that are naturally subject to the Pine. (134–35, emphases in original)

Although it would be a century and a half before Thoreau specifically identified the phenomenon of forest succession, Beverley has already begun to recognize the significance of this mechanism of environmental change for land management decisions.

Addressing the other side of Virginia's double prospect, the environment's capacity to improve familiar English cultivars, Beverley again stresses the importance of labor. On the authority of Banister, he reports for example "that Apples from the Seed, never degenerate into Crabs, or Wildings there, but produce the same, or better Fruit than the Mother-Tree, (which is not so in *England,*) and are wonderfully improved by Grafting and Managing; yet there are very few Planters that graft at all, and much fewer that take any care to get choice Fruits" (314).[33] He brings such observations to bear on the emerging debate over American degeneration (which would come to preoccupy Thomas Jefferson), noting for example that "it was formerly said of the Red-Top Turnip that [in Virginia] in three or four years time, it degenerated into Rape; but that happen'd merely by an Error in saving the Seed; for now it appears, that if they cut off the top of such a Turnip, that has been kept out of the ground all the Winter, and plant that top alone without the Body of the Root, it yields a Seed, which mends the Turnip in the next sowing" (293). Thus while no "*English* Plant, Grain, or Fruit . . . miscarries in *Virginia*; but most of them better their kinds very much, by being sowed or planted there," Virginia's natural capacity for improvement nonetheless requires careful work (293, emphases in original).

Conspicuously absent from Beverley's survey in Book II of the variety of Virginia's flora, indigenous or imported, wild, cultivated, or naturalized, is one of the most prominent of its species, tobacco. (He would mention it in Book III, as we shall see.) Beverley ignores Banister's extensive account of this "unstable sort of staple commodity," although he certainly had access to it.[34] Information on tobacco cultivation was increasingly disseminated during the late seventeenth century in both scientific and promotional literature, such as the *Letter from John Clayton . . . to the Royal Society* (1688) or George Alsop's popular *Character of the Province of Maryland* (1666). The promoter Alsop had confined his remarks to the sequence of seasonal work and information on the tobacco trade as currently managed, subjects that could add little to Beverley's program for improvement.[35] Clayton, on the other hand, had begun to identify the importance of nitrogen and to develop other ideas, such as a scheme for draining swamps in which the resulting fields would, he claimed, produce larger plants and maintain soil fertility for thirty to forty years.[36] Thus while ideas were available contemporarily for experimentation with tobacco, Beverley deliberately ignores them. In fact he puts Virginia's double prospect for improvement into explicit contrast with the tobacco monoculture in a summary passage: "No Seed is sowed there, but it thrives, and most Plants are improved, by being Transplanted thither. And yet there's very little Improvement made among them, nor anything us'd in Traffique, but Tobacco" (314).

The Calculus of Compensation

The tobacco monoculture failed to make best advantage of Virginia's environmental capacities as Beverley understood them. An alternative model for human society's engagement with these capacities preoccupied Beverley in Book III of the *History*, which is devoted to a reconstruction of precolonial Indian culture. We recall that the New England Puritans viewed the Indians' relationship to the land in terms of lack: the Indians "inclose noe land neither have they any setled habitation nor any tame cattle to improve the land by."[37] Beverley inverts such comparisons to find the colonists lacking:

This and a great deal more was the natural Production of that Country, which the Native *Indians* enjoy'd, without the Curse of Industry, their Diversion alone, and not their Labour, supplying their Necessities. The Women and Children indeed, were so far provident, as to lay up some of the Nuts, and Fruits of the Earth, in their Season, for their further Occasions: But none of the Toils of Husbandry were exercised by this happy People; except the bare planting a little Corn, and Melons, which took up only a few Days in the Summer, the rest being wholly spent in the Pursuit of their Pleasures. And indeed all that the *English* have done, since their going thither, has been only to make some of these Native Pleasures more scarce, by an inordinate and unseasonable Use of them; hardly making Improvements equivalent to that Damage. (156, emphases in original)

Although Beverley finds that the colonists have done positive harm to the environment, he does not simply mourn the loss of paradise. Rather, he introduces a calculus of compensation, according to which some kinds of "Improvements" could make up for environmental "Damage" done by the colonial economy.

This calculus of compensation had been written into the georgic almost from the beginning, in Virgil's revision of Hesiod's *Works and Days*. Where Hesiod had described a steady decline from the Golden Age through the present, Virgil found something positive in that loss. Virgil argued that when Jove loosed the wolves and dried up the rivers of wine, bringing the Golden Age to an end, humankind was compelled to study nature in order to develop agriculture, navigation, metallurgy, meteorology, and so on. As Beverley's English contemporary John Dryden translated Virgil's point, then "various Arts in order did succeed, / (What cannot endless Labour urg'd by need?)."[38] Careful labor could produce the good life, for according to the well-known paean to rural virtue in the second of the *Georgics*,

Happy the Man, who, studying Nature's Laws,
Thro' known Effects can trace the secret Cause:
His Mind possessing, in a quiet state,
Fearless of Fortune, and resign'd to Fate.[39]

In Beverley's application of the calculus, the Indians must stand in for the denizens of the Golden Age, yet that positioning is complicated by Beverley's own ethnographic investigations. For one thing, the environment is evidently not always bountiful so the Indians endure periodic want, "girding up their Bellies" when "they happen to have nothing to eat" (181). And while Beverley claims that the Indians lived "in their enjoyment of Plenty, without the Curse of Labour," in fact he describes them as doing a good deal of work (233). They felled trees, cleared land for planting, ordered and tended their fields, gathered wild fruits, nuts, and herbs, hunted, fished, made canoes, prepared food, and so on. The process of making "*peak*" or wampum from mollusk shells seems particularly laborious: chipping, drilling, grinding, polishing and sometimes etching the pieces before stringing them into belts or attaching them to clothing, pipes, tomahawks, and so on (227–28). Although Beverley observes and records all this labor, he is reluctant to identify it as such. Their farming, he claims, "took up only a few Days in the Summer" (156). This reluctance derives from his dissatisfaction with the colonial economy, in contrast to which the Indians' easy production of their sustenance and culture seemed a more harmonious mode of environmental engagement. Beverley saw the colonists labor to produce tobacco in abundance, and saw the market turn that abundance to lack. Thus he contrasts the colonists' tobacco production with that of the Indians, who "let it all run to Seed, only succouring the Leaves, to keep the Sprouts from growing upon, and starving them; and when it was ripe, they pull'd off the Leaves, cured them in the Sun, and laid them up for Use. But the Planters make a heavy Bustle with it now, and can't please the Market neither" (145). Beverley's readers would easily recognize the contrast, since their process involved laboriously starting the seeds in special beds, transplanting the seedlings to the fields, weeding, hilling, picking and killing insects, topping the plant to prevent it from going to seed, and elaborate harvesting and curing processes.[40] The Indians, without a market to please, labor more moderately to produce good tobacco, pruning the plants to keep suckers from "starving" the main leaves, and simply drying and storing the crop.

An index of the success of the Indians' economic-environmental arrangements was their sociability. Beverley found the life of their towns attractive, especially as compared to the requisites of tobacco planting, which had caused the colonists to fall into an "unhappy Form of Settlements, altogether upon Country Seats, without Towns" (118). Where each tobacco planter required large tracts of land, Indian farmers worked small plots. Fertility on these plots was sustained through the practice of multicropping beans together with corn and other plants. Beans fixed much of the nitrogen taken up by the corn, which is only about half as much as that required by tobacco.[41] Tobacco culture required another important environmental feature as well. Since the finished crop was heavy and had to be transported to market, each plantation needed ready access to a river as well as a supply of timber for building the hogsheads that were used as shipping containers. This too encouraged dispersed settlement patterns. The Indians, in contrast, live

altogether by Cohabitation, in Townships, from fifty to five hundred Families in a Town, and each of these Towns is commonly a Kingdom. Sometimes one King has the command of several of these Towns, when they happen to be united in his Hands, by Descent or Conquest; but in such cases there is always a Viceregent appointed in the dependent Town, who is at once Governour, Judge, Chancellour, and has the same Power and Authority which the King himself has in the Town where he resides. This Viceroy is oblig'd to pay his Principal some small Tribute, as an acknowledgment of his submission, as likewise to follow him to his Wars, whenever he is required. (174)

As the topic of settlement patterns opens onto the question of sociopolitical organization here, we see that the Indian towns (like the beavers' "admirable oeconomy") embody good social order and hierarchical political relations. Beverley's use of the ethnographic present tense represents these relations as eternally stable, in implicit contrast to the great unrest the colony had experienced during Bacon's Rebellion and subsequent lesser episodes.[42] Beverley thought that economic diversification would enable nucleated settlements and greater population densities which would for a time check the planters' need for more land, remedy the economic ills of tobacco culture, and encourage political sociability. It would thus compensate for the destructive "Alterations, I can't call them Improvements" the colonists "have made at this Day" (156).

Another form of compensation would be an increased capacity for the economic self-sufficiency of the colony, a point to which Beverley devotes considerable attention.[43] At present, he notes with dismay, the Virginians ship "the very Furrs that their Hats are made of" to England first for manufacture, they let "most of their Hides lie and rot" while they import shoes and other leather goods, and "they are such abominable Ill-husbands, that tho' their Country be over-run with Wood, yet they have all their Wooden Ware from *England*; their Cabinets, Chairs, Tables, Stools, Chests, Boxes, Cart-Wheels, and all other things, even so much as their Bowls, and Birchen Brooms, to the Eternal Reproach of their Laziness" (295). Similarly, because of the their "unfortunate Method of . . . Settlement, and want of Cohabitation, they cannot make a beneficial use of their Flax, Hemp, Cotten, Silk, Silk-grass, and Wool, which might otherwise supply their Necessities" (319). By the end of the century, Jefferson would count this lack a virtue. "Never" did he "wish to see our citizens occupied at a work-bench, or twirling a distaff"; abhorring urban manufacturing centers, he exhorted, "let our work-shops remain in Europe."[44] Jefferson agreed with Beverley that tobacco culture had a detrimental effect on land and society, but by Jefferson's time, a growing European market for wheat would provide the Virginians with an alternative staple. Beverley attempts to envision an escape from a staple economy altogether, in which Virginia would become economically self-sufficient through a balance of various kinds of agriculture, manufacturing, and trade.

Pastoral and Georgic

The calculus of compensation responded to economic dissatisfactions by proposing that improvement could in large measure remedy them. The alternate response to these dissatisfactions was nostalgia for a Golden Age, a response that gains expression in Beverley's idealization, however complicated, of Indian society. The calculus, then, is the point at which pastoral and georgic split off from each other and as such reveals pastoral's dependence on georgic. In Virgil's poem of the earth, the farmer himself experiences this split after the year's harvest is in, as he keeps holiday by the fire, drinking and sporting. This season of leisure and consumption without production recalls stories of Saturn's reign, before the losses imposed by Jove, when "the good old God his Hunger did asswage / With Roots and Herbs, and gave the Golden Age."[45] Imagining everlasting ease temporarily obliterates the hard reality of the farmer's life. Pastoral develops such "intervals of bliss" into a permanent dissociation of aesthetic from practical modes of being in the environment.[46] Thus in pastoral, the landscape as object of beauty and space of leisure is screened off from the labor of creating and maintaining that landscape.[47] The screen is never quite secure, however. Even in precolonial Indian culture as Beverley describes it, the pastoral is always under a vague threat of disruption. To this threat Beverley attributes the Indians' custom of worshiping the evil powers. As an Indian guest explains, "God is the giver of all good things, but . . . they are showr'd down upon all Men indifferently." It is to no purpose to fear or worship God, but on the other hand "if they did not pacify the Evil Spirit, and make him propitious, he wou'd take away, or spoil all those good things that God had given, and ruine their Health, their Peace and their Plenty" (200–201). Perhaps the Indians' worship practices, which in Beverley's account take up a good deal of their time and effort, are a form of work to conserve their Golden Age.

This understanding of pastoral's continual but often unrecognized dependence on georgic inflects even the leisured or aestheticized representations of colonial life in the *History*, as if the georgic refuses to retreat behind a pastoral screen. In one such moment, Beverley remarks that "for their Recreation, the Plantations, Orchards, and Gardens constantly afford 'em fragrant and delightful walks," thus conflating what we would ordinarily take to be points on a continuum from productive to leisured space (308). A plantation affords a pleasant walk to view the progress of the crops. Even a garden, ordinarily the least production-oriented of the three kinds of cultivated space Beverley discusses, can induce the economic awareness generally repressed by the pastoral:

The Almond, Pomgranate and Fig, ripen there very well, and yet there are not ten People in the Country, that have any of them in their Gardens, much less endeavour to preserve any of them for future spending, or propagate them to make a Trade.

A Garden is no where sooner made than there, either for Fruits, or Flowers. Tulips from the Seed flower the second year at farthest. All sorts of Herbs have there a perfection in their flavour, beyond what I ever tasted in a more *Northern* Climate. And yet they han't many Gardens in the Country, fit to bear that name. (316, emphasis in original)

Virginians might have heard tales of the seventeenth-century speculation in tulips from the Dutch merchants with which they had sometimes traded. Although the bubble burst in 1637, the market soon recovered and tulips remained a valuable commodity.[48] Perhaps a projection of a Virginia tulip trade accounts for Beverley's optimism in claiming that seed would produce a flowering bulb in two years, for ordinarily it takes six to seven years. In any case, the present moment seems to offer better prospects for future spending and trade in orchard crops such as almonds. Beverley also finds orchards to be pleasant spaces, and again his aesthetic interest soon opens onto economic concerns:

The Fruit-Trees are wonderfully quick of growth, so that in six or seven years time from the Planting, a Man may bring an Orchard to bear in great plenty, from which he may make store of good Cyder, or distill great quantities of Brandy; for the Cyder is very strong, and yields abundance of in [*sic*] Spirit. Yet they have very few, that take any care at all for an Orchard; nay, many that have good Orchards, are so negligent of them, as to let them go to ruine, and expose the Trees to be torn, and barked by the Cattle. (314)

Again, Virginia's natural advantages are evident in this lack of improvement, the cider yielding an "abundance" of alcohol for distillation, but the colonists neglect those advantages. The result is both economic and aesthetic "ruine."

Here we might ask who neglect their orchards and who do not, for this question concerns the prospects for the diversification that Beverley would promote. Wealthy planters, anticipating those "great quantities of Brandy," could direct servants or slaves to care for apple and peach trees (planting, fencing, grafting, pruning, and so on) and to harvest and manufacture their produce into beverages. Tenants, who operated a large proportion of Virginia farms at this time, would probably not have been so well motivated to make such improvements. Leases on new lands were usually generous, but when a tenant had improved the land, the landlord could charge higher rents or sell the land, thus forcing the tenant to move on.[49] Small holders—and some remained, even after the consolidation of land in the hands of the gentry during the last decades of the seventeenth century—did not have time for, or interest in, even relatively modest projects such as orchards. They certainly would not have been able to embark on more laborious diversification projects.

Even the wealthier planters, however, found that the tobacco monoculture was structurally predisposed against diversification. Governor Berkeley had recognized that tobacco failed to generate capital for new projects. This lack of capital was, if anything, more acute in Beverley's time. It is true that even during the three worst decades of stagnation in the tobacco economy, from 1680 to 1710, there were short-term bursts of demand.[50] However, planters large and small responded to these momentary price increases by overproducing, hoping to get ahead of the market, which in turn soon drove prices back down. When tobacco prices were relatively good, planters had no incentive to diversify. When prices fell, they may have had the incentive but lacked the capital.[51] This structural predisposition against diversification was exacerbated by the fact that tobacco was both crop and currency. As George Alsop noted, tobacco was "the current Coyn" of the Chesapeake region, and would "sooner purchase Commodities from the Merchants, then money."[52] Beverley worries that the planters "now have very little Money" in the form of specie, which caused great "hardship" (285). All exchanges, even trivial ones, were transacted through the medium of tobacco. Any new investment capital for any industry would have to be produced first from the environment in that form. Tobacco thus encouraged a monocultural attitude toward the land even for those who may have hoped to escape the monoculture.

The problematic role of tobacco as both crop and currency may account for Beverley's particular interest in the Indians' *peak* and other forms of worked shells. Drawing on another of Banister's manuscripts, "Of the Natives, their Habit, Customes, & Manner of Living," Beverley adds to Banister's observations on the manufacture of *peak* a discussion of its valuation.[53] *Peak*, Beverley says, "past with them instead of Gold and Silver, and serv'd them both for Money, and Ornament" (227). That made from conch shell of a "dark colour" is "the dearest," valued by English traders "at eighteen pence *per* Yard, and the white *Peak* [also from conch shell] at nine pence." Other configurations are "much more valuable" still, while "another sort . . . is as current among them, but of far less value; and this is made of the Cockleshell, broke into small bits with rough edges, drill'd through in the same manner as Beads, and this they call *Roenoke*" (227, 228). Contrasted with tobacco, these worked shells bear fixed values in exchanges among Indians as well as in relation to English currency: "These sorts of Money have their rates set upon them as unalterable, and current as the values of our Money are" (228). This stability contrasts with Beverley's observation in Book IV on the recent fluctuation of currency in the colonies: "the Neighboring Governments all around, are allow'd to enhance the rate of it with them, to above thirty *per Cent.* more than the Intrinsick Value" (285). The result, he fears, will be a drain on specie, which is already scarce, and further decline in tobacco prices. Now if specie fluctuates (and with it the value of tobacco and labor), so must the value of *peak* fluctuate in relation to specie. Yet that is not how Beverley tells it. Rather, he emphasizes the stability of *peak*, its absolute value.

Such stability is especially curious because it would seem relatively easy to make as much *peak* as one wanted, given that the raw materials, various mollusk shells, are readily available in the Virginia environment. Like the production of tobacco, the production of *peak* required only the application of skilled labor to nature. Yet, evidently in contrast to *peak*, the unit valuation of tobacco decreased as more labor was applied and production volume increased (especially given the static demand after 1680). Thus to counteract the normal laws of supply and demand in the case of *peak*, there must be some external mechanism regulating its production and/or exchange, thereby insuring its stable valuation. Such regulation evidently comes through a structure of circulation without exchange. The Indians, Beverley observes, wear these worked shells "instead of Medals before or behind their Neck, and use the *Peak, Runtees* and Pipes [yet another variety of shell beads, in strings, "much more valuable" than other forms] for Coronets, Bracelets, Belts or long Strings hanging down before the Breast, or else they lace their Garments with them, and adorn their *Tomahawks*, and every other thing that they value" (228). The attachment of these worked shells to other items of "value" is a sign of their valuation, but distribution is fixed by a preexisting social hierarchy and functions to maintain that hierarchy. As Herman Melville would observe tattoos to function among the Polynesian islanders in *Typee*, so *peak* functions here:

The People of Condition of both Sexes, wear a sort of Coronet on their Heads, from 4 to 6 inches broad, open at the top, and composed of *Peak*, or Beads, or else of both interwoven together, and workt into Figures, made by a nice mixture of the Colours. Sometimes they wear a Wreath of Dyed Furrs; as likewise Bracelets on their Necks and Arms. The Common People go bare-headed, only sticking large shining Feathers about their Heads, as their fancies lead them. (162)

As the value of *peak* and other worked shells never fluctuates, class status among the Indians remains ever fixed, the two sites constituting a reciprocally determining relationship of value.

Yet even while the fluctuation of tobacco prices contrasts with the apparently stable valuation of *peak*, *peak* and tobacco function similarly to produce social value. For the Indians, *peak* constitutes cultural capital. That is, it signifies and maintains social differentiation in a culture in which, according to Beverley, nobody struggles for daily necessities. Tobacco, too, constituted cultural capital in Virginia. However much an individual planter might worry about price fluctuations and his own consumption and production patterns, sociopolitical stability in general had become linked to tobacco culture. The planter's status was measured in large part by the amount of land he controlled. The seasonal rhythm of labor on these lands in itself "promoted social cohesion," since at any time of year, one planter knew what all others were doing or having their laborers do.[54] And as we have seen, political stability developed in the aftermath of Bacon's Rebellion. Particularly during the 1680s and 1690s, the decades of economic stagnation immediately preceding the composition of the *History*, the gentry consolidated their dominance. Ironically, then, the tobacco culture that Beverley criticizes was producing the very sort of stable, hierarchical sociopolitical relations for which he so admires the Indians and the beavers. The gentry, the only class in a position to enact Beverley's diversification program, were precisely those who, on the one hand, had benefited most from the tobacco monoculture and, on the other hand, could not redirect their capital into diversification projects without risking their place in Virginia's sociopolitical hierarchy.

This consolidation of the gentry class shapes the *History*'s pastoral moments. Beverley's admiration for the supposedly Golden Age state of Indian society no doubt derives in part from its embodiment of gentry-class values: the Indians' devotion to what Beverley perceived as leisure activities (such as hunting), their stable, hierarchical polity, and so on. Similarly, the one moment of the *History* in which Beverley's account of the colonists' pleasure in nature is *not* directly inflected by economic concerns provides a clear index of gentry-class values. In this moment the georgic seems to vanish completely behind a pastoral screen:

all their Senses are entertain'd with an endless Succession of Native Pleasures. Their Eyes are ravished with the Beauties of naked Nature. Their Ears are Serenaded with the perpetual murmur of Brooks, and the thorow-base which the Wind plays, when it wantons through the Trees; the merry Birds too, join their pleasing Notes to this rural Consort, especially the Mock-birds, who love Society so well, that whenever they see Mankind, they will perch upon a Twigg very near them, and sing the sweetest wild Airs in the World. (298)

Here nature itself, in the person of the mockingbird, shows the love of sociability that Beverley had so admired among the Indians and beavers and that he desired for the colonists. The pleasures of woodland sounds become those of a chamber concert with its typical instruments and vocalists—a social event that, if yet relatively infrequent in the Virginia gentry's parlors, was familiar enough to Beverley and his readers through their cultural connection to English life. And prior even to Beverley's figural cultivation of nature here, nature has already been materially cultivated so as to enable these figures. The brooks that play the opening notes of the "Consort" are not located out in the wilderness (although even there the environment had been managed through indigenous practices), but are readily accessible, at the edges of fields or meadows or gardens. The "shady Groves" that shelter such brooks have been planted as orchards or have been produced from old-growth woodland by the cutting of firewood and timber and the clearing of obscuring, brushy understory by browsing livestock (and prior to that, by the Indians' practices of burning the forest understory and clearing new fields). Such managed woodlands thus provided the colonists with pleasant seats from which to hear the natural concerts. This is to say nothing of the more formal spaces such as the garden of William Byrd I, which had been planted to attract the hummingbirds that Beverley says, later in this passage, "sported about me so familiarly, that with their little Wings they often fann'd my Face" much as a flirtatious daughter of the gentry might have done with her fan (299).

Tobacco culture enabled the formation of the class that appreciated gardens and parlor concerts, a class that was beginning to find reflections of itself in the less obviously cultivated parts of the environment as well, on similar, leisured terms. This class was beginning to develop a pastoral aesthetic specific to the plantation environment. But what of the others oppressed to varying degrees by that class, the small holders, tenants, servants, and slaves? If they could not join an ill-fated expedition such as Nathaniel Bacon's in hopes of improving their lot, perhaps they too could enjoy the song of the "Mock-birds" as they worked in the fields, growing tobacco for another's gain. Thus if Beverley recommended a change in economic-environmental practices that might have cut against his class interests, he did so unwittingly. Virginia planters would eventually come to recognize the economic disadvantages of tobacco, shifting their emphasis to wheat and corn in response to increasing European demand.[55] The Virginians would find an alternative use of their environment, but without really altering the class structure that tobacco had produced and without taking full advantage of the prospect of diversity emphasized by promoters from Hariot through Beverley. And the shift from tobacco to grain, which enabled an intensification of land use, would soon exhaust the soil in its turn.[56]

During this transformation, the increasing use of slaves encouraged a pastoral conception of culture.[57] However, a minor poetic tradition in specific imitation of Virgil's *Georgics* flourished briefly during the eighteenth century. These staple colony georgics—notably Charles Woodmason's "Indico" (1758), James Grainger's *The Sugar-Cane* (1764), and George Ogilvie's *Carolina; or, the Planter* (1776/1791)—had to deal directly with the use of slave labor, something that could be evaded in the pastoral mode.[58] Writing before slavery had fully replaced indentured servitude, Beverley addresses the issue somewhat disingenuously, arguing "that the work of their Servants, and Slaves, is no other than what every common Freeman do's" (272). Fifty years later Woodmason justified slavery, by now the primary source of labor, simply on the grounds of economic necessity, remarking that Africans were naturally well suited to hard work in the hot sun. Had he elaborated his account of the cultivation of indigo at greater length, it is possible he would have presented the ambivalence that troubled Grainger's and Ogilvie's larger efforts.[59] Grainger devoted the last of the four books of *The Sugar-Cane* to the management of slaves, curiously interspersing advice to planters on what tribe of Africans was best suited to what task, what diseases to expect and how to cure them, and so on, with pleas for emancipation, or, at least, for kinder treatment of slaves. Ogilvie attempted to envision an independent yeomanry as the basis of republican civilization in the South, but at the same time he could not describe the actual operations of creating and maintaining a rice plantation—the material reality of the georgic—as being undertaken by anyone but slaves. *Carolina* thus closes with a pastoral screen, a bountiful landscape nearly absent of human labor. Ogilvie's Muse projects a vision of the diverse commodity environments that animated the earliest colonial promoters' texts. She

Sees ev'ry winding Valley wave with corn,
Sees purple Vineyards ev'ry hill adorn;
Sees yonder Marsh, with useless reeds o'erspread,

Give to a thousand looms the flaxen thread;
And Hemp, from many a now neglected field,
Its sinewy bark to future Navies yield.
Nor shall Tobacco balk the Planter's hope,
Who seeks its fragrance on th'irriguous slope.
Around each field she sees the Mulb'ry grow,
Or unctuous Olive form the frugal row;
Beholds our hills the precious Thea bear,
And all the crops of Asia flourish here.[60]

This picture of agricultural diversification contrasts with the establishment of the rice monoculture which had been the primary topic of Ogilvie's poem. Earlier in Part II of the poem he had described in detail the labor of building irrigated rice fields, but here such georgic specificity is absent. Nature transforms itself into commodities; if further production is required, nature gives its plenty directly to machines that will complete the work. In this economy of nature, there is some human intellectual input—the "enlight'ned Rustic joins" lime, sand, and clay "Until the chymic process yields him more / Substantial riches than transmuted ore" (lines 703, 705–6)—but nobody actually seems to plant, cultivate, or harvest the ground thus prepared.

As the staple colony georgics' increasing unease regarding the topic of labor indicates, the split between practical and aesthetic ways of being in the environment, which Beverley had observed and tried to reintegrate but without addressing its origins in the class structure of tobacco culture itself, only widened with the entrenchment of slavery. Other Americans, however, would soon imagine a free georgic culture in the great West. The conflicts that emerged in the formation of that culture are the subject of the next chapter.

Chapter 5

Ideologies of Farming
Crèvecoeur, Jefferson, Rush, and Brown

On the eve of the American Revolution, J. Hector St. John de Crèvecoeur's farmer James of Pennsylvania explained the sociopolitical structure of the American colonies to his English correspondent:

Some few towns excepted, we are all tillers of the earth, from Nova Scotia to West Florida. We are a people of cultivators, scattered over an immense territory, communicating with each other by means of good roads and navigable rivers, united by the silken bands of mild government, all respecting the laws, without dreading their power, because they are equitable. We are all animated with the spirit of an industry which is unfettered and unrestrained, because each person works for himself. . . . We have no princes, for whom we toil, starve, and bleed. We are the most perfect society now existing in the world. Here man is free as he ought to be.[1]

Thomas Jefferson would soon, and more famously, turn farmer James's description into a prescription for the future. "We have," Jefferson remarked,

an immensity of land courting the husbandman. . . . While we have land to labour then, let us never wish to see our citizens occupied at a work-bench, or twirling a distaff. Carpenters, masons, smiths, are wanting in husbandry: but, for the general operations of manufacture, let our work-shops remain in Europe. It is better to carry provisions and materials to workmen there, than bring them to the provisions and materials, and with them their manners and principles. The loss by the transportation of commodities across the Atlantic will be made up in happiness and permanence of government.[2]

Although the loyalist James shows greater interest in the freedom of the individual subject than does Jefferson the revolutionary, both regard an agrarian economy as particularly conducive to the public good. The idea was, as we know, widely held. In 1783, clergyman and president of Yale College Ezra Stiles gave a speech on the rising glory of America, explicitly linking such an economy, founded in "a free tenure of lands," to the ideal republic envisioned in James Harrington's utopian *Oceana*, stating that this ideal had long been "realized" and its political effectivity "verified in

New-England."[3] Loyalist and patriot, Pennsylvanian, Virginian, and New Englander alike agreed that America's past blessings and future promise depended on agriculture.[4]

As Henry Nash Smith and others have observed, the image of the yeoman farmer provided an important locus of American self-definition at this time.[5] This image would increasingly come into conflict with rationalizations of the slave system.[6] Yet even in the North and the West, the nature of farming was itself already in question. Soon after Crève-coeur, Jefferson, and Stiles each grounded America's political virtue on an agrarian base, others such as Benjamin Rush complicated their agrarian optimism. If Americans were "all tillers of the earth," as farmer James had claimed (*L*, 41), Rush introduced critical distinctions, arguing that "it is proper to apply the term of *farmers*" to only *one* class of those who grew crops, managed woods, and raised livestock on American soil.[7] Debates over land use had existed from the earliest days of colonization. We have seen that John Smith criticized Virginia's tobacco monoculture from its very beginnings and that Robert Beverley elaborated this critique. As Jefferson would note, Virginia was shifting from tobacco to grain production during the latter part of the eighteenth century. Beneath this local issue of crop selection, however, lay a larger, nationwide concern over farming methods.

Farming in the eighteenth century was not a single, uniform activity, but rather included a range of diverse and conflicting practices. One of the most easily overlooked aspects of agriculture even today is its class structure. In the premechanized era, a considerable amount of farm labor was supplied by landless men and women. In addition to wage and slave labor, tenant farming was prevalent throughout colonial America and persisted long after the Revolution; in some areas, 30 to 50 percent of farm householders were tenants.[8] Different farming practices interacted with economic structures to produce distinct social categories. One important farming method, practiced with some variation from the first years of American colonization on, involved logging in the winter, burning the slash in the spring, planting a grain (usually corn) for three or four years in succession, meanwhile clearing new land for crops the following years, using old fields for pasturage, and moving on when the fields ceased to support a good harvest. This "backwoods" method was primarily subsistence oriented.[9] Another, more intensive, sedentary method also developed. This method involved the use of green, mineral, and animal manures, diversified production with an emphasis on other grains (especially wheat) and flax, and the rotation of crops; here wage or slave labor were often used. Primarily profit oriented, this method involved considerable participation in the market for agricultural produce.[10] Individuals who practiced either method may or may not have held title to the

land to which they devoted their labor. A large landholder, often a speculator, found that if his tenants practiced the first method, and thereby
improved the land, parcels could then be sold or rented at a substantial profit to those who practiced the second method. The first method
was also attractive to the small farmer on the frontier, who often found
that he could more easily sell an improved farm than agricultural produce. On the other hand, a small farmer might wish to achieve the second
method of cultivation as rapidly as possible and remain on one plot of
land, rather than moving on as a practitioner of the first method would
do. The choices were determined significantly by the local markets for
land, labor, and agricultural produce. Different farming practices and
different positions with respect to the land, labor, and produce markets
grounded different ideologies.

In addressing this conflict over farming methods in the late eighteenth
and early nineteenth centuries, the literature of agrarian improvement
developed a discourse of rural virtue that linked economic intensification (sedentary farming methods and market embeddedness) to national
political stability. There are several reasons why this literature gained such
force at this time. Its production and dissemination depended on, and
arguably contributed to, the development of print culture and a public
sphere.[11] The scarcity of new land along the eastern seaboard encouraged
both agricultural improvement there (as those who remained faced soils
exhausted by generations of cultivation) and territorial expansion (as
those who could not get land in the East moved out to unsettled lands). As
early as 1758, for example, the *American Magazine* ran a monthly column
entitled "The Planter," which promoted agricultural improvement as a
means of increasing profitability and discouraging outmigration. By the
1790s, land scarcity in the East had become acute.[12] As Carolyn Merchant
has shown in the case of New England, at this time the land crisis presented farmers with two choices: migrate west to continue a traditional,
subsistence-oriented mode of production, or intensify production methods to engage with emerging markets for agricultural produce.[13]

Farming methods, thus linked to market concerns, bore ideological
implications. Jefferson's *Notes on the State of Virginia* and Crèvecoeur's
Letters from an American Farmer, while differing in their political orienta-
tions, similarly oversimplified the rural class structure, often minimizing
the increased labor required for intensification, in order to promote the
growth of markets. Benjamin Rush, in contrast, gave a more explicitly
class-conscious analysis. In his "Account of the Progress of Population,
Agriculture, Manners, and Government in Pennsylvania," a number of
topics of concern to agrarians coalesced into a stadialist theory of frontier
settlement that linked the progress of American civilization to increasing economic-environmental intensification. Although this progressive

theory of rural virtue was soon criticized by Charles Brockden Brown, who would later argue for an aristocratic structure of rural management in which powerful landlords controlled vast acreages and mediated all market engagements, it nevertheless came to embody the terms of assessment for the relation of economy to environment into the nineteenth century.

*   *   *

In 1758, "Agricola," a correspondent to the "Planter" column in the Philadelphia *American Magazine*, described a land crisis in Pennsylvania. He observed that declining soil fertility and want of timber for fencing was compelling farmers to sell up or default on their debts and move on. These farmers were attracted to Southside Virginia or North Carolina, where the frontier was not so threatened by the "Indians and French" as it was in the north and where they might find "fresh land, shorter winters, and easier purchases and quitrents" than in Pennsylvania.[14] Thus even "the safer part of the province" would soon "be ruined by the loss of inhabitants." Agricola likened these safer parts to a "sieve": "for tho' thousands of strangers were constantly imported they only shoved out the ancient inhabitants; and even many of the Newcomers removed to other provinces" (489). The land, in Agricola's estimation, seemed to have reached its carrying capacity: possibilities for new environmental inputs, in the form of soil fertility and timber, were declining. Population in forced population out, but outmigration was exacerbated by environmental decline. Pennsylvanians might soon see a return to an older, less efficient land system, as unfenced, exhausted lands would revert to "common[s]" (487). To remedy the farmers' depletion of timber resources, Agricola argued that the customary rail fences might be replaced by live fence rows; he recommended planting black walnuts closely in a line and cropping the saplings at seven feet to encourage dense growth. Declining yields on those fenced lands, though, were a more difficult problem. Here Agricola recommended a course of improvement that agrarian writers would soon develop in greater detail: irrigation of corn and flax to increase yields, a scientific system of crop rotation, and the use of cover crops, animal manure, and mineral dressings to restore fertility. Moreover, he proposed that farmers form agricultural societies "to converse about every method of improving the lands" and "to make new experiments," which might be reported in periodicals such as the *American Magazine* (489). The resulting improvements would support greater population density. This program required an increase in the amount of labor applied to a unit of land. Farmers would have to hire wage laborers or engage tenants to supply some of that labor. Carrying out the program of intensification Agricola recommended, then, would result in an increasingly complex and stratified rural class structure. This complexity and stratification would complicate the program of Jeffersonian agrarianism in the early Federal era.

Jeffersonian agrarianism did not take the form of a retreat from the market, as is sometimes inferred from Query XIX of Jefferson's *Notes on the State of Virginia*.[15] Rather, it was based on a distinct perception of America's potential place in the world market for agricultural produce. Jeffersonians did not debate Federalists over the difference between self-sufficiency and modern commerce; rather the parties contended over two different versions of market development.[16] Jefferson observes that, given the particular "circumstance" of Americans' relations to the environment, it was natural for them to "rais[e] raw materials, and exchang[e] them for finer manufactures than they are able to execute themselves" (*N*, 170). Indeed, he argues in Query XXII that with the conclusion of peace, "our interest will be to throw open the doors of commerce, and to knock off all its shackles, giving perfect freedom to all persons for the vent of whatever they may chuse to bring into our ports, and asking the same in theirs" (*N*, 180). That is, Jefferson wishes to avoid not a commercial economy, but rather an economy heavily oriented toward manufacturing, as is clear from the placement of his discussion of rural virtue under the head of "Manufactures." Yet he knows that even so some manufactures are necessary, such as the ironworks described in Query VI, which specifically support agriculture. He will not be so impractical as Thomas More, whose Utopians needed to trade with other nations for iron.

While Jefferson addresses the topic more systematically than does Crèvecoeur, their visions are similar in many respects. Both see farming as the primary source of independence and social stability. Even Crèvecoeur's Nantucket Islanders value their allotment of grazing rights, which are hypothetically convertible from "right[s] of commonage" to the possession of a "future freehold" (*L*, 93). Interestingly, Crèvecoeur's farmer James, loyal subject of King George III, stresses land-based freedom at least as strongly as does Jefferson. Finding himself the owner of "a good farm" and "free from debts," James rhetorically asks, "where is that station which can confer a more substantial system of felicity than that of an American farmer, possessing freedom of action, freedom of thoughts, ruled by a mode of government which requires but little from us?" (*L*, 25). Jefferson's equally famous representation of American farmers in Query XIX of the *Notes* is directed less toward individual freedom than toward "happiness and permanence of government," a point driven home by his fearful vision of an anarchic urban proletariat (*N*, 171).

Although it is usually read as a paean to the freehold farmer, Jeffer-

son's picture of "those who labour in the earth" lacks economic specificity (*N*, 170). That is, like much of late eighteenth- and early nineteenth-century agrarian writing, the *Notes* construct a pastoral opposition
between urban and rural that tends to obscure the realities of the rural
class structure. At this time, much of the white population of Virginia
were tenant farmers rather than freeholders, and another substantial portion were landless agricultural laborers.[17] There was also a significant division among ownership of the means of production, the richest 10 percent of landowners owning half of the land and consequently controlling
most of the wealth.[18] Jefferson takes this class structure for granted in
his agrarian manifesto, assuming political leadership on the part of the
large landowner, political quietism on the part of the small landowner,
and powerlessness on the part of the landless.

Jefferson grounds his confidence in the stability of the rural class structure in the assumption that after the war the market for agricultural produce will expand, allowing the class structure to reproduce and in the
process refine itself. He narrates the progress of the market (which we
shall see is characteristic of other agrarians as well). Jefferson notes with
satisfaction that the "culture" of tobacco "was fast declining at the commencement of this war and that of wheat taking its place" (*N*, 173). Tobacco culture will inevitably decline, he argues, because "those employed
in it are in a continued state of exertion beyond the powers of nature
to support. Little food of any kind is raised by them; so that the men
and animals on these farms are badly fed, and the earth is rapidly impoverished" (*N*, 173).[19] Here Jefferson may be alluding to slavery, which he
wanted to abolish not merely on humanitarian grounds but, as we infer
from the Query XVIII, for fear of insurrection. His words apply equally
well, however, to the situation of the tenant farmer who plants too much
tobacco in order to meet his rent and taxes. For the promotion of a stable
agrarian society, wheat is a more suitable staple than tobacco, Jefferson
argues, because "besides cloathing the earth with herbage, and preserving its fertility, it feeds the labourers plentifully, requires from them only
a moderate toil, except in the season of harvest, raises great numbers of
animals for food and service, and diffuses plenty and happiness among
the whole" (*N*, 173). The reference to "labourers" in Jefferson's account
of the rural economy includes any combination of slaves, wage laborers,
tenants, and freeholders.

The important point for Jefferson is not so much the class structure
itself, which he takes for granted, as the relations among choice of crop,
the reproduction of labor and reproduction of the means of production
(the fertility of the land), and the production of surplus value. He goes on
to argue that the freeing up of tobacco land will additionally permit the
raising of horses ("an article of very considerable profit"), cotton, hemp,

and flax (*N*, 174). His table of export values shows that in 1758 these four commodities combined to account for less than 1 percent of the total value of Virginia's exports, in contrast to tobacco, which accounted for 59 percent, but he hopes the proportions will change. Although wheat comprised just 23 percent of 1758 exports, it would, as Jefferson predicted, replace tobacco extensively in the 1780s in response to the increasing European demand for grain.[20] Jefferson focuses on export values rather than on total production because the growth of this surplus provides his only justification for proclaiming, "let our work-shops remain in Europe" (*N*, 171).

Assertions that America's business was agriculture did not originate with Jefferson, of course. From the Hakluyts on, the New World was considered a vent for the English goods that were to be exchanged for raw produce. We have seen the difficulties encountered by John Smith and Robert Beverley, for example, in attempting to promote even the most rudimentary of manufactures. *American Husbandry* (1775), a compendious, colony-by-colony account of American agricultural practices with suggestions for more efficient management, anticipates Jeffersonian agrarianism in many respects. This five-hundred-page analysis, published anonymously in London but written "by an American," as the title page advertises, concludes with a proto-Jeffersonian proposal that manufacturing be excluded from America. The author, like Jefferson, points to the urban proletariat as a locus of political instability, arguing that the desire for political independence will arise in those areas where manufacturing becomes profitable enough to draw population off the land. For both, the key to maintaining social stability is the cultivation of staple crops. But where their programs for land use and economic relations are nearly identical, Jefferson and the author of *American Husbandry* seem to differ radically as to political end—the former, of course, advocating independence from Great Britain and the latter arguing that the colonial relationship will necessarily continue indefinitely given the agricultural base of the American economy. What is common to both, despite apparent differences, is an emphasis on market agrarianism as a structure of sociopolitical control.

A similar, if much briefer plan for the American economy appeared in the first agricultural treatise written in America, Jared Eliot's *Essays upon Field Husbandry in New England* (1748–59). Remarking that "a Staple Commodity is of great Importance to a Country," Eliot specifically advocated the draining of wetlands as especially promising for the cultivation of hemp: "If we can raise more than to supply our own Occasions, we can send it Home" to England.[21] The author of *American Husbandry* is considerably less optimistic two decades later, arguing that in "the northern colonies . . . the climate will not produce staples of value enough to purchase manufactures."[22] However, a preventative to political restlessness is possible in "the establishment of new colonies in such a climate as will yield staples," which would draw off surplus population—a proposal for reversing economic entropy that, as we have seen, had been a familiar topos since More's *Utopia* (*A*, 541). Thus anticipating one of Jefferson's most important acts as president, the author advocates "the acquisition of Louisiana . . . to supply that necessary quantity of fresh land which will be wanting to prevent the surplus population applying to any other profession than agriculture" (*A*, 542). As a means to an essentially similar sociopolitical end, Jefferson noted "we have an immensity of land courting the industry of the husbandman" and asked, "Is it best then that all our citizens should be employed in its improvement, or that one half should be called off from that to exercise manufactures and handicraft arts for the other?" (*N*, 170).

We have seen that Jefferson makes no explicit mention of wage laborers or tenants in his account of rural virtue. Even so, he does not envision a "classless state," as Leo Marx and others have suggested.[23] Rather, he describes a basic division between wealthy and poor white Virginians (the laboring and tenant classes evidently being contained in the latter category). The division is manifested in agricultural practices: "The wealthy are attentive to the raising of vegetables, but very little so to fruits. The poorer people attend to neither, living principally on milk and animal diet. This is the more inexcusable, as the climate requires indispensably a free use of vegetable food, for health as well as comfort, and is very friendly to the raising of fruits" (*N*, 158). The poor ought to grow peas, and both rich and poor ought to grow apples, but the basic occupation of agriculture will continue to reproduce the social and political relations outlined in Query XIX. That the economic hierarchy might admit some social permeability—at least for those "twenty of the best geniusses [who] will be raked from the rubbish annually" by means of public education (*N*, 153)—does not change the existence or the desirability (from Jefferson's perspective) of the class structure as such.

Benjamin Franklin had described a similar, and similarly stable, rural class structure in the North with a trio of poems in the 1755 issue of his almanac, *Poor Richard*.[24] The first of these, evidently a paraphrase of Horace's second Epode (*Beatus ille*), retains the original's praise of rural virtue, describing a "happy swain" who in "studying Nature grows serenely Wise," but eliminates its descriptions of farming activities: pruning, harvesting, shearing, and the like (*P*, 469).[25] The following two poems introduce a class division into the rural scene while obscuring the origin of that division in the question of labor. "The Farmer," who is set in contrast to both the "Beggar" and the "Great Man" of the city, is "far remov'd from Slavery, as from Pride." He has "No shining Heaps of massy Plate" but lives independently (we never see quite how) on "his old paternal Fields," where bird songs "Invite to sacred Thought, and lift the Mind / From low Pursuits, to meditate the God!" (*P*, 470–71). In "Rural Life in a Higher Class," the landlord, subject of the poem, commands a more extensive view of a more plentiful landscape than does the small farmer. Twelve lines, for example, enumerate the flowers in his garden and trees in his grove and orchard. He also is shown to have a power that the small farmer does not, since he transforms his environment into an object of beauty: "There from his forming Hand new Scenes arise, / The fair Creation of his Fancy's Eye," including garden, grove, orchard, field, pasture, temple, mansion, with wild fields (roses, honeysuckles, and so on) beyond (*P*, 473). Absent here are the wage laborer or the tenant, who actually do the work of forming these scenes. In fact it is a convention of eighteenth-century agricultural writing that all labor is attributed to the agency of the owner. Poor Richard advised that "the Master's Eye will do more Work than both his Hands" (*P*, 474). Jared Eliot, in describing a ditching operation performed when he was sixty-two and presumably beyond very much hard labor, refers indiscriminately to "I," "we," and "the Labourer," finding no conflict in thus subsuming the subjectivity of labor (*F*, 25).

Crèvecoeur, like Jefferson, Franklin, and the author of *American Husbandry*, assumes that an agricultural economy will produce social and political stability in America, but goes further in representing farmers as a homogenous, classless group in the early letters.[26] "Some few towns excepted," says James, "we are all tillers of the earth," and this geographical equivalence is aligned with socioeconomic equivalence:

Lawyer or merchant are the fairest titles our towns afford: that of a farmer is the only appellation of the rural inhabitants of our country. . . . There, on a Sunday, [one] sees a congregation of respectable farmers and their wives, all clad in neat homespun, well mounted, or riding in their own humble waggons. There is not among them an esquire, saving the unlettered magistrate. There [one] sees a parson as simple as his flock, a farmer who does not riot on the labour of others. (*L*, 41)

Yet "farmer" here must denote not only landowners large and small, but wage laborers and tenants as well, if that is the only title applicable to "rural inhabitants." According to Crèvecoeur, an immigrant begins as a laborer, and is very well treated during this time, but does not remain in that position for long. Consider the story of Andrew the Hebridean, who is supposed to typify the immigrant's experience. The immigrant counts in Crèvecoeur's narrative only insofar as he becomes a freeholder:

He purchases some land; he gives all the money he has brought over, as well as what he has earned, and trusts to the God of harvests for the discharge of the rest.

His good name procures him credit; he is now possessed of the deed, conveying to him and his posterity the fee simple and absolute property of two hundred acres of land [this is roughly half the size of James's own holdings], situated on such a river. What an epocha in this man's life! He is become a freeholder, from perhaps a German boor; he is now an American, a Pennsylvanian, an English subject. (*L*, 58)

His identity as an American farmer is complete, that is, at the moment he is bound into the markets in land and agricultural produce through a structure of debt, a manner more inextricable, hence more secure, than that of the wage laborer.

However, Crèvecoeur's story of Andrew the Hebridean, which is meant to typify the process of Americanization, is not quite the story of a freeholder. Andrew is in fact a tenant and remains one through the four years during which Crèvecoeur charts his fortunes. At first, Andrew wants to buy some land, but does not have sufficient capital or and credit. The landlord-speculator whom he approaches will not sell him the one hundred acres in question, but says he "will do better" by leasing it to Andrew for thirty years on the following conditions: no rent the first seven years; an obligation to plant fifty fruit trees and drain seven acres of swamp in the first three years; after seven years, rent of $12.50 per year (*L*, 77). These are generous terms. The period of the lease is much longer than the customary five to seven years. If Andrew wants to be released from his obligations, the landlord will pay him for the improvements he has made to that point, according to a jury's valuation. Andrew "may sell the lease" but not the land itself, so he does not hold "the fee simple and absolute property" of this tract, which Crèvecoeur states elsewhere is a fundamental precondition of his becoming "an American" (*L*, 79, 58). For the landlord—who assumes that Andrew will build a house and outbuildings and will eventually clear or drain the specified amount of land—Andrew's tenancy is a means to hold, improve, and draw a profit on land that would otherwise only cost him in taxes or quit-rents. Additionally, in a market where labor is scarce and labor requirements vary seasonally, tenancy provides an efficient means to bind labor power to the landlord's holdings.[27] If Andrew vacates early, the landlord will have a good farm to sell, or to rent again at higher rates, to be further improved.

For Andrew, tenancy is a means to accumulate capital for entry into the landowning class, a step up the socioeconomic ladder from his beginnings in America as a wage laborer. Yet if he was a typical tenant, his prospects for entry into the landowning class were not as good as Crèvecoeur implies. According to a study of tenancy in colonial Chester County, Pennsylvania, for example, by the middle of the eighteenth century, "few persons who climbed the tenurial ladder from laborer to farm tenant were able to acquire capital or credit early enough in life to buy improved land in the county and then retire their debts without help from their families or by income from a trade" such as milling or innkeeping. For the vast majority of tenants, migration westward offered the best economic opportunity.[28] At the time, southwestern Pennsylvania would have been a likely choice. If, in moving there, a hypothetical Andrew avoided tenancy and bought land (by no means the norm at this time, since landowners comprised only one-fourth to one-third of the total population and newcomers were more likely than old residents to be landless),[29] then he would be encumbered with a mortgage, the very thing from which his first landlord had saved him by refusing to sell him land. He would in any case have to deal with another land speculator who might pressure him into tenancy as the first had done. If he bought land, in order to pay his mortgage he would have to depend on the market in agricultural produce. This market, though small, did exist in all but the most remote areas. In southwestern Pennsylvania in 1796, downriver trade was profitable for the 16 percent of landowners who produced at commercial levels. Another 63 percent produced enough over subsistence to enter local markets, but these were much more likely to be barter than cash. A great deal of this surplus was produced by tenants for the profit of landlords, the few who traded downriver.[30] The lives of many Andrews were determined by the structure of land speculation and tenancy.

Although the writers discussed so far sometimes note a distinction between large and small landowner, for the most part they tend to minimize the importance of this distinction and to elide tenancy and wage laboring altogether, containing all farmers in a single category, the "yeoman" or "freeholder" who is a synecdoche for all Americans. However, complicating any simple picture of America as a nation of yeomen was the existence of a class of migratory subsistence farmers who represented an indeterminate place in the socioeconomic structure, being neither wage laborers nor, in important respects, landowners amenable to the agrarian design. Where agricultural intensification required an increased application of labor to land (labor that was often elided in the literature of improvement), the backwoods farmers represented an alternative to intensification. Many such farmers were squatters or tenants, but even if they held land outright, they were characterized by their separateness from the market and by their "living without government" (A, 200). Crèvecoeur calls them "our bad people" and predicts their rapid displacement by, or infrequent transformation into, civilized agrarians. Anticipating the stadialist settlement theory of Benjamin Rush, he explains that

remote from the power of example and check of shame, many families exhibit the most hideous parts of our society. They are a kind of forlorn hope, preceding, by ten or twelve years, the most respectable army of veterans which come after them.

In that space, prosperity will polish some, vice and the law will drive off the rest, who, uniting with others like themselves, will recede still farther, making room for more industrious people, who will finish their improvements, convert the log-house into a convenient habitation, and, rejoicing that the first heavy labours are finished, will change, in a few years, that hitherto-barbarous country into a fine, fertile, well-regulated, district. (*L*, 47)

Crèvecoeur's farmer James himself imagined such a narrative of progress as he thought about moving west among the Indians to avoid the turmoil of the Revolution, during which "our civil government" could no longer "shed [its] blessings on our husbandry" (*L*, 39). In Letter XII, James says he will bring portable grain mills with him, build plows, and "persuade" the Indians "to till a little more land than they do, and not to trust so much to the produce of the chase" (*L*, 210). He has observed, however, that on moving to the back country, men "degenerate" in manners and morals (*L*, 52): "Once hunters, farewell to the plough," since the "eating of wild meat . . . tends to alter [the] temper" of even formerly civilized farmers (*L*, 51, 52). Thus he will encourage "industrious motives" in his own children by keeping accounts of their production, "giv[ing] each of them a regular credit for the amount of it to be paid them, in real property, at the return of peace" (*L*, 212). If the economic realities of frontier life, "toiling for bare subsistence on a foreign land," will not encourage intensification, James will thus by both material and symbolic means bring the agrarian economy to the backwoods (*L*, 212).

Where Crèvecoeur explicitly locates backwoodsmen in "the Carolinas, Virginia, and many other parts" (*L*, 54), Jefferson does not seem to recognize them as a distinct class. We can perhaps read a division between backwoods farmers and agrarians into Jefferson's distinction between the wealthy and the poor. Yet if this suggests an implicit goal of bringing Virginia's back settlers into line with the agrarian ideal, for the most part Jefferson simply ignores any farmer who does not participate directly in the market. Looking into the future, he describes even the future farmers of "the western country on the Mississippi, and the midlands of Georgia" as fully embedded in the market for produce: they "will be able to undersell" Virginia and Maryland in tobacco, obliging the latter to shift to grain, flax, and livestock production (*N*, 173). In this way, when Virginia and Maryland no longer "hav[e] such quantities of land to waste as we please," the present "indifferent state" of agriculture will be improved (*N*, 92).

Other representations of backwoods farming appear after the Revolution in the works of writers more intent on investigating the rural class structure than were either Jefferson or Crèvecoeur. Benjamin Rush in particular identifies three "species" of settlers in a letter to English physician Thomas Percival in 1786; this letter was later published in his *Essays*

(1798) as "An Account of the Progress of Population, Agriculture, Manners, and Government in Pennsylvania."[31] In this essay, each "species" (class here takes on a quasi-biological existence as the scientist Rush naturalizes the social phenomenon he inscribes) is identified by a profile of traits and practices bearing clear implications for American ideology. The three occupy points on a chronological continuum, indicating stages from extensive to intensive cultivation and culminating in the establishment of ideal agrarianism. The evaluative aspect of Rush's account, which discouraged backwoods farming and promoted intensification, had practical political implications for the state of Pennsylvania at this time. According to documents surrounding the Treaty of Fort Stanwix (1784), the Iroquois would retain hunting rights on ceded lands in western Pennsylvania "untill [those lands] are improved," at which point those rights no longer obtained.[32]

The settler who first begins this improvement process is, according to Rush, "generally a man who has outlived his credit or fortune in the cultivated parts of the State" (E, 213). He does not start out a raw immigrant, like Andrew the Hebridean, but has already attempted the American agrarian success story and failed. He is usually "a tenant to some rich landholder" and presumably has been one before (E, 215). His agricultural practices are those of backwoods farming: girdling trees (an old method, common on Virginia tobacco land, quicker even than logging to clear land for a first crop), primarily planting corn, not remaining long on a single tract. Crèvecoeur had claimed that backwoodsmen "contract the vices" of the Indians (L, 53). So, too, Rush remarks that "as he lives in the neighbourhood of Indians, he soon acquires a strong tincture of their manners," such as a propensity for "violent" fits of labor "succeeded by long intervals of rest" (E, 214). Yet for Rush this formation is determined by the interaction of social structure with innate character. He does not speak, as does Crèvecoeur, of any alteration of temper caused by eating wild meat, or any other such purely environmental-physiological causal mechanism. Rush's first settler remains only "two or three years" on a given piece of ground. Civilization inevitably progresses and "above all" the first settler "revolts against the operation of laws. He cannot bear to surrender up a single natural right for all the benefits of government, — and therefore he abandons his little settlement" and moves on (E, 215). Rush estimates that some individuals of this class "have broken ground on bare creation, not less than four different times in this way, in different and more advanced parts" of Pennsylvania (E, 215).

Where Rush is concerned with backwoods farmers in Pennsylvania and Crèvecoeur with those in Virginia and the Carolinas, others found in New Jersey a similar class, who "exhaust the old [land] till it will bear nothing more, and then, not having manure to replenish it, nothing remains but taking new land to serve in the same manner" (*A*, 105). The backwoods farming method was said to be a problem pervading all of American agriculture at this time.[33] So argued John Spurrier, whose treatise *The Practical Farmer* (1793) was dedicated to Jefferson. As do Rush and Crèvecoeur, Spurrier criticizes the emulation of Native American practices:

The farmers in general, in this country seem to have studied the cultivation of no grain but maize or Indian corn. . . . It suits the Indians, as they have such a plenty of land, but being of a roving disposition they are not longer in a place than just to have two or three crops, and then remove to another spot. That cultivation may suit some of the farmers here, as well as the Indians (from whom they learned) as long as they can do like them; that is when they have wore out their land, to remove to another place; but when this country increases in population, and gets thicker inhabited, the case will be altered.[34]

By 1819, however, the case was evidently not yet altered, according to John Lorain, who at that date published a promotional tract, *Hints to Emigrants*, to encourage settlement in Pennsylvania rather than on the prairies, where an abundance of federally-administered land was becoming available in the wake of the government's dispossession of the indigenous inhabitants. Lorain, himself a Pennsylvania farmer, also wrote an agricultural treatise, *Nature and Reason Harmonized in the Practice of Husbandry*.[35] In this treatise, he argues that while the backwoods method has the merit of providing great immediate fertility, the "Yankee" method of permanent occupation, crop rotation, and intensive manuring ought to supplant it after the first crop. So important is the choice of farming method that he proposes that "poor" farmers, whom he specifically characterizes as tenants, ought to be compelled by their leases "to farm properly."[36] Intensive manuring, among the most important of these proper practices, could be accomplished by two means, both requiring capital investment and thus participation in the market. A large investment in cattle could be recovered by selling dairy products if a market was available. Use of green manure crops required an investment in seed and an investment in time to enable cleared land to be taken out of direct production while the manure crop matured; these could be recovered through the sale of increased grain yields. But such practices are too seldom implemented, Lorain argues. The frontier farmer has been taught "by precept and example, to build a cabin, clear land, plough and crop perpetually, until the grounds are so much exhausted as no longer to produce crops worth half the value of the labor bestowed upon them. After this very extensive and inconsiderate injury has been done to the soil, these cultivators remove further back, in the fruitless search of a soil that will never wear out."[37] Lorain misinterprets the intentions of many of these farmers, who were not interested in calculations of labor value but were, in their semi-

nomadic practices, "preserving their traditional lifestyle through migration."[38] Assuming a profit orientation among all farmers, he argues that
Illinois is too far from "a good market for the produce of the land," a place
where prices are low and "labour quite as high, or higher" than in more
thickly settled areas. Even if the farmer hires no labor, "yet, if he estimate
his labour, and that of his family, at a fair price, (and this he certainly
ought to do, in a country where labour is more valuable than the same
amount of money,) and to this add the interest of his capital, he will soon
see, that farming, under the circumstances noticed above, is a very bad
business, when compared with what might be done elsewhere."[39] Lorain
goes on to argue that Pennsylvania land can bear yields of wheat as high
as that of Illinois (20 bushels per acre), provided that the farmer "possess
a sufficient capital to keep a good stock of cattle and to cultivate the soil as
it should be."[40] That Lorain would soon be proved wrong on this point, as
prairie farms produced yields hitherto unheard of (without manuring),
is unimportant in this context. What is important is that he identifies part
of the economic foundation of two incompatible agricultural practices
and argues that farming ought to be so thoroughly governed by market
considerations that even a farm family's labor ought to be measured in
dollars, rather than in terms of its mere ability to sustain itself.

Despite the agrarian improvers' critiques, economic factors did not
always permit a choice of practices. Given the scarcity of markets for agricultural produce in frontier regions, farmers west of the Appalachians
generally farmed at a subsistence rather than a market level because they
found that their "best and perhaps only marketable product" was an improved farmstead.[41] They worked to build houses, barns or sheds, and
fences, and to clear forest, not to increase their production of crops and
livestock. Even small landholders were potentially speculators, their connection to the land market eclipsing their connection to the produce
market and encouraging transient occupancy patterns.[42] Market forces
encouraged similar practices in both freehold and landlord-tenant structures. Recall that Andrew the Hebridean, while never able to own the land
he works, was permitted to sell what improvements he could make in the
way of buildings, clearings, and so on, if he chose to move. Rush assumes
that tenants are not so empowered, but similarly observes the speculative
endeavors of small landowners: "If our first settler was the owner of the
spot of land which he began to cultivate, he sells it at a considerable profit
to his successor; but if (as is oftner the case) he was a tenant to some rich
landholder, he abandons it in debt; however, the small improvements he
leaves behind him, generally make it an object of immediate demand" (E,
215–16). Since large landowners found tenancy financially advantageous,
a "symbiotic relationship between tenancy and speculation" emerged in
frontier areas.[43] In western Pennsylvania, the locus of Rush's analysis, op-

portunity for land speculation peaked in the early to mid 1790s, soon after the date of Rush's letter to Percival, but held strong for some time thereafter.[44]

One of the few positive representations of backwoods farmers during this period appears in John Filson's promotional tract, *The Discovery, Settlement, and Present State of Kentucke* (1784). This text is best known for its appendix containing the supposed autobiography of Daniel Boone. Where the Boone narrative focuses on the slaughter of Indians, the main text describes the agrarian settlement made possible by that slaughter and by the "four natural qualities necessary to promote the happiness of a country, viz. A good soil, air, water, and trade."[45] A substantial portion of the text is devoted to discussions of transportation routes. Holding to a theory of agricultural practice that Lorain and Spurrier would disapprove of, Filson argues that Kentucky land "will produce about thirty bushels of wheat, and rye, upon a moderate computation, per acre. . . . These accounts of such amazing fertility may, to some, appear incredible, but are certainly true. Every husbandman may have a good garden, or meadow, without water or manure, where he pleases" (*D*, 25). Although the Kentuckians use backwoods farming practices (not manuring their fields), in their social and political practices they would not seem to be backwoods farmers according to the prevailing contemporary definition. According to Filson, these first Kentuckians are "polite, humane, hospitable, and very complaisant. . . . As yet united to the State of Virginia, they are governed by her wholesome laws, which are virtuously executed, and with excellent decorum. Schools for education are formed, and a college is appointed by act of the Assembly of Virginia, to be founded under the conduct of trustees in Kentucke, and endowed with lands for its use" (*D*, 29). Churches have also been established, and thus "from these early movements it is hoped that Kentucke will eminently shine in learning and piety, which will fulfil the wish of every virtuous citizen" (*D*, 30). Filson uses the Boone narrative to reinforce this image. It begins with a vision of civilization already accomplished: "we behold Kentucke, lately an howling wilderness, the habitation of savages and wild beasts, become a fruitful field; this region, so favorably distinguished by nature, now become the habitation of civilization" (*D*, 49). The conclusion of the Boone narrative delineates the nature of that civilization: "Let peace, descending from her native heaven, bid her olives spring amidst the joyful nations; and *plenty, in league with commerce,* scatter blessings from her copious hand" (*D*, 81, emphasis added).

We find then, in turn-of-the-century agricultural literature, conflicting representations of backwoods farmers. The reason lies at least partly in the particular positions of the respective authors. Rush and Filson both want to promote a market orientation, but Filson's text on the whole supplies more encouragement to land speculators, no doubt because Filson was himself a speculator with a personal interest in stimulating the western land market. Since the structure of land speculation and tenancy encouraged nonintensive, backwoods farming practices in western Pennsylvania, it must have done so in Kentucky as well, where, after the opening of the Virginia land office in 1779, speculation was rampant.[46] It is tempting to conclude that Filson's settlers are not tenants or backwoodsmen at all, but rather commercial farmers. This is unlikely however, given the interplay of market forces in land and produce, which encouraged speculation and transient occupancy patterns.[47] Considering the dependence of land speculators on tenancy to improve the land, it is quite probable that Filson's law-abiding, pious, ambitious Kentuckians are being represented as ideal tenants, the sort that speculators might hope to engage.[48] Since Rush is not writing as a speculator, he can afford to represent the backwoodsmen more negatively—especially since his stadialist theory predicts that they will eventually disappear. He is not even so generous as Crèvecoeur, who calls them "a kind of forlorn hope" since "prosperity will polish some" (as it had done for farmer James's father) even as "vice and the law will drive off the rest" (L, 47).

Rush's second "species of settler," a midpoint in the development of intensive, civilized agrarianism, is "generally a man of some property"; he pays one-third or one-fourth down in cash for a three hundred- to four hundred-acre tract (E, 216). Since we know that he has replaced the first settler, we can assume that he has purchased the land either from the state of Pennsylvania (in which case the first settler would have been a squatter) or, equally likely, from a speculator (in which case the first settler may have been either tenant or squatter).[49] But the second settler is not industrious and so cannot meet his mortgage. His farming is primarily subsistence oriented: he "by no means extracts all from the earth, which it is capable of giving," raising "but little more than is necessary to support [his] famil[y]" (E, 217, 222). This may be because he "sometimes drinks spiritous liquors to excess" and "delights chiefly in company." He "will spend a day or two in every week in attending political meetings," time that could be better spent farming; as a result, "he contracts debts which . . . compel him to sell his plantation, generally in the course of a few years, to the *third* and last species of settler" (E, 217, emphasis in original). Given this burden of debt, we might expect him to degenerate into the first species. Rush does not, in any case, pursue his fortunes any further, for the point of the chronological scheme of displacement is the permanent settlement of the third species. In this way, the market economy, as manifested directly in the debts that cause the second settler to sell up and move on, thus ensures its own maximization by driving off those who cannot, or will not, participate in it.

Although the second settlers do participate in the market for land, Rush finds their full participation in the market economy complicated by the production of one anomalous commodity. He points out that the second settler "raises a quantity of wheat and rye: the latter is cultivated chiefly for the purpose of being distilled into whiskey" (*E*, 216). The virtuous third class of settler, as we will see, will have none of the second settler's whiskey: "beer, cyder, and home made wine are the usual drinks of his family" (*E*, 219). The latter drinks are made on each farm, only for home consumption. Unlike whiskey, their production does not distract the farmer from the marketing of grain and fiber staples. Beer and cider connote temperance as well, there being an important moral distinction here between fermented and distilled beverages, to which Rush attached political significance.[50] In a passage that takes on greater weight with the 1798 publication (soon after the Whiskey Rebellion) Rush remarks on the second settler's resistance to taxation: "with high ideas of liberty, he refuses to bear his proportion of the debt contracted by its [i.e., liberty's] establishment in our country" (*E*, 217). This antitax ideology emerges directly from material conditions. Whiskey was primarily an item of barter, produced for local consumption. Distilleries were numerous but small; for example, in Washington County, Pennsylvania, 500 stills were in operation in 1790, or one for every ten families.[51] Since the whiskey excise was imposed at the point of production, rather than at the point of purchase, the small distiller had no means of raising money for taxes on whiskey that was not sold for cash. Ironically, though, whiskey would seem to be an ideal product for the emerging market agrarianism that Rush envisions. Since it occupies only one-sixth of the volume of the grain from which it has been distilled, it was more easily and profitably transported over long and difficult trade routes.[52] Rush's temperance views proscribe any consideration of this means of economic development.

In the third and final stage of settlement, Rush links the "complet[ion]" of "civilization" to market-oriented practices (*E*, 221). He states that "it is to the third species of settler only, that it is proper to apply the term of *farmers*" (*E*, 221, emphasis in original). One of this class is "commonly a man of property and good character—sometimes he is the son of a wealthy farmer in one of the interior and ancient counties of the state" (*E*, 218). This farmer diversifies his crops; "convert[s] every spot of ground" he can to productive use, to hay meadow if not to crop land; plants a large garden and orchard (answering Jefferson's call for the cultivation of more vegetables and fruits); and builds permanent stone buildings (again, answering Jefferson) (*E*, 218). Like Jefferson's yeomen, he participates in the market for agricultural produce where the first and second settler does not, thus promoting what Rush perceives to be the public good. For example, "it was from the produce of these farms, that those millions of dollars were obtained from the Havanna after the year 1780, which laid the foundation of the bank of North America, and which fed and cloathed the American army, till the peace of Paris" (*E*, 220). As a result of his privileged position with respect to the market, the third settler both wants and can afford government, which Rush views primarily as a protector of property rights: "in proportion as he encreases in wealth, he values the protection of laws: hence he punctually pays his taxes towards the support of government" (*E*, 219–20).

The market generating this wealth seems to consist of only two agents: the landowner-producer and the consumer. That is, in specifying that the third settler's "sons work by his side all the year and his wife and daughters forsake the dairy and spinning wheel, to share with him in the toils of harvest," Rush ignores the large amount of wage labor used on such farms (*E*, 219). We have already seen that he takes a dim view of the tenant class, however necessary this class was as a preliminary stage in the establishment of market agriculture. The admission that the intensive agriculture he so admires in fact requires the existence of a permanent wage-laboring, dependent class would complicate his social vision, in which "benevolence and public spirit . . . are the natural offspring of affluence and independence" (*E*, 220). This elision of the wage labor necessary for intensification is marked in an otherwise relatively class-conscious analysis.

Rather than entering into immediate social relations, Rush's ideal agrarians evidently form their social identity according to the structure of mediation that Myra Jehlen identifies as typically American: "The connections between men come indirectly through their common connection to the land." Yet the question of "American incarnation" is more complicated than this, as we have seen, and works differently for different classes.[53] One difference is evident for example in the contrast between Rush's third settler—who works "alone" (or rather with the help of invisible hired laborers) and devotes some of his profits to the establishment of churches, schools, and other material icons of civilization—and the second settler—who spends much of his time in the company of others without perceiving the need for these mediating structures. Not only do the second settlers drink together and foment revolutionary politics (thus threatening to emulate the urban proletariat that Jefferson so abhorred), they also perform much of their labor communally. The "want of money" deriving from their subsistence orientation, according to Rush, makes it "necessary for them to associate for the purposes of building houses, cutting their grain, and the like:—This they do in turns for each other, without any other pay than the pleasures which usually attend a country frolic" (*E*, 222). In contrast, "the virtues which direct [the third settler], are industry and oeconomy. Idleness—extravagance—and ignorance fly before him" (*E*, 225). Even farmer James, Crèvecoeur's sober Quaker, approved of the "frolic" accompanying communal labor such as house-raising (*L*, 80). For Rush the communal ideology of the backwoodsmen is negatively valued because their labor practices themselves "aris[e] from necessity, and the peculiar state of society in which these people live.—Virtue should, in all cases, be the offspring of principle" (*E*, 222). Rush's first and second classes of settlers engage in communal labor on the land without pay for their own mutual benefit, and only so far as required for their subsistence. They make social connections with each other directly through that labor. The most "civilized" class, on the other hand, find their social and political identity only in their connection to the market, where the interaction of commodities replaces human interaction. Their connection to the market alone warrants the particular form of their connection to the land. The market itself is the foundational social institution—schools, churches, and the like being mere epiphenomena of the market, funded by the profit generated by intensification. Thus the market figures as the ultimate guarantee of "freedom"—and there is no longer a need for political association to ensure "freedom" (as in the case of the second settler). The material structure of engagement with the land itself becomes a secondary issue.

It seems curious that none of the texts discussed so far directly addresses the prevalence of squatters in frontier areas, since squatting by definition poses an affront to market ideology. Even in avoiding the land market, however, squatters did economically benefit landowners. By clearing fields and undertaking other improvements, they performed the same services as tenants or laborers. On the other hand, in their emulation of Native American farming practices and occupancy patterns, squatters were perceived as not being dedicated to the *permanent* improvement of the land. As we have seen, a central assumption of land tenure in this country has been that the right to occupy land derives from laboring on it so as to improve it. This assumption, coupled with the fiction that Native Americans were not farmers, legitimated the expropriation of their lands.[54] While Filson does not mention Native American agriculture and Jefferson and Crèvecoeur minimize its cultural importance, other eighteenth-century agrarians do admit it; but it is the wrong kind of farming from their perspective, a kind practiced by the white backwoodsman as well. This nonintensive method of agriculture would leave the land unchanged in the long run *if* it were not subsequently occupied by sedentary farmers. When a field no longer supported a high yield of corn, it was left to return to forest, whereby fertility would be restored. It would eventually be completely reforested, as anyone who has hiked in a second-growth forest (without being consciously aware that it was once clear-cut) will recognize. Meanwhile, the field provided edge lands that supported an increased population of deer and other animal sources of food. In dealing with both Native American and white practitioners of this farming method, the agrarians assume a narrative of displacement and progress. Of course they do not advocate killing backwoodsmen as if they were Indians, but they do assume a similar migration westward in the face of expanding civilization and its visible sign, the market. Yet contrary to the agrarians' narratives of class displacement, some squatters stayed on their lands rather than moving on, claiming right by improvement. As early as 1750, in some areas of Pennsylvania, squatters were brought into the land market by the legislation of preemption rights, according to which a squatter's improvement of land gave him first right of purchase.[55] In Kentucky, a preemption law came into force with the opening of the Virginia Land Office in 1779. As a result, a squatter there might suddenly become a small-scale speculator, since preemption permitted a claim of 1,400 acres.[56] On federally administered lands, beginning with the Land Ordinance of 1785, government policy did not tolerate squatters, but attempts to prevent or remove them often proved ineffective. Squatters formed claims clubs to protect their access to land at federal auction, while local political pressures secured various exemptions, leading to the Preemption Acts of 1830 and 1841.[57] In this way, as contemporary agricultural writers well knew, squatters were eventually brought into the land market and/or forced off the land.

The year after Rush published his account of Pennsylvania settlement in his collected *Essays*, Charles Brockden Brown satirized it in his frontier gothic, *Edgar Huntly* (1799). Where Rush's scheme had provided a specific program for the Jeffersonian goal of orderly westward expansion, grounding political stability in the stadialist development of agrarian virtue, Brown undermines that ground. Brown's rejection of Jeffersonianism by the early 1800s is well known.[58] We can read this rejection as beginning with *Wieland*, but in any case it is clear in *Arthur Mervyn*, where in Part II of the novel Arthur reverses the trajectory of Part I: he abandons his hundred acres, rejects the farmer's daughter, and leaves the countryside for good, interested now only in the manners and social institutions of the city. In the early 1800s, Brown went on to write a series of anti-Jeffersonian pamphlets. In *Edgar Huntly*, which he wrote between Parts I and II of *Arthur Mervyn*, Brown worked up to this position by taking aim at Rush. We recall that Huntly, in making his way back to the settlement of Solebury after his horrendous experiences in the wilderness, comes across three farmsteads in turn. These farmsteads correspond significantly to Rush's three stages of frontier settlement. In the first, Huntly finds a mere hut, "consist[ing] of a few unhewn logs laid upon each other," which "had been erected by a Scottish emigrant, who not being rich enough to purchase land, and entertaining a passion for solitude and independence, cleared a field in the unappropriated wilderness, and subsisted on its produce," as we would expect of Rush's first species of settler.[59] This squatter, however, had since "disappeared," perhaps killed by Indians (*H*, 200). In any case, the progress of civilization would seem to have gone backwards here, for the hut has long been occupied by the Lenape Old Deb (also a squatter), who had refused to be removed westward with the rest of her nation. Where Deb had formerly been rather sociable, frequently visiting Solebury, she now restricted her rambles to the wilds, in the company of "her guardian wolves" (*H*, 201). This much, while complicating Rush's scheme, does not yet necessarily controvert it. The next farmstead Huntly encounters on his way back to Solebury represents an improvement on the Scot's hut and clearing. The dwelling is "small and low" but is built of boards (albeit rough-sawn) rather than logs; near it is a small apple orchard (*H*, 196). Most of these details correspond to Rush's description of the second settler's farmstead, as does the contrast between the independence of the Scot and the sociability of the inhabitants of the second farmstead, who offer Huntly "hospitable entertainment" as Rush's second settlers would be glad to do (*H*, 196). Finally, nearest to Solebury, Huntly finds a house with glazed windows (distinctly a luxury), built of boards that "had undergone the plane, as well as the axe and saw," and "embellished with mouldings and a pediment"; he infers from these and other "tokens that this was the abode not only of rural competence and innocence, but of some beings, raised by education and fortune, above the intellectual mediocrity of clowns" (*H*, 217). Yet here, when confirmation of Rush's narrative of rural progress is apparently complete, Brown undercuts that narrative's assumptions. The third farmer turns out to be a drunkard who lives "a wild and ruffian life" that is "little in unison with the external appearances of the mansion" (*H*, 218). The place has a commodious barn, and other evidences of a good estate, but so debauched is the owner that in a fit of rage he has banished his wife and child to this barn just moments after an Indian attack. Huntly, who had hoped from the appearance of the place that he "could claim consanguinity with such beings" as inhabited it, concludes, "here then was no asylum for me" and continues on the road toward town (*H*, 217, 220). Thus disrupting Rush's reified understanding of the rural class structure, Brown uses details borrowed from Rush's writings to dissociate morality and social stability from economic individualism as represented by the market-oriented third settler.

Having thus criticized even the tempered republican possibilities in Rush's ideas on agrarian development, Brown would later move further to the right as he sketched his own views. In "A Specimen of Agricultural Improvement" and "A Specimen of Political Improvement," two fragments published in the *Literary Magazine* in 1805, he tells the story of Sir A——, who marries the orphaned heiress of a 25,000-acre estate in Scotland, fires the corrupt steward, and takes up the management of the estate himself.[60] Sir A—— divides the existing fifty-acre farms in half, but the new system of cultivation he introduces, which substitutes new crop choices, crop rotation, and manuring for the former long-fallow system, increases the productivity of these farms by a factor of five. The wastes are improved as well: moors are enclosed for pasture or cropland or planted to timber, and fens are drained for meadow—while the tenants lose the rights to these commons by which they had (inefficiently, to Sir A——'s mind) supported themselves. Thirty years into this program of intensification, the new order of the landscape, with its "neat and substantial dwellings and barns, the fields . . . completely hedged, or fenced, or ditched," gives visible evidence of his accomplishments.[61] The population of the estate has increased fourfold and the revenue ninefold. Sir A—— invests some of his new revenue in creating new parishes and schools and in rebuilding a town that will soon be "the most beautiful in Europe" ("A," 92). He undertakes all these improvements not for himself, Brown says, "but as they were subservient to the general good."[62]

Yet Sir A—— has been able to accomplish this program only through the exercise of "unlimited authority" over the occupants of the land ("A," 91). The lords of the estate historically had "never . . . alienate[d] any portion" of it, employing only "tenants at will" whose leases were never "for a longer term than a year" ("A," 90). Sir A—— continues this policy, for even the practice of "granting leases of considerable duration," which might give tenants some limited freedom in land management decisions, would "undermine" the "true foundation" of his "power," thus threatening to "destroy" the "harmony of his system" ("P," 127). He admits tenants only "under strict conditions as to the mode and objects of their cultivation" ("A," 88). If they do not fulfill these conditions, or if they commit any other infraction, they are simply dismissed. "In judging his people," Sir A—— is "bound down by no laws, either written or prescriptive" ("P," 127). Rather, his tenants' "life, liberty, and property" are "held, in fact, by no other tenure than their lord's pleasure" ("A," 91). Brown clearly admires this "despotic" power, tantamount to "political tyranny," since it "render[s] the will of Sir A—— absolute" in effecting his program ("A," 91; "P," 126). Ironized echoes of the Declaration of Independence are unmistakable ("property" here translating into "the pursuit of happiness," as most of the founders understood it to do) as Brown argues the benefits of a system in which a landlord's power stands in for and exceeds the power of a republican state. Such a structure of control was lacking in Rush's narrative and in other accounts such as Lorain's, which could only argue that farmers ought to be compelled by their leases "to farm properly." [63] According to Rush, individuals would respond or not, depending on their inherent virtues, to free-market conditions, maximizing efficiency through intensification; by increasing the market embeddedness of numerous individual owner-operators, intensification would theoretically produce sociopolitical stability. Brown disavows any such notion of inherent virtue, characterizing the laboring classes as naturally "a race of tipplers and idlers" who are reformed only through Sir A——'s strict supervision and subject to immediate dismissal if his program of "new modelling the rising generation" failed in a given instance ("P," 122). Brown thus dispenses with the possibility of agrarian republicanism entirely, seeing the only hope for stability and productivity not through direct engagements with the land and produce markets, but rather in a system of universal tenancy, in which such engagements are mediated only by the landlord, who controls the labor market absolutely.

*   *   *

The discourse of rural virtue during the late eighteenth and early nineteenth century worked to naturalize the market by arguing that the environment itself would naturally encourage intensification, the development of a market economy, and its supposedly concomitant sociopolitical stability.[64] Filson, we recall, claimed that Kentucky possessed the "four *natural* qualities necessary to promote the happiness of a country, viz. A good soil, air, water, and *trade*" (*D*, 107, emphases added), while Rush regarded the ever-increasing engagement with these qualities as the inevitable progress of civilization. By representing backwoods farming as an abuse of the land, rather than as a sustainable practice that put a low limit on population density, agrarian theorists developed an implicit environmentally based rationale for economic intensification, thus linking land closely to market concerns. However, backwoods farming was also affected by market relations to a large extent: specifically, by a strong, often speculative market in land, a limited market for agricultural produce above local subsistence, and a relative scarcity of wage labor that increased with distance from thickly settled areas, which, among other things, encouraged short-run tenancy or squatting. Given these market determinations, then, nonintensive backwoods farming could not be dismissed out of hand as an unnatural response to the environment. Facing the ideological complications thus posed by the backwoods farmers, agrarian theorists employed a variety of strategies. They marginalized the impact of the speculator-tenant structure on farming practices and market relations (Jefferson, Crèvecoeur, Franklin, Spurrier, Filson, Rush).[65] They excoriated nonintensive farming practices and antimarket ideologies and proposed backwoods farming's eventual disappearance as a natural effect of the market (Crèvecoeur, Spurrier, Lorain, Rush). Or, they ignored altogether the existence of antimarket, backwoods farmers as a class (Jefferson, Franklin, Filson). By these means, they attempted to effect the disappearance of a significant oppositional ideology and to deny the legitimacy of communally organized agricultural production and politics, promoting a market orientation by means of a discourse of rural virtue.

Yet it was Brown, more presciently than Jefferson, Rush, or the other agrarian improvers, who anticipated certain important developments in rural capitalism. Today (despite the promise once shown by upper-Midwestern populism, which held that a communitarian political economy was the only hope of the independent owner-producer) the agricultural economy is characterized by the increasing consolidation of large tracts under centralized corporate direction, agricultural production being carried out not by tenants, as in Brown's story of Sir A——, but by wage laborers who similarly have little control over or stake in the ongoing management of the land. The few remaining owner-producers are managed less directly by the financial institutions who supply their operating capital and by the agribusiness conglomerates who are their only market connections, but they are externally managed nonetheless. Unlike Sir A——, these conglomerates do not even reinvest some of their revenues in community services.[66]

In antebellum America, alternative rural economies still existed, however. The next chapter will examine the implications for "civilization" of one such economy among the Cherokees.

Chapter 6

Cherokee "Improvements" and the Removal Debate

In an era that saw forced or coerced removals of many indigenous Americans from their homelands, the Cherokees' was the only case to gain a large measure of white support. Ralph Waldo Emerson, for example, although generally unconcerned over the fate of indigenous peoples, wrote a letter of protest to President Martin Van Buren asking, "Will the American government steal? Will it lie? Will it kill?"[1] A key to the Cherokees' enlistment of white support was their ability to tap into an American discourse that identified the rural as a site, source, and refuge of civic virtue. This discourse of rural virtue, as we have seen in the previous chapter, was established in a rhetorical battle against backwoods farming waged during the early years of the republic. The marks of rural virtue were sedentary farming, which improved the land, and embeddedness in market relations, which was enabled by that improvement. In the terms of this discourse, Indians were, on the one hand, characterized as savages whose land was not cultivated, not "improved," and thus could not ground American political virtue. On the other hand, the virtue of the rural was potentially extended to the Indians in arguments that they ought to be removed westward, where they and the land could simultaneously be cultivated.

In countering this logic to argue against removal from their homeland, Cherokees drew on images which were familiar to whites through the discourse of rural virtue but which had roots in Cherokee agricultural traditions as well. Their deployment of such georgic imagery in a counternarrative of improvement mounted significant critiques of both the dominant white image of the Indians' "savagism" and the idealization of the "middle landscape" as white property.[2] The counternarrative accurately represented certain aspects of the Cherokees' relation to their land in the pre-Removal era, such as their impressive agricultural productivity. However, it elided other aspects, such as the persistence of communal labor practices and the conception of land as a national heritage, rather than as individual, alienable property; for these continuations of traditional culture could have been seen as evidence of savagism.

Colonization had brought about transformations in the Cherokees' two primary economic-environmental activities in the precolonization era: farming and hunting. Farming had been a significant means of subsistence prior to colonization. During the eighteenth century, farming declined as men took exclusively to hunting. Participating in a colonial market for furs and skins, they came to embody the hunter-savage role preconceived by Europeans. By the century's end, however, hunting was less economically viable than farming. In the nineteenth century, the resurgence of farming among Cherokee men, as well as its continuation by women, provided a significant new means of cross-cultural self-definition. Whereas in the eighteenth century the Cherokees had explained themselves to whites using the image of the hunter, to argue against the land cessions that would disable the hunting activities that had become so economically useful to whites, in the nineteenth century, spokesmen such as Elias Boudinot, John Ridge, and David Brown presented the Cherokees as good farmers, again in hopes of holding onto the nation's land. This picture of Cherokee agrarianism affronted the white Georgians, who found it easier to argue for the removal of transient hunter-savages than of sedentary farmers. If pro-Removal whites accepted the georgic image of Cherokee culture, they could no longer base their arguments on the claim that Indian "savages" were not making the best use of the environment and its capacities to ground "civilization."

When the Cherokees succeeded to some extent in focusing public attention on the issue of land use, the opposing whites—as well as some, such as Jeremiah Evarts, who took the Cherokees' side—tried to shift the focus of the land debate from use to ownership. The white establishment, while divided on the Removal question, was united in defining land as individual, alienable property. The Cherokees, on the other hand, considered land occupancy to be a national matter, within which individual use rights were determined by long-standing tradition that was codified into law in the era of "improvement." Moreover, given population demographics, physical environment, and land laws, Cherokee agriculture during this era was probably more sustainable than that of their white neighbors.

For all these reasons, then, it is clear that the struggle over Cherokee land was a struggle to define basic terms of the human relationship to the natural environment in America. The Cherokees proclaimed that their use of the environment was good according to the terms of valuation contemporarily accepted by most whites. They argued that they had made a productive and sustainable landscape and wanted to continue working it. The United States government's response to this argument indicated that the care of the American land and inhabitants was not, finally, its primary concern. The fact that the discovery of gold on Cherokee land

finally forced the issue of removal merely symbolized the primary importance of individual property relations in the white American conceptualization of land use.

During the Removal era, other white writers with nearer regional investment, such as William Gilmore Simms, mystified the issue of property
relations by returning to the question of land use, attempting to erase the
Cherokees' counternarrative and repair the white discourse of savagism
that their public interventions had unsettled. The Cherokees themselves
had their agri-cultural traditions uprooted, but then reestablished them
in the West—where they would suffer further incursions in the Dawes Act
era. While most turned away from the white public sphere that had failed
to bring them justice, one prominent writer, John Rollin Ridge, worked
out the consequences of forced removal in an allegorical novel of exile
set among agrarian landscapes, gold fields, and mountains that evoked
the Cherokees' ancient homeland. Where the pre-Removal Cherokees
had counted on the political effectiveness of georgic topoi, Ridge drama-
tized the nation's alienation from its traditional environment. Like the
struggle for Cherokee lands in the East, the California gold rush raised
the issue of legal rights to natural resources. Narrating the dispossession
of such rights, Ridge turned to the American landscape to recapitulate
the point that Emerson had made in his letter of protest to President
Van Buren: Removal indicated that the ground for the right to occupy
and use land in America was state violence. Ironically, violence had been
one of the means by which the Cherokees, like other indigenous peoples,
had managed their environment prior to colonization. Warfare had protected the agricultural occupation of land and had created large border
zones between nations in which game was preserved from overhunting.
In the pre-Removal era, diplomacy could have maintained similar rights
to occupation and environmental use, but did not.

Improvement

White public debate over removal, like all questions of Indian policy in
the nineteenth century, took its terms from the ideological binary of savagism versus civilization. This binary, as identified by Roy Harvey Pearce,
worked according to a deconstructive logic: the idea of American civilization depended on its opposition to savagism, and yet the idea of savagism
was itself fundamentally a product of civilization.[3] The discursive means
by which American civilization produced the very savages it needed for
self-definition came to have, as we will see, a quite literal force for the
Cherokees in the eighteenth century. However, in another formulation
of the binary, one coopted by the Cherokee counternarrative, Indians

themselves could participate in the movement of progress, or, in contemporary language, "improvement."

The Cherokee spokesmen were not assimilationists, however, for they insisted on separate nationhood and national sovereignty. In the Cherokee counternarrative, much of what looked to whites like accession to civilization, such as the development of letters, was, from another perspective, an assertion of continuity, a maintenance of national identity.[4] Like their Pequot contemporary William Apess, the Cherokees assumed a primarily political definition of identity, rather than one founded on a notion of inherent or even cultural difference.[5] Like those who in the twentieth century coopted the EuroAmerican mythology of "Mother Earth" to develop a new, pan-Indian identity and to promote critical agendas such as environmental protection, Cherokee spokesmen became skilled at turning white cultural forms to their own purposes.[6] As Arnold Krupat has demonstrated, for example, the 1830 Cherokee Memorials to Congress, which formally petitioned for their right to remain in their homeland, strategically appropriated certain tropes from white legal rhetoric to assert "political equivalences" between Cherokees and white Americans.[7] In general, Cherokee spokesmen proposed their national narrative as a supplement to the white narrative of progress, thereby demonstrating the potential plenitude of, if not American civilization, then civilization in America. The difference in these formulations became the center of the crisis, as Georgians and others particularly interested in Removal found in Cherokee agrarianism a more solid ground of resistance than they had expected from mere savages.

"Improvement" became a key term in the Cherokee counternarrative for several reasons. Important in the general Anglo-American lexicon of the progress of civilization, the term had specific material referents in the practice of agriculture and thus a particular bearing on the central issue, the occupation of land. "Improvements" were the results of any effort to cultivate land: cleared fields or meadows, orchards, granaries, barns, fences, houses, mills, and so on. The image of the yeoman farmer who undertook such efforts at improvement had become an important constituent of United States national identity in the early nineteenth century and, thereby, an image the Cherokees could coopt to demonstrate their resemblance to the whites who lived around them. More than this, however, the Cherokees' development of a modern agrarian economy in the first quarter of the nineteenth century meant the cessation of material assistance (plows, looms, and so on) from the United States government by 1819 and a significant decrease in cash annuities by the 1820s; that is, it argued for Cherokee economic independence.[8] Most important, agriculture was the one feature of "civilization" that pertained directly to the central issue of removal and as such was the only feature to be formally recognized in the Removal Act of 1830 itself. The Act says nothing about Christianity, literacy, constitutional government, and so on among the Cherokees, for these could easily be elided. However, the Act was predicated on an exchange of lands and so had to address the issue of land use, which it did by stating

That if, upon any lands now occupied by the Indians, and to be exchanged for, there should be such *improvements* as to add value to the land claimed by any individuals of such tribes or nations, it shall and may be lawful for the President to cause such value to be ascertained by appraisement or otherwise, and to cause such ascertained value to be paid to the person or persons rightfully claiming such *improvements*. And upon the payment of such valuation, the *improvements* so valued and paid for, shall pass to the United States, and possession shall not afterwards be permitted to any of the same tribe.[9]

This language belies Andrew Jackson's claim, made only a year earlier in his first State of the Union address, that the lands in question were "tracts of country on which they have neither dwelt nor made *improvements*."[10] While Jackson was intent on removing Indians, he used the logic of improvement to ease the legal strictures on land ownership by whites: in the same year that he signed the Removal Act he also signed the Preemption Act which gave squatters on public land who had fulfilled "the fact of cultivation . . . and possession" first rights to purchase 160 acres.[11]

Thus "improvement"—with its double force of the progress of civilization in general and the agricultural use of land in particular—became the key node of ideological antagonism, the site where it became evident that relations between the Cherokee nation and the United States and Georgia were, in the end, only a question of military force. Two Memorials to Congress, one from the General Council and another from "native citizens of the nation," make this abundantly clear. The Council's Memorial asserts that Cherokees "ardently desire to remain in peace and quietude upon their ancient territory, and to enjoy the comforts and advantages of civilization" because "their only and best hopes of preservation and advancement in moral and civil improvement is to remain where their Great Father [not Andrew Jackson of course, and the pointed irony of using the President's preferred term of address is unmistakable here] alone placed them. There they wish to pursue agriculture, and to educate their sons and daughters in the sciences and knowledge of things which pertain to their future happiness."[12] The linkage between the ongoing processes of "pursu[ing] agriculture" and "moral and civil improvement" (cultivation in both its contemporary senses) appeals directly to white culture's idealization of the Jeffersonian middle landscape. The Council goes on to argue that "the power of a State may put our national existence under its feet, and coerce us into her jurisdiction; but it would be contrary to legal right."[13] The citizens' Memorial continues to protest this exercise of mere power and concludes by again linking the Cherokees' improvement to their home lands: "Divest them of their liberty and country, and you sink them in degradation, and put a check, if not a final stop, to their present progress in the arts of civilized life."[14] Removal, that is, would regressively translate the counternarrative of improvement into the dominant white terms of savagism.

The counternarrative articulated in the Memorials had a long history. We can begin to trace that history by examining what is perhaps the most familiar Cherokee text from the pre-Removal era, Elias Boudinot's 1826 "Address to the Whites." Speaking at the First Presbyterian Church of Philadelphia, hoping to secure donations for a school and printing equipment, Boudinot assures his audience that the Cherokees are a good investment, for "the nation is improving, rapidly improving in all those particulars which must finally constitute the inhabitants as an industrious and intelligent people."[15] He points to three features of civilization—letters, Christianity, and constitutional government—that, he says, "must certainly place the Cherokee Nation in a fair light, and act as a powerful argument in favor of Indian improvement" (73–74). Yet these are, as he indicates, "three things of late occurrence" among his people, in some sense the end of the narrative of "improvement" (73). Boudinot begins that narrative by going

as far back as the relinquishment of their towns; when game became incompetent to their support, by reason of the surrounding white population. They then betook themselves to the woods, commenced the opening of small clearings, and the raising of stock; still however following the chase. Game has since become so scarce that little dependence for subsistence can be placed upon it. They have gradually and I would almost say universally forsaken their ancient employment. (71–72)

They "have commenced a life of agricultural labour," although there are some who "would gladly resume their former course of living" if they could (72). As proof of this narrative of improvement among the vast majority, Boudinot gives agricultural statistics, describing how many cattle, plows, looms, mills, and so on the nation possesses. About the Cherokees' life in their "towns" before they "betook themselves to the woods" under the pressure of colonization, Boudinot says very little. Yet his narrative signifies as much by its absences as its presences. He knows, for example, that it is probably wise to avoid any mention of the role of slavery in the Cherokee economy when speaking to Philadelphia Presbyterians who might be divided on the issue. Similarly, his focus on the nation's history only after colonization affirms his white audience's belief in the progress of civilization. To carry such a narrative back prior to colonization would be to tell a story of regression from an agricultural to a hunting economy, and only then the welcome progression from hunting to agriculture. Even so, the nation's precolonial history is evident in the narrative for those attentive enough to hear it. It appears, for example, in Boudinot's concluding image of the Cherokee nation as a Phoenix, "rising from the ashes of her degradation . . . taking her seat with the nations of the earth" (77). This image, soon to become the name of the bilingual newspaper that Boudinot would edit (an important vehicle for the improving/conserving Cherokee syllabary), suggests recovery through continuity, the restoration of past glory, and, as it is used here, the legitimation of national sovereignty. The Phoenix image, that is, implicitly brackets the hunting-savage state as a temporary phenomenon, one in fact caused by white intervention. Moreover, since hunting is undertaken by "all frontier people whether white or red," this employment would seem finally to indicate more similarity than difference between the two peoples (72).

An important aspect of the history that Boudinot tropes for his white audience concerns the persistence and resurgence of an agricultural economy as an important constituent of national culture. Prior to colonization, the Cherokee economy was organized in terms of mixed production, with agriculture primary and gathering and hunting (undertaken between growing seasons) secondary.[16] According to traditional stories, Kana'ti and Selu, husband and wife, spirit of game and spirit of corn, long ago gave these means of life to the Cherokees and continue to watch over them from the upper world.[17] As in the case of the Choctaws and other nearby peoples, this mixed mode of production was economically and environmentally stable, hunting and agriculture being integrated aspects of a dynamic whole.[18] Population density was low, permitting a long-fallow system of cultivation in which old fields were allowed to revert to forest, restoring natural fertility, before being cleared and cultivated again. Warfare, undertaken on a modest scale by European standards, theoretically protected agricultural lands but more importantly in practice created large border zones between nations that preserved the game population.[19]

Colonization and trade altered this sustainable balance by encouraging market hunting. By the middle of the eighteenth century, the Cherokee national economy had become primarily oriented toward export. Hunting for deerskins (now in any season) and for slaves, and gathering marketable herbs such as ginseng, became the primary modes of production; as the transatlantic slave trade increased, slave hunting became less important and deer hunting more important.[20] Where men had once been centrally involved in farming—clearing new fields, plant-ing, harvesting—now they were employed so extensively in hunting as to decrease the agricultural labor supply significantly. Women tradition-ally had been responsible for harvesting some early weeds from the crop fields for foodstuffs and for hoeing the crop during the rest of the grow-ing season.[21] Now they had to do all the work. Under these conditions, Cherokee agricultural production declined. The English were soon sup-plying them with corn, pork, and beef in times of shortage.[22]

During the eighteenth century, then, the white fiction of savagism be-came literalized as Cherokee men, increasingly imbricated in the colonial trading economy yet maintaining a distinct cultural identity, materially enacted the "savage" hunter role in which the whites had cast them. Prior to colonization, hunting had been, as Boudinot says, an "ancient em-ployment," but one among others. As a result of colonization and trade, hunting became a primary means of distinguishing Cherokee from white modes of life—particularly since men were the ones involved in formal-ized cross-cultural interactions, such as treaty and land negotiations, in which comparative national identities were most visible and most at stake. Moreover, the hunter identity provided a base from which to resist land cessions. In 1777, for example, the Cherokee chief Corn Tassel argued in treaty negotiations against the cession of land to North Carolina because white encroachment "spoils our hunting grounds." He went on to explain to the white North Carolinians, "Your stocks are tame and marked; but we dont know ours they are wild. Hunting is our principle way of living. I hope you will consider this and pity me."[23] The Cherokees recognized that this hunter identity was intimately linked with the colonial presence. As chief Skiagunsta put it in 1745, "My people cannot live independently of the English. . . . The clothes we wear we cannot make ourselves. They are made for us. We use their ammunition with which to kill deer. We can-not make our own guns. Every necessary of life we must have from the white people."[24]

The Cherokees soon experienced a crisis of the hunting economy in which they had temporarily found national identity. As Corn Tassel pointed out, the colonists had taken some of the best tracts for cattle and horses, while hogs overran much of the remaining woodland. These fac-tors disrupted the edge environments on which deer depended. While enough forest and edge land remained to support a smaller, although still substantial population, the deer were largely hunted out under encour-agement from the colonists.[25] Despite the rapidly declining deer popula-tion, Cherokee men continued to define themselves as hunters in cultural differentiation from whites.[26] Yet many found that the deerskin trade in-volved them inextricably in debt. Hunters received goods against the pro-ceeds of the following year's hunt. When, as too often happened, the hunt did not cover the debts, Cherokee headmen ceded land to the English as payment.[27] Such cessions reduced the Cherokees' hunting grounds, further diminishing the prospects of maintaining a hunting economy.

As market hunting became unsustainable, the Cherokees, self-identified to the whites as hunters, were viewed as candidates for removal and/or civilization. Usually we think of this configuration of Indian policy as emerging in the early nineteenth century, beginning especially with the Jefferson administration. Soon after the Louisiana Purchase, Jefferson was sounding out the Cherokees about exchanging their homelands for lands in the West, even as he continued the Washington and Adams administrations' policy of encouraging among the men "a taste for raising stock and Agriculture" by providing plows, breeding stock, and so on.[28] Yet some forty years earlier, Henry Timberlake had already proposed removal and agrarian development as solutions to the decline of the local hunting economy. Timberlake, a Virginian army officer who visited Cherokee towns during the Seven Years' War to cement their alliance with the English, observed that the Cherokees were "much attached to the French" because they were more remote, whereas "the English are now so nigh, and encroached daily so far upon them, that they not only felt the bad effects of it in their hunting grounds, which were spoiled, but had all the reason in the world to apprehend being swallowed up, by so potent neighbors, or driven from the country." He then suggests a means by which they could now get along with the English:

Were arts introduced, and the Cherokees contracted into a fortified settlement, governed by laws, and remoter from the English, they might become formidable; but hunting must be then laid more aside, and tame cattle supply the deficiency of the wild, as the greater the number of hunters, the more prey would be required; and the more a place is haunted by men, the less it is resorted to by game. Means might be taken, would the Cherokee follow them, to render the nation considerable; but who would seek to live by labour, who can live by amusement? [29]

Writing in the context of eighteenth-century European wars for empire, Timberlake is interested in the Cherokees' potential value as military allies: they "might become formidable" and form a "considerable" nation occupying a buffer zone, to the west of their current lands, between English settlements and the French or Spanish presence in the Mississippi basin.[30] Even so, he proposes the alteration of their economy, a shift from hunting—to him, a matter of mere "amusement" rather than "labour"—to farming. In fact he believes that the Cherokee have no economy whatever, at least in the European understanding of the term: "The sole occupations of an Indian life, are hunting, warring abroad, and lazying at home. Want is said to be the mother of industry, but their wants are supplied at an easier rate" (99). Yet the very land the Cherokees now occupy is, he observes, enviably well suited to agriculture, "the soil requiring only a little stirring with a hoe, to produce whatever is required of it; yielding vast quantities of pease, beans, potatoes, cabbages, Indian corn[,] pumpions, melons, and tobacco, not to mention a number of other vegetables imported from Europe, not so generally known amongst them, which flourish as much, or more here, than in their native climate" (68). He observes that farming is the work "of women alone," to the English another mark of the savage state (68). Agricultural improvement among the Cherokees remains unimportant to Timberlake unless it supports a warrior nation to the west, allied to the English. One would think that a nation of hunters would be equally effective, if not more so, than a nation of farmers for this purpose, being more skilled with weapons. Perhaps Timberlake's logic is that farmers would become more attached than hunters to a particular tract of land, thus more willing to resist the threat of encroachment from the French or Spanish. Or perhaps he did not think it through this far at all, but instead simply failed to resolve the contradiction between perceptions of Indians as eternal savages and as candidates for civilization. The ambivalence of Timberlake's discourse anticipated the terms of white debate over the Cherokee question in the years to come.

Where the writings of men such as Timberlake and the policy of the United States government continued to identify the fate of the Cherokee nation with the occupations of its men and assumed a gendered division of labor amenable to white bourgeois assumptions about the separation of spheres, Boudinot's narrative of improvement does not explicitly address the issue of gender. We might conclude that this is because, having taken up farming to replace hunting, Cherokee men would not want to admit their apparent feminization. Yet the absence of gender anxiety in Boudinot's text might suggest that other concerns, in particular the sovereignty of the nation, were more important to his purpose in this transnational communication. Gender identity would remain an internal matter.[31] This is not to say that gender was never mentioned in Cherokee communication to whites at this time. John Ridge, responding to Albert Gallatin's request for information on the current state of Cherokee society in 1826, alluded to the history we have traced in reference to Boudinot's narrative, observing economic transformation in men's roles:

There is not to my knowledge a solitary Cherokee to be found who depends upon the Chase for subsistence. Every head of a family has his own farm and House. The hardest portion of manual labor is performed by men & the women occasionally lend a hand more by choice & necessity than anything else. Justice is due to the females of the poorer class of whom I now speak. Duties assigned them by nature as Mothers or Wives are well attended to and . . . cheerfully do they prepare our meals, & for the family they sew, they spin and weave and are in fact a valuable portion of our citizens.[32]

Within the nation, under the pressures of colonization, masculine identity underwent complex transformations. However, these transformations are evidently not something that Boudinot thinks important to share with his white audience. As for Ridge, his account of gender relations takes up only a small portion of his response to Gallatin.

Cherokee women, who had continued to farm all along, were thus largely unrecognized vehicles of cultural continuity, grounding national identity in the land as they came to realize that market hunting was no longer environmentally sustainable.[33] In renewing their ancient commitment to agriculture, Cherokees of both genders adopted English crops, livestock, and technologies. Twenty years before the Jefferson administration began to encourage agriculture among Cherokee men to replace the declining deerskin trade, the women had already begun to augment the traditional food production of corn, beans, and squash with cotton, flax, and sheep to supply new materials for clothing and other uses.[34] Where women readily took to the loom, men more slowly took to the horse-drawn plow, but by 1810, as Boudinot noted, the nation had about five hundred plows, about one for every four families.[35] By 1828, most families had a plow and horses to draw it. Even so, traditional practices, such as the *gadugi*, a system of mixed-gender, communal labor, persisted.[36]

The fact that, continuing through the Removal era, nearly all the prominent public voices among the Cherokees (and among the whites as well, of course) were men's voices explains to some extent why the continuity of agriculture as a feature of Cherokee identity remained obscure. On the rare occasions when women's public voices are recorded, they seem to have identified agriculture as a male activity of recent development. For example, petitioning the National Council in 1817, Beloved Woman Nancy Ward enjoined the men, "don't part with any more of our lands but continue on it & enlarge your farms. Cultivate and raise corn & cotton and your mothers and sisters will make clothing for you which our father the president has recommended to us all."[37] In practice, gender lines were not necessarily so rigidly drawn; Beloved Woman Ward herself, for example, had raised the nation's first large cattle herd.[38] Inheritance laws would probably have tended to concentrate large livestock holdings among men rather than women.[39] Crops were a different matter, however. By 1830, most cotton was still being produced by women, despite Beloved Woman Ward's representations to the Council. In general, men plowed the fields, as they had prepared the fields for planting prior to the colonial era. Both men and women worked the fields together from planting through harvest, except for the small, mixed-blood elite, comprising less than 7 percent of the population, who used slave labor to create the "flattering profit" in the cotton trade that was noted, for example, by John Ridge in his response to Gallatin's query.[40] Those like Boudinot who represented Cherokee agrarianism to the white public were men from the elite, slaveholding class, but the majority of women and men who performed their own labor and retained traditional practices such as the *gadugi* were also against removal. That is, whatever the complexities of gender, race, and class relations in agricultural production within the nation, what mattered most in the Cherokees' public address to whites was national sovereignty. Like white Americans—and that was the crucial point—the Cherokees were a nation of farmers, devoted to their land.

National Property

By the time Boudinot gave his "Address," direct political pressure for removal had been building for over a decade. In 1802, Georgia had ceded its western land claims to the United States in exchange for a promise that Indian title to all lands within state boundaries would be extinguished as soon as this could be done peaceably. As Georgia became more insistent, the United States managed in 1817 to convince some Cherokees to remove to what is now Arkansas. In 1824, President Monroe, in a special message to Congress, responded to Georgia's criticism that he had been dilatory in fulfilling the government's promise to extinguish the Cherokees' title by stating that while removal would be in the best interest of the Cherokees, the United States had no obligation to remove them against their will. Thus giving no comfort to either Georgia or the Cherokees, Monroe argued in his 1824 State of the Union address that the federal government's only course was to continue to persuade the Cherokees to exchange the lands claimed by Georgia for lands in the West.[41] U.S. policy remained ambivalent, for in that same year, Secretary of War John Calhoun proposed that Georgia accept the Cherokees as citizens, although Georgia's Governor Troup refused the proposal.[42]

Perhaps encouraged by the tenor of Calhoun's proposal for citizenship—although disagreeing with its substance which would have eliminated national sovereignty—Cherokees such as Boudinot and John Ridge soon began to issue public statements concerning the situation and prospects of the nation. Notable among these statements is David Brown's 1825 letter to the Richmond *Family Visitor*, which was reprinted in the most prominent newspaper of national circulation at the time, *Niles' Weekly Register*. Brown is more successful than Boudinot at grounding national identity in a particular landscape in a way that would be familiar to whites. Educated, like Boudinot and John Ridge, at the Foreign Missions School in Cornwall, Connecticut, Brown had ample opportunity to become familiar with white literary and landscape conventions, which he deploys to advantage in this text to argue that the Cherokees "*have no more [land] to spare.*"[43] He emphasizes his anti-Removal position by noting the Cherokees' "universal satisfaction" over the recent death of the "despicable" Creek chief William McIntosh, "a traitor to his country" who had signed a Removal treaty (107).[44] The thrust of his argument, however, addresses cultivation and the environment. He begins by comparing the state of the Cherokees who had been persuaded to remove to Arkansas (in 1817–19) with "the improved condition of those on this side of the Mississippi, in a moral, intellectual and religious point of view" (106)—thus suggesting, as the Memorials to Congress would later do, that removal would entail the inverse of improvement, a regression toward savagism. In this comment Brown is probably responding particularly to a provision of the Adams administration's removal plan, just recently formulated, according to which individuals would be induced, by cash incentives, to remove to the newly designated Indian Territory.[45] Brown responds to this threat to national solidarity by describing the beauty and productivity of the Cherokee homeland, showing how it grounds civilization.

Brown begins with a wilderness scene and then moves toward an agrarian middle landscape, thus suggesting a narrative familiar to his white readers, the improvement of the natural environment for human purposes:

A range of majestic and lofty mountains stretch themselves across the nation. The northern part of the nation is hilly and mountainous. In the southern and western parts there are extensive fertile plains, covered partly with tall trees, through which beautiful streams of water glide. These plains furnish immense pasturage, and numberless herds of cattle are dispersed over them. Horses are plenty, and are used for servile purposes. Numerous flocks of sheep, goats and swine, cover the valleys and hills. On the Tennessee, Ustanala and Ganasagi rivers, Cherokee commerce floats. The climate is delicious and healthy; the winters are mild. The spring clothes the ground with its richest scenery. Cherokee flowers, of exquisite beauty and variegated hues, meet and fascinate the eye in every direction. In the plains and valleys, the soil is generally rich; producing Indian corn, cotton, tobacco, wheat, oats, indigo, sweet and Irish potatoes. The natives carry on considerable trade with the adjoining states; and some of them export cotton in boats, down the Tennessee to the Mississippi, and down that river to New Orleans. Apple and peach orchards are quite common: and gardens are cultivated and much attention paid to them. (106)

Brown begins with an elevated perspective, a commanding view or "magisterial gaze" that in white convention legitimated the cultural possession of the landscape.[46] The revelation of the landscape to us enacts a movement that corresponds to contemporary ideas about the evolution of civilization from the state of nature. In the first few sentences the description moves from mountains and forests through open plains to crop fields and a trade network of rivers, environments respectively indicating the hunting, herding, horticultural, and commercial stages of human socioeconomic development.[47] This supposed evolutionary narrative does not, of course, correspond to the Cherokees' own history. Their mixed hunting and horticultural economy had existed for centuries prior to colonization; hunting had been a primarily commercial endeavor during the eighteenth century while herding had been adopted only with the nineteenth-century resurgence of horticulture. However, the movement of Brown's description enables white readers to imagine the evolution of environmental engagement in familiar, stadialist terms, ending in an agrarian commercial present in which "agricultural pursuits, the most solid foundation of our national prosperity, engage the chief attention of the people" (106). In the foreground of the picture, the Cherokees' agriculture harmonizes perfectly with the land's natural beauty. Even the spring flowers bear the nation's name. Brown follows the produce out of the Cherokee landscape, through its trade network of rivers, linking the nation's commerce to that of the United States, but in the end draws back to the nation's interior, to images of its orchards and gardens, and the homes they support: "numerous and flourishing villages are seen in every section of the country" (106). Thus while using landscape conventions familiar to whites, he reorients those conventions to argue against Manifest Destiny by erasing "one of the favorite visual tropes" of contemporary landscape illustration, the "image of the stupefied savage confronting signs of civilization on the march."[48]

Considered in terms of the visual conventions of the picturesque, apart from any sense of narrative movement, Brown's composite landscape represents a balanced sense of land use. The mountains remain forested, the lower hills and plains are partly forest and partly pasture, while the rich bottom lands are planted to corn, cotton, and other crops. The scene thus demonstrates the environmental soundness of Cherokee agricultural practices. As was characteristic of Southeastern indigenous farming generally, hillsides, susceptible to erosion, remain untilled. By contrast, contemporary white farmers used the land more intensively than did indigenous farmers and were less concerned with erosion control.[49] While existing in sustainable balance, the farms were immensely productive: at this time the eastern Cherokees were not only growing cotton for market, as Brown indicates, but were also producing corn and livestock at levels that exceeded the averages for both the Southern region and the United States as a whole.[50] As an editorial preface to Brown's letter suggested, "cotton and cattle will become the great staples of the commerce of the Cherokees—they can raise both with peculiar advantage, and, as cultivators and herdsmen, must become rich."[51] Removal would thus seem to be against their best interests and the United States' interest as well. In Brown's picture, the Cherokees have established themselves as supplements to the white narrative of possession and improvement. Their environment has manifested their destiny.

However, such landscape scenes were open to misinterpretation in one important respect, on the question of property relations. This misinterpretation promoted the Cherokees' public image as a civilized nation, yet it ultimately cut against their hopes of remaining on their land. Where whites assumed land to be alienable property, Cherokee tradition did not allow for such a conceptualization of their physical environment.[52] Our first written record of Southeastern indigenous land practices, the narrative of Hernando de Soto's expedition of 1539–42, identifies the division of land into agricultural plots (as distinct from commons) specifically with productive labor: "The Maize is planted and picked in, each person having his own field; fruit is common for all, because it grows abundantly in the woods, without any necessity of setting out trees or pruning them."[53] De Soto and company may or may not have believed that such a division indicated individual ownership (and they would have understood ownership in more or less feudal terms), but in fact all land was held in common by the nation and was individuated only through use in agricultural production. Produce was the property of each household, although it was extensively and voluntarily redistributed for the welfare of the whole town.[54] If a plot of land were to be regarded as an alienable possession, however, individual Cherokees could then be dispossessed, as was specified in the 1830 Removal Act, which defined the exchange of lands as a set of individual transactions.

Decades before Removal, white colonization put pressure on the traditional inalienability of land, first at the community level as Cherokee leaders ceded large tracts of hunting grounds during the eighteenth century. At the individual level, early in the nineteenth century some Cherokees began to let fields to white farmers on shares. This practice might have been conceptualized through traditional schemata as an instance of individuation through use, the white tenant providing the labor that would make the land produce its crops for the benefit of its Cherokee claimant. Slavery was being integrated into the Cherokee economy on a small scale at this time, probably according to a similar rationale concerning labor.[55] The National Council no doubt realized that rental on shares might bring the long-standing land tradition into question by permitting ongoing white occupancy and perhaps creating a class of quasi-individual landowners among the Cherokees. Thus in 1808 the Council considered legislating a ban on sharecropping. Indian agent Return Meigs persuaded them against such a ban, but as concern over white intruders increased, the incidence of sharecropping declined.[56] In 1817, the Council encoded tradition into positive law, formally defining land as national property: individuals could not sell land because they could not own it. In 1821, in an attempt to discourage voluntary removal, the Council banned emigrants from selling any improvements to anyone, including other Cherokees. Emigrants, should they choose to return to the nation, would forfeit rights of occupancy and use on any lands they abandoned; other Cherokees had to wait three years before taking up such lands and their improvements.[57] The Cherokee Constitution of 1827, which opens by delineating the Nation's boundaries with great geographical specificity, defines all land within these bounds as "the common property of the Nation" (Article I, Section 2).[58] While individual citizens could possess "improvements" to the land, they could not sell these "improvements" to "the United States, individual states," or "individual citizens thereof." "Improvements" could be sold to other Cherokees who remained in the nation, but emigrants forfeited "all their rights and privileges" including the right to occupy land or possess improvements within the nation (Article I, Section 2).[59]

An 1832 editorial in the *Cherokee Phoenix* articulates this understanding of land as a national heritage, rather than a set of individual possessions, specifically in relation to the theoretical underpinnings of white American political discourse:

The natural rights of mankind when they form themselves into a community, for their mutual benefit, consists [*sic*] first, in a liberty to ordain such rules for the conduct of its members, as will conduce to their happiness. Secondly, a right to a country on which to exercise this liberty. They are reciprocal rights, one cannot exist without the other. — This I conceive to be the primary rights of man, and to which all mankind are justly and naturally entitled to. These rights the Cherokees have from time immemorial enjoyed.[60]

Evidently elaborating on a point of Chief Justice John Marshall's majority opinion in *Worcester* v. *Georgia* (March 1832) that the indigenous nations "retain[ed] their original natural rights, as the undisputed possessors of the soil, from time immemorial," the *Phoenix* commentary here refines Marshall's definition of "nation" as merely "a people distinct from others."[61] The *Phoenix* points out that the Cherokees are a "community" that has compacted itself politically, framing laws for the "mutual benefit" and "happiness" of the whole. In both liberal and republican theory— in the writings of John Locke and Adam Smith, of James Harrington and Thomas Jefferson—the political compact was grounded in the individual's right to own property (the two theories differing primarily in their attitude toward civic responsibility and the accumulation of property). This fundamental ground of the white political compact is absent from the Cherokees' statement of rights: the nation enjoys its right to land as a nation, not as a set of individuals, the protection of whose discrete property rights was the liberal or republican state's primary purpose. Yet the *Phoenix* editorial strategically attaches the discourse of natural rights directly to the question of national sovereignty, originating in the communal land practices of "time immemorial," and thereby dispenses with the mediation of national sovereignty through the property rights of the individual subject.

Whites having no intimate knowledge of Cherokee land theory and practice would not, however, have thought of the issue in this way. The editor of *Niles' Register*, for example, interpreted David Brown's letter as demonstrating that the Cherokees have "just ideas of the value of property." [62] The Removal issue became, for this editor, a matter of competing claims to individual possession, in which Cherokee individuals would have the better case than incoming Georgians by right of original and continued occupation and use. Similarly, preconceptions of land as private property had colored William Bartram's late eighteenth-century description of Cherokee farms: "all before me and on every side, appeared little plantations of young Corn, Beans, &c., divided from each other by narrow strips or borders of grass, which marked the bounds of each one's *property*." [63] Thus translated into property even in sympathetic white interpretations of Cherokee agrarianism, the land became conceptually alienable.[64] Yet at the same time, this interpretation of agrarianism, with its assumptions about civilization, increased the public perception of the legitimacy of the Cherokees' national claims to the possession of their land as property, and so made it more difficult to argue for the forced alienation of their land.

In this context, one of the most outspoken white critics of Jacksonian Indian policy, Jeremiah Evarts, took up the questions of occupancy, use, and property. In a series of *Essays on the Present Crisis in the Condition of the American Indians*, published in the *National Intelligencer* in 1829 under the pseudonym "William Penn," Evarts rehearsed the terms of the conflict from the first treaties through the present. In the second essay, he affirms and even extends the counternarrative of improvement developed by Brown and Boudinot:

It has been alleged, that the savage of the wilderness can acquire no title to the forests, through which he pursues his game. Without admitting this doctrine, it is sufficient to reply here, that it has no application to the case of the Cherokees. They are at present neither savages nor hunters. It does not appear that they were ever mere wanderers, without a stationary residence. At the earliest period of our becoming acquainted with their condition, they had fixed habitations, and were in undisputed possession of a widely extended country. They were then in the habit of cultivating some land near their houses, where they planted Indian corn, and other vegetables. From about the commencement of the present century, they have addicted themselves more and more to agriculture, till they now derive their support from the soil, as truly and entirely as do the inhabitants of Pennsylvania or Virginia. . . . They earn their bread by the labor of their own hands, applied to the tillage of their own farms; and they clothe themselves with fabrics made at their own looms, from cotton grown in their own fields.[65]

Among white commentators on the Removal issue, Evarts is unique in identifying the Cherokees as originally farmers. He elides the development and decline of the hunting economy in the eighteenth century, presenting a continuity of agricultural land use to answer any argument that would link right of occupancy to economic structure. This point is directed particularly against the state of Georgia's insistence, ever since its 1802 agreement with the United States, that the Cherokees occupied the land claimed by Georgia only as tenants at will who retained temporary hunting rights.

Continuing this line of argument in a later essay, Evarts constructs a dialogue between the Georgians and the Cherokees in which both sides explicitly state their interests. When the Georgians charge that "you are a vagrant, hunting and savage people" and thus have no right of possession, the Cherokees answer, "but we are not the sort of people that you take us to be," but are and always have been sedentary farmers (126). Although the Georgians' reply depends on a narrative of the progress of savagism to civilization, the Jacksonians' main argument for dispossession, it nevertheless grants a certain validity to the Cherokee counternarrative. The Georgians, echoing the justification for colonization of waste land that we first encountered in More's *Utopia*, object that

you had no business to betake yourselves to an agricultural life. It is a downright imposition on us. This is the very thing that we complain of. The more you work on land, the more unwilling you are to leave it. . . . It is all designed to keep us, the people of a sovereign and independent State, from the enjoyment of our rights. We must refer you to the law of nations again, which declares that populous countries, whose inhabitants live by agriculture, have a right to take the lands of hunters and apply them to a better use. (127)

Thus Evarts shows that the Georgians are illogical in claiming that the Cherokees are hunters while simultaneously admitting that they are farmers who would then have right of possession through use according to the Georgians' own assumptions regarding use.

This much of Evarts's representation is consistent with the Cherokee counternarrative. Elias Boudinot's editorials in the *Phoenix* prior to his resignation in 1832, for example, present a similar characterization of the opposition between the Cherokee nation's public image and the demands of United States Indian policy.[66] In a November 12, 1831, editorial, he recalls the history lesson from his 1826 speech in Philadelphia: "the Cherokees have been reclaimed from their wild habits—Instead of hunters they have become cultivators of the soil" (141–42). Boudinot continues, pointing out Georgia's envious response to its discovery of Cherokee agrarianism:

Well would it have been if the cheering fruits of those labors had been fostered and encouraged by an enlightened community! But alas! . . . No sooner was it known that they had learned the proper use of the earth, and that they were now less likely to dispose of their lands for a mess of pottage, than they came in conflict with the cupidity and self-interest of those who ought to have been their benefactors. . . . They are now deprived of rights they once enjoyed—A neighboring power [Georgia] is now permitted to extend its withering hand over them. (142)

Here Boudinot alludes to the fact that the Georgians, in response to their perception of Cherokee improvement, had passed an Indian Code asserting the sovereignty of state laws over Cherokee lands. He goes on to decry the most recent violation of national sovereignty, Georgia's arrest in early 1831 of missionaries living within the Cherokee Nation who refused to sign a loyalty oath to the state. The missionaries were "chained, dragged away . . . tried as felons, and finally immured in prison with thieves and robbers" (143). Four months after Boudinot wrote these words, the Supreme Court (in *Worcester* v. *Georgia*) upheld Cherokee sovereignty, declaring Georgia laws void, and ordered the release of the missionaries. President Jackson's refusal to enforce the Court's decision, which encouraged Georgia to go ahead with its lottery of Cherokee lands, weighed heavily in Boudinot's reconsideration of his position on Removal.[67]

Evarts wrote prior to Georgia's passage of the Indian Code, the Supreme Court's decisions in key cases, and Jackson's deliberate negligence. Having said all he could to this point concerning the legal issue of sovereignty, he presents yet another argument in his penultimate essay. Approaching the question of property from a new angle, this argument represents an unwitting reversal, undercutting the positive image of Cherokee agrarianism that Evarts had so carefully built up to this point by attempting to weigh Georgia's economic interest against the Cherokees' potential loss and suffering. While the invocation of this moral calculus must, in its address to Jacksonian policy, be considered a rhetorical failure, Evarts's intention was to remedy the envy that both he and Boudinot saw animating Georgia's designs on the Cherokee lands. These lands, he argues, are

far less capable of lucrative cultivation, than the State [of Georgia] is generally. I speak not without some knowledge on the subject; and I have made inquiries of others. Let the representatives in congress from Georgia, if they are personally acquainted with the quality of the land within the Cherokee limits, state frankly how large a part is composed of mountainous and barren tracts, which a Georgian would pronounce utterly worthless; how large a part would produce but moderate crops; and how small a fraction would be considered land of very good quality. Let these things be stated, and it will be found that the Cherokee country is not by any means so valuable, as has commonly been supposed. (179–80)

Evarts does attempt to recover the ground of sovereignty, reminding us that the fertility of the soil "can make no odds as to title," but rests his case on the claim that "the value of the property here at stake is nothing, compared with the feelings of the Cherokees; not to mention the importance of the principles to be decided" (180). Yet even if he is correct about the agricultural value of these lands, the damage is done by admitting the moral calculus in the first place. It should be noted here that in the entire series of twenty-four essays (the bulk of which reprint and analyze various treaties), Evarts never mentions gold. Possession of land, in the absence of any agreement to the contrary, implies mineral rights; if possession is adjudicated on agrarian grounds, the right to gold follows. Yet in admitting the issue of the land's market value, Evarts cannot forestall the public's recollection of the recent discovery of gold in the Cherokee nation. Even so, Evarts's economic argument would be taken up by Chief John Ross to argue against the proposed Removal treaty. Ross evidently believed that when the Georgians discovered that the land was not as valuable as they had thought for agriculture, the state would annex the gold mining region and accept a cash settlement in exchange for giving up its claims to the rest of the Nation, for he petitioned President Jackson to that effect.[68] Boudinot recognized that this belief was unrealistic.

Evarts's account of the value of the Cherokee lands, drawn from first-hand observation and confirmed by John Ross, reflects a difference between Cherokee and white land practices. Much of the land was indeed marginal for agricultural purposes, as Evarts noted. Even so, given demographics, physical environment, and national land laws, the Cherokees' agriculture was more sustainable than that of their white neighbors. Land could be taken out of cultivation to restore its fertility for much longer, without extensive manuring, than land owned individually by white farmers. This difference in sustainability remained largely invisible in statements of the Cherokee counternarrative, although the environmental balance of David Brown's composite landscape hinted at it. During the eighteenth century especially, the Cherokees lost an enormous amount of land through cessions, while epidemics also decimated the population. The situation then was as follows: according to a census conducted by the U.S. government in 1835 to determine population and land use on Cherokee lands claimed by Georgia, 9,780 individuals lived on 13,692 square miles, at a density of 1.4 persons per square mile. Of the more than eight million acres of Cherokee land, the census defined 614,400 acres as tillable, of which 19,351 were currently being cultivated. It is possible that the census underrepresented the amount of cultivated acreage, for when government agents canvassed Cherokee territory in 1836–37 in order to value lands for reimbursement under the Removal Act, they found 35,285 acres of improved fields.[69] Not all of these may have been in cultivation at the time. Yet no matter which of these figures for cultivated land is accurate, it is clear that in addition to eight million acres of non-agricultural land, the Cherokees had an immense amount of potentially tillable acreage in reserve as a check against nonsustainable intensification. The smaller acreage figure (19,351) allows for a theoretical thirty-one-year fallow cycle. That is, as new acreage is brought into tillage to replace old fields that have lost fertility, assuming stable population figures it would take thirty-one years for the nation to cycle through all of its tillable land. During those thirty-one years, an abandoned field would grow into woods and natural fertility would be restored, meanwhile providing forage land for livestock. Compare this to the typical white farmer's land use at this time. The most common size of a white, Midwestern farm in antebellum America was 80 acres; Southeastern farms were generally smaller unless the owner used slaves.[70] The 1835 census indicates that the average Cherokee family had 14.2 acres in cultivation at any given time.[71] 453 total acres of tillable land per family were available in the national reserve. A white family with the same 14.2 acres in cultivation but with only 80 total available could count on a fallow cycle of only five years (in the unlikely case that all 80 were tillable, less if not). This is one-sixth as long as the Cherokee family's thirty-one years, and not nearly enough to restore a field's fertility. With the larger 1836–37 estimate of cultivated acreage (35,285 acres), the average Cherokee family would be able to have 26 acres in production at a given time and at this rate could count on a seventeen-year fallow cycle. At this same rate, a white farmer owning 80 acres and cultivating 26 at a time could count on only a three-year cycle; this farmer would rapidly exhaust the land unless he resorted to extensive manuring.

Cherokee land practices in the pre-Removal era, then, did not encourage intensification. As we have seen, Cherokee farmers produced more corn and livestock than did white farmers at the time. They did so not because they cultivated all land more intensively, but rather they opposite: like other Southeastern indigenous farmers, they planted only the lands that provided the highest yields and let marginal lands alone.[72] With the adoption of stock raising, a portion of these marginal lands provided forage for cattle and hogs. Nor was this sensitivity to sustainability exclusive to the indigenous peoples of the Southeast. The Seneca leader Red Jacket, for example, also knew the wisdom of holding large tracts of fallow land in a national reserve. Responding to the Monroe administration's request for land cessions in 1819, Red Jacket argued, "You told us that we had large and many unproductive tracts of land. We do not view it so. Our seats we consider small; and if left here by the Great Spirit we shall stand in need of them. We shall want timber. Land after the improvements of many years wears out. We shall want to renew our fields; and we do not think that there is any land in any of our reservations, but what is useful."[73]

A white farmer who had a mortgage or was trying to pay rent on 40 or 80 acres did not have the option of long-fallow farming as the Cherokees did. Instead, maintaining a given level of production required intensification—more labor, more manuring, moving onto marginal lands such as hillsides or swamps, and so on. If fertility diminished too much, the white farmer either bought more land or moved out and took new land to the west. In contrast, pre-Removal Cherokee land laws and practices necessarily assumed a closed frontier. Yet within delimited boundaries (given a stable population) the Cherokees could have sustained their production indefinitely at pre-Removal rates. When a field became exhausted, there was plenty of tillable land in the national reserve without tilling hillsides or draining wetlands. National land law allowed Cherokees to take up any land not currently cultivated by another farmer. Since they did not have to buy this land—in fact, could not buy it—unlike white farmers they could work these new fields without needing to use some of the surplus produce to pay off a mortgage. And, in contrast to white agriculture at the time, no Cherokees needed to resort to tenancy or wage labor to make a living from the land.[74] The fact that nobody could own the land meant that anybody could work it freely and less intensively than in a system in which land itself has a cash value. Moreover, in theory, if substantial population growth were at some future point to require intensification, the long-standing existence of national land laws may at least have checked the potential for the socially irresponsible exploitation of land permitted by private property systems.

Partly because of actual contemporary differences between Cherokee and white land laws and practices, georgic imagery did not occupy a central position in the Cherokee nation's *internal* debates over the Removal Treaty. The counternarrative of "improvement" was, after all, externally motivated: it was a means of enlisting white support. Thus allusions to the counternarrative in the *Phoenix* seem primarily oriented toward the numerous non-Cherokee readers of that paper.[75] In August 1831, for example, the *Phoenix* reported that "not less than one thousand beeves will be driven from this Nation for the northern markets this season, besides those taken into Georgia and South Carolina." The *Phoenix* offered the marketing of these cattle, which were raised by "(as the expression is) . . .

the common Indians," as counterevidence to a malicious claim made by a white Georgian in the *Macon Telegraph* that the Nation was "on the point of starvation, some of them subsisting on sap and roots."[76] The *Phoenix* had already satirized this claim, stating that if the *Telegraph*'s correspondent could

> inform the public what sap it is, and what roots, which have the virtue of preserving life three weeks, the world will be indebted to him for the discovery. Civilized Ireland, where we are told many persons die of hunger, may be induced to erect a monument to his memory. He could not mean esculent roots we presume. The only roots we have heard of some families digging are the pink and snake roots [for medicinal purposes], but we have not heard of their subsisting on them.— But to be serious. . . . On account of the drought last summer very little corn was raised, & many are in fact suffering.[77]

White farmers suffered similarly under similar circumstances. Agricultural items in the paper intended primarily for the nation's internal readership assume, by contrast, a wholly practical tone. For example, the *Phoenix* printed agriculturalist John Taylor's directions for preventing wheat smut and gave advice on harvesting oats gleaned from the *Detroit Courier*.[78]

However, both the pro- and anti-Treaty parties did employ the counternarrative in internal debates when it could be used to advantage. In his Annual Message to the General Council in 1834, for example, John Ross successfully addressed the majority of the Cherokees' attachment to their land by characterizing the western Indian Territory, for which they were to exchange their homelands, as vastly inferior: "The insalubrity of the climate, the inadequacy of fertile lands, the scarcity of water & timber requisite for the comforts of civilized life, are considerations which will make the permanency of their residence where they are allocated, doubtful."[79] Elias Boudinot, on the other hand, had argued against Ross that to remain would be to face "*submission to the laws of the States* by taking reservations" and held up "the fate of our poor brethren, the Creeks, to be a sufficient warning to all those [i.e., the Ross party] who may finally subject the Cherokees to the laws of the States" (177, emphasis in original). The Creek nation, that is, had accepted "reservations," individual allotments as private property, and had thus lost most of its land (in a prefiguration of the Dawes Act). As early as 1806, the United States had proposed a system of allotment to the Cherokees, knowing that a great deal of land would thus become available for white possession.[80] Cherokees were being evicted from their farms under the Georgia land lottery, but Boudinot warned that to hope for redress from Georgia courts was, in fact, to admit of the applicability of Georgia's jurisdiction, with its construction of land as individual, alienable property.[81] By contrast, the Treaty of New Echota maintained the Cherokee tradition of national, rather than individual possession of the lands in Indian Territory until the Dawes Act stipulated otherwise.[82]

In their last appeal to Congress before U.S. forces removed them, the Cherokees reprised the agrarian topos that had figured so centrally in their arguments. Their Memorial of Protest, submitted to Congress June 22, 1836, gives several stories of the loss of farms, thus illustrating Georgia's hypocrisy in its claims to have enacted its statutes controverting Cherokee sovereignty out of "real humanity to these Indians."[83] Particularly evocative is the story of the Nation's principal chief John Ross. Returning home to find his family dispossessed of their farm through the Georgia land lottery, Ross

went out into the yard, and saw some straggling herds of his cattle and sheep browsing about the place. His corn crop undisposed of. In casting a look up into the wide spread branches of a majestic oak, standing within the enclosure of the garden, and which overshadows the spot where lies the remains of his dear babe, and most beloved and affectionate father, he there saw, perched upon its boughs, that flock of beautiful peafowls, once the matron's care and delight, but now left to destruction and never more to be seen.

The georgic mode turns elegiac as the Ross family nostalgically recollects, from "some place of refuge within the limits of Tennessee," their life on their old farm.[84]

Land, Law, and Violence

Following the passage of the Removal Act, pro-Removal whites such as William Gilmore Simms returned to the question of land use to mystify the issue of property relations. An image of the comparative barrenness of the Cherokee homeland considered as agricultural property, which Evarts had developed and which John Ross had attempted to use strategically in his negotiations with Jackson, gave Simms the setting for his quite successful first novel, *Guy Rivers*.[85] Here, such imagery worked to erase the Cherokee agrarian counternarrative at the very time (1834) when the Treaty of New Echota was being negotiated. Simms's story of the gold rush opens on a scene "in the upper part of the state of Georgia, a region at this time fruitful of dispute, as being within the Cherokee territories" (13). This first sentence contains the novel's only mention of the Cherokees; hereafter they are figured only indirectly, in the land's lack of civilization and improvement. Their absence implies that, in 1834, the removal of an uncivilized people has already been accomplished.[86] The "long reach of comparatively barren lands" in Cherokee territory, "fruitful" only of "dispute," Simms finds "garnished with a stunted growth, a dreary and seemingly half-withered shrubbery, broken occasionally by clumps of slender pines. . . . All around, as far as the eye may see, it looks in vain for relief in variety. There still stretch the dreary wastes, the dull woods, the long sandy tracts, and the rude hills that send out no voices, and hang out no lights for the encouragement of the civilized man" (13–14). Not only effacing Cherokee agriculture in particular, but even suggesting the difficulty of cultivating this land under any circumstances, Simms continues, as if to refute point by point David Brown's 1825 description of the same environment: "The ragged ranges of forest, almost untrodden by civilized man, the thin and feeble undergrowth, the unbroken silence, the birdless thickets, —all seem to indicate a peculiarly sterile destiny" (13). However, the environment does yield the wants of civilization in another respect: "Nature, thus, in a section of the world seemingly unblessed with her bounty, and all ungarnished with her fruits and flowers, seemed desirous of redeeming it from the curse of barrenness, by storing within her bosom" a great trove of "mineral treasures" (14). Simms will go on to criticize the white gold seekers drawn to this waste as lawless backwoodsmen, but not because they have usurped the Cherokees' rights to this gold. Indeed, the possibility of Cherokees' possessing mineral rights is not addressed at all, even though this issue caused a good deal of unrest and resulted in Georgia's passing a resolution stipulating that the Cherokees had no such rights, being only tenants at will, and forbidding them to extract any gold. Rather, Simms notes only the white backwoodsmen's refusal, in their single-minded pursuit of gold, to entertain the agrarian dreams that should belong to them as members of the white race: their "perverted heart, striving with diseased hopes, and unnatural passions, gladly welcomes the wilderness, without ever once thinking how to make it bloom like the rose" (14). Simms's account of the Georgia Guard similarly effaces the possibility of any Cherokee agency with respect to either mining or agriculture. The Guard, a private militia hired by the state but with no accountability for its actions, was formed in 1830 ostensibly to stop gold mining by squatters so as to save the gold for the white claimants who would move in as soon as the Cherokees were removed. In fact the Guard sided with whites against Cherokees in all disputes, arresting John Ross, confiscating the nation's printing press, and committing numerous other acts of harassment.[87] Simms, however, refashions the Guard into the representative of law and order in the territory, replete with legal documents and "the great seal of the state" of Georgia (175). Their conflict is not with any Cherokees, since none appear in the novel, but rather with the white squatters who are mining gold without holding title or mineral rights. One of the squatters tears up a legal parchment bearing the state seal. These outlaws, Simms emphasizes, are the antithesis of farmers, for even the better of them "could not bear the slow process of tilling, and cultivating the earth—watching the growth and generations of pigs and potatoes, and listening to that favorite music with the staid and regular farmer, the shooting of the corn in the still nights, as it swells with a respiring movement, distending the contracted sheaves which enclose it" (103). Simms's affectionate lingering on the music of the corn indicates the direction of his sympathies. Thus at the end of the novel, after many adventures, the hero takes the heroine out of this wilderness and back to the paternal plantation in South Carolina; other "worthy villagers" go west to take lands in the Mississippi basin; the villain commits suicide (487). We assume that some squatters remain, but we do not see them. The land is emptied and returned to its apparently natural wilderness state (again, no Cherokees are mentioned); it is now ready for what Simms would regard as lawful white settlement and agricultural improvement under the aegis of the state of Georgia which could grant legitimate titles.

Where Simms imaginatively possessed the north Georgia landscape during the period of the Removal negotiations, the most prominent Cherokee writer of the antebellum era, John Rollin Ridge, would deal with the trauma of dispossession in a novel also set during a gold rush, *The Life and Adventures of Joaquín Murieta* (1854). The Cherokee counternarrative had attempted to ground justice in the land, but Ridge was forced to confront that narrative's failure. Thus *Joaquín's* story of violent displacement recapitulates the issue at the heart of Cherokee removal: rights to natural resources. In California, Mexicans first showed Yankees how to operate gold mines. When the great profitability of these mines became apparent, however, the state of California passed a tax law that made it unprofitable for anyone but U.S. citizens to mine gold; Mexicans who persisted in working their claims were driven off by Yankee vigilantes.[88] This time there was no attempt by the federal government to nullify an oppressive state law, as there had been in *Worcester* v. *Georgia.* Joaquín is driven off his mining claim by "a band of lawless men" who "would allow no Mexicans to work in that region."[89] We next see Joaquín "cultivating a little farm on the banks of a beautiful stream that watered a fertile valley, far out in the seclusion of the mountains. Here he might hope for peace." Again though, "a company of unprincipled Americans—shame that there should be such bearing the name!—saw his retreat, coveted his little home surrounded by its fertile tract of land, and drove him from it, with no other excuse than that he was 'an infernal Mexican intruder!'" (10). Displaced by whites who desire his gold claim and his farm, Joaquín becomes a figure of national allegory.[90]

Joaquín also suggests Ridge's personal history of double displacement, first from the Georgia gold fields and then from his Arkansas farm. In 1836, his grandfather and father, Major Ridge and John Ridge, prominent signatories to the Treaty of New Echota, had taken their slaves to

Indian Territory, just in advance of forced removal, and established a new plantation. Rollin Ridge, after witnessing the killing of his grandfather and his father in 1839 by members of the Ross party, fled to Arkansas with his mother to live among another group of Cherokees who had been established there for two decades. He studied law, but found the practice tedious. Settled on a farm in Arkansas, he began writing newspaper articles such as "The Cherokees—Their History—Present Condition and Future Prospects," which proposed that the Cherokee Nation be admitted to the Union as a separate state. In 1849, he was provoked into killing a member of the Ross party and was forced to flee Arkansas. He soon joined a party of Cherokees headed for the California gold fields and continued to write, for example supplying accounts of life in the mining camps to the New Orleans *True Delta*.[91] Settled on a 160-acre farm in the new California community of Marysville, he pursued a literary career. He contributed poems and sketches to various California periodicals, edited several newspapers, became involved in California politics, and found, in current accounts of the celebrated outlaw, a story that resonated with both personal and national history.

Engaging with this story, Ridge turns, as the pre-Removal Cherokees had done, to white conventions of landscape representation as potential ground for justice and law. He had already published a number of Romantic poems depicting nature as a space of rejuvenating retreat.[92] Bringing this EuroAmerican literary mode into conjunction with the political concerns of his narrative, he returns to the question that had occupied his compatriots in their struggle against the state of Georgia. Early on in the novel, when Joaquín and his crew have to flee their first encampment among the Mexicans, they ride into the coastal range west of Mount Shasta. Their view of the mountain, an emblem of permanence which "serves at a distance of two hundred miles to direct the course of the mountain-traveler, being to him as the pole star to the mariner," occasions a poem of retrospection. While the outlaws remain in the coastal range, the poem's perspective is taken "from the Sacramento Valley at a distance of one hundred and fifty miles"—that is, from near Marysville, whence the outlaws have just fled, and where Ridge himself had recently settled (23).[93] A sense of loss even touches the poem's opening images of sublime grandeur, in Mt. Shasta's estrangement from human presence: "We may not grow familiar with the secrets / Of its hoary top, whereon the Genius / Of that mountain builds his glorious throne!" (24). This Genius, "with his gaze supreme," looks out, "still watchful of the fertile Vale," on "the guarantee of health and happiness" of those below:

> In the middle of his furrowed track, the plowman,
> In some sultry hour, will pause, and, wiping

From his brow the dusty sweat, with reverence
Gaze[s] upon that hoary peak. The herdsman
Oft will rein his charger in the plain, and drink
Into his inmost soul the calm sublimity. (24, 25)

But the terms of that "guarantee" are open to question. The sublime mountain is set apart from the Sacramento Valley and is not contiguous, geographically or aesthetically, with the Valley's agrarian landscape. It is this landscape from which Joaquín has been doubly displaced, first from his own farm and then from the nearby Mexican encampment. Thus Ridge goes on to suggest the conditional nature of the "guarantee," questioning the perceptual linkage of natural with social law that has up to this point provided the poem's governing topos:

And well this Golden State shall thrive, if, like
Its own Mount Shasta, sovereign law shall lift
Itself in purer atmosphere—so high
That human feeling, human passion, at its base
Shall lie subdued; e'en pity's tears shall on
Its summit freeze; to warm it, e'en the sunlight
Of deep sympathy shall fail—
Its pure administration shall be like
The snow, immaculate upon that mountain's brow! (25)

With that ambivalent pronouncement, the poem closes. What had a moment ago been a peaceful agrarian landscape—farmer and cowhand pausing from their labors, "little children playing on the green"—is revealed to be a site of "human passion." Subduing that passion, the law cannot be altered through "sympathy," however "deep."

We would expect law to be an important topic in the novel.[94] Ridge's ambivalence here has its source not only in Cherokee history generally, but in his personal history as well, as he works through the trauma of witnessing the killing of his father and grandfather. The execution of John Ridge and Major Ridge at the hands of the Ross party was justified in principle under Cherokee law, which stated that anyone involved in the sale of Cherokee lands without popular sanction would be put to death (a law that, ironically, Rollin Ridge's father had helped to frame in 1829). As Major Ridge remarked on signing the Treaty of New Echota, "I have signed my death warrant."[95] Rollin Ridge's wish to avenge these killings bears on the revenge theme in *Joaquín*.[96] His personal history also bears on the topic of law in the novel, for while Joaquín's tragedy is the failure of "sovereign law" to "subdue" the "human passion" of the Americans who have oppressed him, Ridge's own desires for revenge—and so analogously Joaquín's—have their warrant in traditional Cherokee law as well, and again, in a way intimately connected with his personal history. The ancient blood law required retribution whenever one Cherokee killed another under any circumstances. Major Ridge played a central role in amending the law in 1796 to cover only cases of premeditated murder; under the Cherokee reorganization of 1819, the National Council transferred the administration of this law from the clans to the state.[97] Even if Ross's state authority to execute members of the Treaty party was doubtful, given the factionalism of the post-Removal Cherokees, Major Ridge's remark that the Treaty was also his death warrant gave it some legitimacy. Rollin Ridge's desire for revenge had no current legal legitimacy whatever, but either instance could, depending on interpretation, have been required by Cherokee law at some point in the not too distant past. Either, but not both: if the execution of the Treaty signatories was legal, retribution would not have been legal, and vice versa. California law, too, in the apostrophe to Mount Shasta, seems to admit of similar ambivalence, as indicated by the conditional "if" of the concluding simile. If the "pure administration" of California law was "like / The snow, immaculate upon that mountain's brow," it involved the removal of everything human from its consideration.

As the human landscape had failed to ground justice for the pre-Removal Cherokees, neither can the nonhuman landscape, sublime Mount Shasta, provide any realizable model for human law. That wilderness landscape becomes, instead, an aesthetic object distanced from questions of political, legal, and economic practice. The novel's disruption of any perceived linkage between law and land thus recalls and elaborates on the Cherokees' experience in dealing with Georgia and the United States. The court had theoretically granted them protection and limited sovereignty, but the executive had refused to enforce it and had later removed the body of the nation at bayonet point. This experience had shown them that the ultimate ground of the law was not nature, improved or unimproved, but human violence. This is the lesson of Joaquín's death as well, for he is not brought to trial but is, nevertheless, legally executed. A bill authorizing the organization of "a Company of Mountain Rangers in order to capture, drive out of the country, or exterminate" Joaquín and his crew is "passed and signed by the Governor," and the company is soon organized (145). Joaquín is killed at Arroyo Cantoova, the "fine tract of rich pasturage, containing seven or eight thousand acres, beautifully watered, and fenced in by a circular wall of mountains through which an entrance was afforded by a narrow gate or pass" (28). While Joaquín did not intend Arroyo Cantoova for a permanent settlement, it was a fine place to keep the stock he raided from white ranchers, until, "having completed his revenge, and, having accumulated an equivalent for the fortune of which he had been robbed by the Americans, he would retire into a peaceful portion of the State of Sonora, build him a pleasant home, and live alone for love" of his dear Rosita (29). But the agrarian-domestic hope is denied him, and he meets a violent death.

Joaquín is well suited to allegorize the history of the Cherokees precisely because he is not an Indian.[98] A Mexican rancher, he is oppressed by American prejudice but is not encumbered with the burden of "savagism" that most contemporary whites loaded onto any Indian whatever, even the agrarian Cherokees.[99] Thus his character is freed from Indian stereotype to exemplify the true nature of the Cherokee loss. This was not quite the tragic fate emplotted in the dominant narrative about Indians, as identified by Krupat and Pearce—a white ideology of the necessary accession of savagism to civilization. Rather, it was a tragedy of positive law, in which the right to occupy and use land is revealed to be finally grounded not in economic-environmental considerations, but in violence, the right of conquest: white Americans, not Indians, are the savages here. In this, Ridge's novel thematically recapitulates the National Council's assertion in their 1830 Memorial to Congress that "the power of a State may put our national existence under its feet, and coerce us into her jurisdiction; but it would be contrary to legal right, and the plighted faith of the United States' Government. It is said by Georgia and the Honorable Secretary of War, that one sovereignty cannot exist within another, and, therefore, we must yield to the stronger power."[100] The horror that Rollin Ridge witnessed as a child, the killing of Major and John Ridge, devolved from that larger tragedy of yielding to the stronger power. Linking their fates to the rule of the U.S. government by signing the Treaty of New Echota, they knew they had no choice but to accept its foundation of violence. They knew too that violence had been an important aspect of the Cherokee world prior to colonization, but that the terms had now changed. Warfare had been a cultural technique for environmental management, maintaining borders and checking the possibility of counterproductive intensification in hunting and agricultural land use. European warfare was different, however, promoting not sustainable balance but total conquest.

The Cherokee Loss

Prior to Removal, the Cherokees had selectively appropriated certain terms of the white discourse of national identity to try to ground justice in the land itself. Although they succeeded aesthetically, they failed politically. In fact, their aesthetic success may have worked against them, as whites eyed greedily the beautiful, fertile agricultural environment that the Cherokees showed they had built—even if Jeremiah Evarts had belatedly tried to suggest that this environment was not quite so beautiful and productive after all. Politically, in the largest sense, the Cherokees' loss depleted the American environmental heritage by removing a significant model for conceptualizing land use in terms of the public good. If they had not been removed, Cherokee farmers, counting on plenty of tillable acreage in a national reserve, without the complications of property ownership, could have provided a historical model for sustainable agriculture. In the antebellum era, this conceptual loss was not particularly apparent. As the Cherokees themselves presented the issue to the white public at the time, the question seemed to be not how to use a particular environment but rather who got to use it. Subsequently, however, agrarian capitalism's increasing intensification—its emphasis on maximizing productivity and private profit on individually owned parcels of land—has worked against public goods such as social justice, health, and sustainable land use.[101]

This is not to idealize the Cherokees in retrospect. A conflict between the slaveholding minority and the vast majority who undertook their own labor and worked the land less intensively would surely have erupted in their homeland, as it did in Indian Territory, with the coming of the Civil War. And we cannot know how their economy and legal system would have responded to the intensifications of agrarian capitalism in the United States during the rest of the nineteenth century and into the twentieth, had they been permitted to remain. Rather, it is simply to point out that different understandings of agriculture as a national project—different relations among individuals, the state, the economy, and the environment—might have generated different models of agricultural production in the long run. If the physical environment is defined as a national trust, rather than an aggregate set of individual possessions, a nation might more effectively determine its use for the public good than the United States has been able to do.[102]

Chapter 7

"Co-Workers with Nature"
Cooper, Thoreau, and Marsh

Why not control our own woods and destiny more?
Thoreau, "The Dispersion of Seeds"

For Americans unfamiliar with the Cherokee georgic, Removal could be written off as yet one more instance of the inevitable disappearance of a primitive mode of life. Robert Beverley had much earlier described a loss of "Native Pleasures" resulting from colonization and had proposed a calculus of compensation in which a georgic society, through diversified economic engagement with the natural environment uniting beauty and use, might hope to repair the loss. Differing valuations of this loss are registered in our literature as early as the conflict between Thomas Morton and the Plymouth colonists. In *New English Canaan* (1637), Morton found the Indians to embody a native civility lost to the English, whereas William Bradford saw Morton and his Indian crew forsaking good work and good order for mere pleasure, idleness, and disruption. Late colonial and Federal-era agrarian writers found such "Indian" traits to characterize white backwoods farmers as well, who were supposed to have lacked the industry to produce at market levels. These writers followed Edward Johnson in celebrating increasing market embeddedness as the foundation of sociopolitical stability and the public good. Yet the image of the "Indian" persisted as a means of registering dissatisfactions with the results of particular economic engagements with the environment (dissatisfactions that today are registered for example in our appreciation of wilderness as a place of escape and recreation). In the antebellum era, an important locus of this appeal to the primitive was James Fenimore Cooper's Leather-Stocking Tales, which gave "Indian" values a white spokesman in Natty Bumppo, thus bringing them respectably into dominant American discourses. While the Cherokees were strategically arguing that in certain respects they were "white," Cooper imagined translating an "Indian" relationship to the environment into white terms, thus finding a positive valuation where William Gilmore Simms, for example, found a negative one.[1]

In the first of the Leather-Stocking Tales, *The Pioneers* (1823), Cooper set up an environmental debate, attaching various positions to various characters. Readers could identify (or not) with Judge Temple, the proto-conservationist who lacks environmental knowledge; the laborer Billy Kirby or the scientific improver Richard Jones, who would, in different ways, thoughtlessly exploit natural resources; or the white Indian Natty Bumppo, who speaks for the wilderness.[2] The judge's daughter, Elizabeth, gives yet another perspective, the one perhaps most familiar to Cooper's genteel Eastern readership. Elizabeth shows a fine appreciation of landscape aesthetics, but little understanding of the relationship between the form of a landscape and its capacity to sustain human life and culture, as she interrupts her father's account of the early "starving-time" to ask, "But . . . was there actual suffering? where were the beautiful and fertile vales of the Mohawk? could they not furnish food for your wants?"[3] Through the interaction of these characters, Cooper took it upon himself to educate such a readership in the relationship of economy to environment.[4]

The environmental debate in *The Pioneers* goes in two directions. On the one hand, Cooper imagines the possibility of an escape from economy altogether in the figure of Natty, who—if we do not look too closely at the fact that he gains his livelihood as a market hunter—seems to embody a nonexploitative relationship to the natural environment. On the other hand, within the terms of the settlement economy, Cooper addresses issues of law, property, and practical environmental management. In presenting this debate, he evokes the systems-theory approach to the relationship between economy and environment first envisioned by the Hakluyts and their cohort. Cooper fears that expansion will force the economy up against its environmental limits in America, anticipating a reiteration of the entropic scenario that the Hakluyts' program of colonization had attempted to prevent for England. Eventually, Cooper says, "the evil day must arrive, when their possessions shall become unequal to their wants" (16). Against that day, he investigates the social ecology of the settlements, hoping to derive its compatibility with nature. His inability to resolve the debate he poses is nowhere more strongly evident than in the hollow sound of the novel's last sentence, where we suddenly find Natty's values accommodated to those of the settler culture: "He had gone far towards the setting sun,—the foremost in that band of Pioneers, who are opening the way for the march of the nation across the continent" (456).

In *Man and Nature* (1864), George Perkins Marsh unpacks the contradiction underlying the doubly directed environmental debate in *The Pio-*

neers. Cooper had posited nature as the source of all value and had criticized the settler culture's incompatibility with that value, even as he wanted to value settler culture positively in its own right. Where Cooper imagined a hypothetical compatibility with nature in the solitary "Indian" mode of environmental engagement represented by Natty, Marsh locates the question of compatibility on a deeper level, in the origins of human identity as such. He argues that "the earth was not, in its natural condition, completely adapted to the use of man" but rather inevitably requires certain interventions to support human life.[5] Where Cooper imagined Natty as offering an escape from economy (even if he is ultimately recontained by it), Marsh proposes a resolution that depends on importing the category of economy to conceptualize nature itself and our relation to it, thus anticipating modern sustainable economic theory. It is a matter of getting human systems, which can be altered, to match environmental systems, which cannot. Thus Marsh reaches back through the history of the American georgic tradition to an idea formulated in the 1610 *True Declaration of Virginia*, "God sels vs all things for our labour."[6] He sees that the exchange relation has been unequal in practice, leading to the drawing down of nature's value: nature cannot repay human labor with the "incredible vsurie" the *Declaration* had imagined.[7] The use of input and output capacities had proceeded to the point where they might soon become insufficient to support human life. Exceeding this point would result in environmental apocalypse.[8] Marsh's return to the entropic scenario described by the Hakluyts and their cohort thus gives that scenario a global scope, encompassing the whole of the human species. As the reversal of entropy in any system is possible only through importing some capacity for work, Marsh envisions a restoration of nature's value through the same agency that had diminished it: human labor. He argues that we must become "co-worker[s] with nature in the reconstruction of [its] damaged fabric" (35). Marsh's global program bears comparison here with the local program developed by Thoreau in his late work on forest succession, in which he urges Concord farmers to cooperate with the "steady and consistent endeavor of Nature" to manage their woodlots.[9] The beneficiary of the cooperative labor envisioned by Marsh and Thoreau is not, as it had been for the Jamestown company, the private individual so much as the environment itself and its capacity to sustain human life into the future.

In thus developing a critical perspective on the American georgic tradition from within, Marsh necessarily investigates the fundamental relationship between humankind and nature—the terms, as my epigraph from Thoreau puts it, of "our destiny." Marsh asks "the great question, whether man is of nature or above her" (465). Philosophical accounts outside the georgic tradition have often addressed the question of our relation to nature through the category of perception.[10] Yet so long as our focus remains perceptual, what we actually do in the world and how we do it may remain secondary issues.[11] Marsh instead approaches this fundamentally human question of being through the category of labor—the history of what we have done in the world and how we have done it—to make recommendations regarding practices. This approach in turn opens onto larger questions of agency, the organization of these human practices. Through what structures, Marsh asks, can we implement ecological knowledge, be it gained through scientific study or through "the common observation of unschooled men" (such as Natty Bumppo and Billy Kirby), so as to foster the public good now and for the future (52)? This is the motivating question of the American georgic—one that we are still asking today, but too often without recalling the georgic's most important insight, that labor is life.

Use, But Don't Waste

We have seen that in *Nature*, Emerson put forth a landscape aesthetic dependent on a position of social alienation: "you cannot freely admire a noble landscape, if laborers are digging in the field hard by."[12] The aesthetic that Cooper attributes to Natty Bumppo is curiously similar to Emerson's, and like his, provides no workable model for a human community's relationship to the environment. Cooper particularly remarks on Natty's solitary appreciation of "the hand of God" in a "wilderness" scene familiar to us from Thomas Cole's 1826 painting *Falls of the Kaaterskill* (294).[13] It is true that in his younger days, Natty sometimes had "weak spells, when [he] felt lonesome," which he cured by looking down "at the ways of man" from the distant perspective of a mountaintop. With the wisdom of age, however, he no longer feels "such longings," but rather "relishe[s]" only purely "nateral" scenes such as the Falls because they bear no sign of human life: "the hand that made the 'Leap' never made a mill!" (293).

The environmental conflict in *The Pioneers* is generally thought to pit Natty's "wilderness values," as evidenced for example in this scene, against the social law of Judge Temple and the settlers.[14] In framing the issue in this way, however, we have too willingly granted Cooper's elision of the fact that the fundamental conflict is not so much between the settlement economy and the wilderness as between two economies that depend on different kinds of environmental input. Like the eighteenth-century Cherokees, Natty is a market hunter. Early on he explains, "The time has been, when I have shot thirteen deer, without counting the fa'ns, standing in the door of my own hut" (22). If in this instance he followed his own environmental maxim, "use, but don't waste," he must have sold the deerskins for leather (248). Throughout the novel, Natty expresses values consistent with his occupation, frequently arguing that settlements such as Templeton interfere with his economy. As he puts it during the pigeon-shoot episode, "Wasn't the woods made for beasts and birds to harbour in? and when man wanted their flesh, their skins, or their feathers, there's the place to seek them" (248). He sees that the settlements have made the game scarce:

I must go low toward the Pennsylvany line in sarch of [beavers], maybe a hundred mile, for they are not to be got here-away. No, no—your betterments and clearings have druv the knowing things out of the country; and instead of beaver-dams, which is the nater of the animal, and according to Providence, you turn back the waters over the low grounds with your mill-dams, as if 'twas in man to stay the drops from going where He wills them to go. (387–88)

Human engineering (building mills to grind grain) has supplanted the beavers' supposedly more providential work at staying the waters' courses, threatening what Natty takes to be a more natural economy in which he harvests beaver pelts. Although, as the Cherokees learned during the eighteenth century, overhunting could decimate the game population as well, Cooper limits the representation of the hunting economy to one man (temporarily two, counting the young Effingham, for John Mohegan no longer hunts but makes baskets and brooms) and thus does not show it running up against its own inevitable environmental limit. In *The Prairie* (1827), this economy again concerns only one man, the lone trapper, Natty.

However, as we see in Natty's alignment of his access to beaver pelts with the dictates of "Providence," Cooper is reluctant even to recognize the hunting economy *as* an economy. Rather, he identifies a purely hunting and trapping mode of life with Indians—the "habits of the 'Leatherstocking'" being "nearly assimilated to those of the savages"—who are themselves dissociated from labor (85). John Mohegan, for example, is said to lack "the muscular appearance, that labour gives to a race of men" (86). Natty and Mohegan thus provide the illusion of escape from economy altogether, a promise of everlasting abundance that the settlers' practices threaten to upset. Cooper's characterization of them as solitary outsiders, rather than as members of a complex society, fosters this illusion.

That Cooper postpones to distant "ages" the "evil day" when the settlers' "possessions shall become unequal to their wants" makes the threat no less real (16). Yet he would not describe the social ecology of Templeton in such great detail if he thought the case were hopeless. Rather, he places his hopes for the accommodation of economy to environment in the protoconservationist Judge Temple. Inquiring into both Temple's philosophy of management and the environmental history of the Otsego Lake region, we will find that matters do not always turn out as Cooper imagined. Judge Temple fails in his projects for want of environmental knowledge, although in a larger sense we might say that Cooper succeeds by pointing us to the importance of social-ecological analysis in three key instances: the pigeon shoot, the fishing episode, and the visit to Billy Kirby's sugarbush.

As an instance of the conflict between Natty's values and those of the settlers, the pigeon shoot is more dramatic for us than it could have been for Cooper's original audience, since we know the eventual fate of the passenger pigeon. We should recognize here that there is a practical reason for the shoot and also that (as I will discuss below) agricultural land use did not cause the pigeon's extinction. Judge Temple's cousin, Richard Jones, notes that the birds will "overrun our wheat-fields, when they come back in the fall" (244). At spring planting, the birds consume the seed in the fields.[15] As Billy Kirby puts it, "if you had to sow your wheat twice, and three times, as I have done," you would have no qualms about the shoot (246–47). Temple agrees, remarking that "we have happily frightened the birds from this side of the valley," and takes an additional perspective that contrasts him directly with Natty (250). Temple regards the shooting as sport, but afterwards he regrets "that he has purchased pleasure at the price of misery to others" (250). Natty of course speaks against such "wasty ways" (248). He wants only one bird to eat—but rather than taking one already dead, he kills yet another with a brilliant wing shot. This exhibition is not so much a demonstration of his environmental ethic as it is an answer to Billy's challenge "for a single shot" (247). Natty has a reputation to maintain; he has, he reminds us, often killed loons before they can dive and performed other such exploits (248). His livelihood depends on the marksmanship so impressively (albeit a bit luckily) demonstrated here. The settlers believe that their livelihood depends on killing the pigeons. The suffering that disturbs both Temple and Natty would seem to be a matter of numbers.

The fishing episode seems more straight forward at first. The bass that the settlers net in such wasteful numbers do not pose a threat to their economy, as do the pigeons, but in fact contribute to it, providing food in a lean season. The settlers' overfishing is simply, as Temple describes it, "a fearful expenditure of the choicest gifts of Providence" (259). Ever the sportsman, Temple prefers the "pleasure" of "playing with the hook and line" for "salmon-trout"; he wishes that the settlers would "be more saving of the game" for this pleasure as well as less "prodigal" in their own net-fishing (252, 260). Natty's position on this question derives from his occupation as market hunter, for he allows that if the bass "had fur, like a beaver, or you could tan their hides, like a buck, something might be said in favour of taking them by the thousands with your nets; but as God made them for man's food, and for no other disarnable reason, I call it sinful and wasty to catch more than can be eat" (266). Judge Temple suggests that in this case he and Natty "agree in opinion. . . . A net of half the size [typically used] would supply the whole village with fish, for a week, at one haul" (266). Natty disagrees, however, objecting to the entire structure of legal regulation: "you fish and hunt out of rule; but to me, the flesh is sweeter, where the creater has some chance for its life" (266). Natty twists the issue here, for his indigenous method of spearfishing at night with a jacklight is more deadly than Temple's genteel angling, though neither of the two will generally kill more "than can be eat" no matter what the season.

The exchange serves a larger purpose, however, in foregrounding Temple's frequently expressed interest in game laws. The settler's net-fishing is entirely legal, as Cooper notes at the beginning of this chapter: "the season had now arrived when the bass-fisheries were allowed by the provisions of the law, that Judge Temple had procured" (251). Such a law was in fact passed in 1798, five years after the events in *The Pioneers* are supposed to take place. It may be that Cooper was vague about the dates, but in any case since his father William had no doubt worked to pass the law, as Cooper states of his fictional counterpart here, it is worth considering in detail.[16] The Preamble states that "it has become necessary to guard against the destruction of the fish in Otsego Lake at a season of the year when they are of little or no value." With this evidently economic end in mind, the law prohibits fishing with a "net or seine in the waters of Otsego Lake at any time between the twenty fifth day of May and the first day of October," punishable by a ten-dollar fine plus court costs.[17] The law is curious, for it could not have protected the fishery. Judge Temple explains that nature itself has afforded the "bass" in particular, the lake's greatest resource and the one sought most eagerly by the settlers, a kind of protection:

if there can be any excuse for destroying animals in this manner, it is in taking the bass. During the winter, you know, they are entirely protected from our assaults by the ice, for they refuse the hook; and during the hot months, they are not seen. It is supposed they retreat to the deep and cool waters of the lake, at that season; and it is only in the spring and autumn, that, for a few days, they are to be found, around the points where they are within reach of a seine. But, like all the other treasures of the wilderness, they already begin to disappear, before the wasteful extravagance of man. (260)

Temple here gives an accurate account of the habits of the Otsego "bass," actually the lake whitefish, although he does not go into the behavioral causes that render the law ineffective. The whitefish moves into the shallows in late fall to spawn and remains there until spring, when it seeks cool depths as the shallows warm. The 1798 law, however, bans netting when the fish are inaccessible (Otsego is 166 feet deep) and permits it when they are particularly vulnerable, at spawning time and in early spring just after ice-out.[18] Other important species (such as lake trout, another fall-spawning, coldwater fish) would be similarly affected. No wonder Cooper thought that the fish "begin to disappear." Temple's law evidently sanctions the waste that he claims elsewhere to deplore, although he may not be fully aware of its potential environmental effects.[19] If the pigeon-shoot episode pits settlement and wilderness values in direct conflict, the fishery regulation by contrast seems to fail within the terms of the settlement ethic itself, expressly for want of environmental knowledge.

It is ironic then that the passenger pigeon became extinct while the whitefish population remained stable in Otsego Lake until the 1990s. Judge Temple expresses concern over the whitefish, but not even Natty could predict the demise of the passenger pigeon. When Natty observes that agricultural land use generally diminishes the game population, he is primarily concerned with marketable species such as deer and beaver. No market yet existed for passenger pigeons. The bird was little affected by settlement until railroads made it possible to ship fresh game quickly from rural to urban areas. Logging decreased the pigeons' nesting sites, but habitat destruction was not the key factor in extinction; grain fields, in fact, provided an abundant new food source. Rather, market hunters dealt the pigeon its death blow.[20] In this case, the hunting economy reached the limit of its environmental capacities. The Otsego whitefish by contrast, which Cooper thought threatened as early as 1793 by the settlers' wasteful fishing, remained abundant despite heavy commercial fishing pressure.[21]

The subsequent histories of the passenger pigeon and the Otsego whitefish thus raise the issue of social ecology, although not quite in the way Cooper predicts as he analyzes the economic-environmental engagement of 1790s Templeton from the perspective of 1823. Cooper undertakes another such investigation in the visit to Billy Kirby's sugarbush. Richard Jones, who experiments with unusual agricultural improvements (mineral salts to cure hog mange, brick chips for poultry gravel [163, 188]), has been urging Temple to "introduce a little more science into the manufacture of sugar" among his tenants (221). We gather that Temple has been unsuccessful in the sugar business, as William Cooper had been. Temple's daughter Elizabeth defensively points out that "the world is of the opinion that Judge Temple has tried the experiment fairly, though he did not cause his loaves to be cast in moulds of the magnitude that would suit [Richard's] magnificent conception," thus disappointing the merchants as Cooper's father had done (222). This is no wonder, for Temple's ideas on sugar production appear ridiculous:

"I hope to live to see the day, when farms and plantations shall be devoted to this branch of business. Little is known concerning the properties of the tree itself, the source of all this wealth; how much it may be improved by cultivation, by the use of the hoe and the plough."
"Hoe and plough!" roared the Sheriff;—"would you set a man hoeing round the root of a maple like this . . . . Hoeing trees! are you mad, 'duke?" (222)

As Richard points out, there was no need to cultivate this native tree (which can even regenerate in its own shade). Nor could this resource provide the primary income for "farms and plantations," as Cooper implicitly reminds us through the presence of Mr. Le Quoi, who has observed cane sugar production in the West Indies. In New York, sugaring was a common by-employment of small farmers and tenants on estates such as Temple's/William Cooper's, undertaken at a time of year when there was little other work to do. Most settlers with access to maples produced enough sugar for home consumption, as the indigenous inhabitants before them had done. William Cooper failed, however, to turn domestic to commercial production, for the settlers could not produce a sufficient quantity and quality of sugar. His failure was clear by 1792, the year before Temple visits Billy's sugarbush.[22] Perhaps, unlike William Cooper, Judge Temple has not given up on this project. Even so, his conversation with Billy offers little encouragement. Billy is a good source of woodland environmental knowledge in general, for he knows such arcane facts as how to use walnut bark for mosquito repellent (230). Yet when asked how to discern the quality of a sugar maple tree, he only replies cryptically that "there's judgment in all things" (226). He does allow that he never taps "a stunty tree, or one that hasn't a good, fresh-looking bark; for trees have disorders like creaturs" (226–27). Richard draws an analogy with medicine, examining the skin of the patient. Billy judges that this analogy "an't far out of the way. It's by the look of the thing, sure enough," but supplies no more details (227). He knows the weather, tree selection, tapping methods, "when and how much to stir the pot" in which the sap is evaporated, and so on: "It's a thing that must be larnt" (226). Yet he does not divulge the fine points of his trade or how he "larnt" them. Nor does he offer any suggestions on how to produce at the market level sought by Temple.

As in the fishing episode, then, we see that Temple has an interest in environmental management, but wants knowledge. Billy has environmental knowledge, but apparently no interest in management—nor in being managed. He would as soon fell a maple tree as tap it for sugar, if the

pay were better and if the work meant no "abatement of a tittle of his independence" (190). This raises another issue regarding the maples. Billy
hopes that the price of ashes is still good. Temple replies approvingly,
"Thou reasonest with judgement, William. . . . So long as the old world is
to be convulsed with wars, so long will the harvest of America continue"
(229). Yet where hunters like Natty, as well as the agrarian settlers, need a
certain amount of potash to keep them in gunpowder and soap ashes too
are an important local commodity (glass, dyes, and other uses less so),
Temple is concerned with the question of scale. He worries that "we are
stripping the forests, as if a single year would replace what we destroy"
(229). Like William Cooper, Temple wants to conserve maples "not as
ornaments" but rather "for their usefulness" (229). William, we know, believed that their long term value for sugar production outweighed their
immediate value as ash or firewood, but still turned from sugar to potash
because the former could not bring enough revenue to cover production and shipping costs. By 1792, the year before the events depicted
in *The Pioneers*, his shift to potash was effectively complete, and he encouraged burning the trees that he had previously tried to protect.[23] His
son (who again, as in the fishing episode, may have been vague about
the chronology) does not go on to follow Judge Temple's fortunes in the
sugar business. While he leaves open the possibility that some combination of Temple's interest in conservation, Richard's science, and Billy's
local knowledge might yet encourage the development of this sustainable
industry, he makes no optimistic predictions.

Temple's "consoling reflection" on this episode, however, concerns
not the local tradeoffs involved in the social ecologies of sugar and ash
production, but rather the larger question of how to regulate any such
ecology. Leaving the sugarbush, he says that "the hour approaches, when
the laws will take notice of not only the woods, but the game they con-
tain also" (229). Here questions of resource use run up against the laws
of property, foreshadowing the way the game laws drive the final conflict
of the novel. All along, Richard Jones has been urging Judge Temple to
forbid all hunting on his lands. Temple has expressly given Natty permission to hunt, however, recognizing a right to game deriving from prior
occupancy. Yet the conflict that begins with the episode in which Natty
cannot resist killing a buck out of season (even though "the venison is
lean now, and the dumb things run the flesh off their own bones for no
good" [295]) arises not from this local and immediate sense of property
rights, but rather from the larger structure of property brought forth by
the game laws. Unlike a feudal system in which the landlord owned the
deer in his park, the American system of game laws regulate the killing
of deer regardless of land ownership. In dictating when any person may
or may not kill a deer, such laws in effect construe deer as the property of

the state.[24] A law prescribing the season for deer hunting was passed by the New York legislature in 1788, and so would presumably be in effect for the events of *The Pioneers*.[25] If Temple owned the buck in question there would be no conflict (he had given Natty hunting rights), but since the quarrel is between Natty and the state, Temple has no choice but to pass sentence.

Temple in fact holds conflicting opinions regarding the game laws, which register his (and William Cooper's) conflicting positions as landowner and conservationist. In a scene set at the Bold Dragoon tavern, Temple argues for a return to a quasi-feudal structure in which game is the property not of the state, but of the landlord: "I hope to live to see the day, when a man's rights in his game shall be as much respected as the title to his farm" (160).[26] In such a day, he would not feel compelled to sentence Natty for killing a buck on his land. Yet in the same conversation he commends the New York legislature for passing "an act . . . to prohibit the killing of deer in the teeming months. These are laws that were loudly called for, by judicious men; nor do I despair of getting an act, to make the unlawful felling of timber a criminal offence" (160). Imposing a season on deer hunting infringed on the quasi-feudal rights to game that Temple desires. His remark on a timber law is even more puzzling, since there would seem to be no need to outlaw something already "unlawful." A certain kind of timber law could constrain his economic freedom to use the maple trees on his property for sugar, firewood, or ashes as he sees fit; it could, that is, infringe on rights conveyed in "the title to his farm," as game laws would infringe on "a man's rights in his game." The salient difference between the two cases is the fact that deer can migrate across property boundaries. Thus game laws protect the rights of the public at large in aiming to preserve their future access to game. No similar structure of rights extends to access to maple trees, for trees are part of an individual parcel of land in a way that the deer are not; that is, they are not public property, the use of which is regulated by the state. Thus one way to think about Temple's "consoling reflection" is that if local economics cannot encourage the preservation of resources such as maple trees, a larger structure in which those resources are not the absolute property of an individual landowner might regulate their use for the larger public good. Under such a structure, sugar production might thrive, but William Cooper might well have gone bankrupt, his individual capacity to accumulate capital and manage the land he owned being seriously impeded.

Unpacking Temple's hypothetical extension of the game laws to other resources such as "the woods," we recall an even more extensive structure of property regulation in effect at this time: the Cherokees' system of land tenure, whereby the soil itself was the common property of the nation and was individuated not through absolute possession but rather through use in agricultural production. This system preserved land as a resource equally available to all members of the nation. However, a national system of resource ownership would infringe on an individual's property rights in a capitalist economy. In the absence of such a system, management of sustainable economic engagements with the environment evidently depends the enlightened self-interest of property owners.

Labor Is Life

Most of the settlers in 1790s Templeton/Cooperstown had emigrated from New England under pressure of an agricultural crisis: increasing population, decreasing farm sizes, and soil exhaustion.[27] Those who remained in New England responded to the crisis either by intensifying agricultural production (according to methods examined in Chapter 5) or by developing industrial production. Both modes of intensification, Carolyn Merchant argues, encouraged a bifurcated conceptualization of the environment, in which nature was regarded instrumentally on the one hand, as "an abstract order of mechanical forces," and emotionally or spiritually on the other, as "a mother who embodied moral law."[28] George Perkins Marsh, responding to the environmental degradation wrought by a half-century of such intensification in New England, attempted to reconcile this split. He wanted to draw from the mechanistic and moralistic views of nature a synthetic understanding of environmental limits that would inform a program of cooperation with the order of nature.

Marsh approaches this reconciliation through the topic of labor, first dispelling the illusion offered by Cooper's Natty. For Marsh there is no westering escape from economy, no historical Eden, no possibility of a golden age in which we might simply live off nature's ever-ripe bounty. On the contrary, he posits that "labor is life," for "the earth was not, in its natural condition, completely adapted to the use of man, but only to the sustenance of wild animals and wild vegetation" (15, 38). Human life and culture thus require "a certain measure of transformation of terrestrial surface, of suppression of natural, and stimulation of artificially modified productivity" (38). The historical results of such labor are evident in the traces that herding, horticultural, and industrial societies leave on the land, but even in the "savage" state prior to the inception of herding and farming (for like many of his contemporaries Marsh adhered to a stadialist theory of cultural evolution), human beings work to alter their environment so as to assure their continuance in it. If "the wandering savage" hunts certain animals for food, "he compensates this loss by destroying also" the predator species, "protecting the feebler quadrupeds and fish and fowls, which would otherwise become the booty of beasts and birds of prey" and thus unavailable for human use (40).

Marsh had seen however, both in his native Vermont and on his travels abroad, the abuse of this principle of compensatory intervention amounting to "an almost indiscriminate warfare upon all the forms of animal and vegetable existence" (40). In response to humankind's overintensification of environmental engagement, nature "avenges herself upon" humankind "by letting loose upon her defaced provinces destructive energies hitherto kept in check by organic forces" (42). Nature's revenge takes the form of diminished environmental capacities. "Another era of equal human crime and human improvidence," Marsh argues, "would reduce [the earth] to such a condition of impoverished productiveness, of shattered surface, of climatic excess, as to threaten the deprivation, barbarism, and perhaps even the extinction of the species" (43).

The evidence of power in both humankind's environmental transformations and nature's potential for destructive energies raised "the great question, whether man is of nature or above her" (465). Environmentalists may well recoil at the apparent arrogance of this question—for of course we are "of" nature and the environmental crisis has arisen precisely because we have thought we are not.[29] Yet Marsh's consideration of the question through the category of labor is worth pursuing. Marsh had evidently begun with a predetermined answer, stating early on that "though living in physical nature, [humankind] is not of her," but rather "is of more exalted parentage, and belongs to a higher order of existences than those born of her womb and submissive to her dictates" (37). As preliminary evidence for this claim, he adduces "the fact that, of all organic beings, man alone is to be regarded as essentially a destructive power" (36). In the absence of human intervention, nature repairs any temporary disruptions caused by such events as "geologic convulsions" to reestablish "a condition of equilibrium" (29).[30] Change, of course, occurs within local environments, but in the absence of human intervention, the topography, climate, and distribution of species "are subject to change only from geological influences so slow in their operation that the geographical conditions may be regarded as constant and immutable" (35). Animals may temporarily disrupt a local balance, as for example the beaver, which seems (as Robert Beverley had observed) almost humanlike in some of its actions. However, a beaver pond will eventually revert to bog and then solid ground, become reforested, "and thus the interrupted harmony of nature is at last rëestablished" (32). Marsh does note dynamic processes, reporting, for example, on new research identifying a regular "order of succession" of forest trees (122). Here he calls for further study, since the European scientific literature has demonstrated that this order appears to "move in opposite directions" in Denmark and northern Germany, regions of roughly similar climate (122). However, in general Marsh de-emphasizes such evidence of unpredictable dynamism in natural processes in order to identify humankind as the primary agent of environmental change.

Rather than understanding humankind's role as improving raw nature ultimately to bring forth an orderly world ordained by God—a view we have seen most fully expressed in Johnson's *Wonder-Working Providence*[31]— Marsh observes that human action often turns the "harmonies of nature" to "discords" (36). He notes, for example, that the deforestation and agricultural impoverishment of the Mediterranean region that began during the Roman empire, while not theoretically irreversible, are practically so without an alteration of the mode of human life there: "the wounds [man] inflicts upon the material creation are not healed until he withdraws the arm that gave the blow" (41). Human beings could move on like the beavers, allowing natural reforestation to begin, but in practice they do not. It is curious then that Marsh criticizes the American backwoods farming method—which with its semimigratory practices and low population density was environmentally sustainable (see Chapter 5)—for exhausting the soil (233). His real target in this critique should be subsequent settlement by those who follow the pioneers, a pattern that did not permit reforestation and the natural restoration of fertility. All human engagement with the environment, he argues, "should be so conducted as not unnecessarily to derange and destroy what, in too many cases, it is beyond the power of man to rectify or restore" (35). That is, he wants to demonstrate that the environmental ethic Cooper had attributed to Natty Bumppo (use, but don't waste) is not specific to a wilderness condition, but rather must apply to human society in general: "Man has too long forgotten that the earth was given to him for usufruct alone, not for consumption, still less for profligate waste" (36).

The propensity to waste provides a fundamental distinction between humankind and the rest of nature. Other animals "hunt only as long as they feel the stimulus of hunger . . . and they do not wastefully destroy what they cannot consume. Man, on the contrary, angles to-day that he may dine to-morrow," and in the process many fish are lost (106). The very recognition of waste, however, reveals the possibility of its cessation. We have seen that in the originating era of the American georgic tradition, the elder Richard Hakluyt developed a conceptual transformation of the category of waste, seeing therein the potential for productive resources. Marsh shares this vision, recommending reforestation as a means of restoring the natural norms of temperature and rainfall and preventing soil erosion and siltation. He also notes other, nonagrarian instances of transformation, such as recent progress in "the utilization of waste . . . from metallurgical, chemical, and manufacturing establishments" (37). However, he most often decries the residue of nonproductive waste, for example those fish that are simply lost in an inefficient harvest and transportation system. This waste is specifically the unintended result of economic planning, of moving resources from place to place to make them available for human consumption. The phenomenon of waste, that is, indicates the future-directedness of human life. Marsh thus proposes that our capacity of foresight in environmental engagement is what finally distinguishes human from other environmental activity. Human action upon nature "differ[s] in essential character" from that of other animals "because, though it is often followed by unforseen and undesired results, yet it is nevertheless guided by a self-conscious and intelligent will aiming as often at secondary and remote as at immediate objects" (41). Marsh then mobilizes this will for moral ends, proposing that the "duties which this age owes to those that are to come after it" include a "self-forgetting care for the moral and material interests of our own posterity" (279).

We might object that this species-specific capacity for foresight, which contains the theoretical seed of the self-regulation that Marsh urges, is itself natural, providing evidence that humankind is "of" nature. The structure of Marsh's book explores this objection by moving from the predetermined answer at the beginning (humankind is "above" nature) to the open question (whether humankind is "of" or "above" nature) at the end. Marsh's primary concern however, as he explained to his publisher, was to preserve the category of agency on which his program depended: he needed to posit that "man . . . is a free moral agent working independently of nature" because that position gave the only hope of altering practices.[32] Yet the indeterminacy at which he finally arrives—"of" or "above"—is really a matter of both/and. Through consciousness of history, we ought to be able to think into the future consequences of present actions. "Even now," he warns, we are "breaking up the floor and the wainscoting and doors and window frames of our dwelling, for fuel to warm our bodies and seethe our pottage" (52). Arguing that we need to begin practicing "a better economy" even before "the slow and sure progress of exact science" can work out all the details, Marsh through this figure of the earth as our built dwelling returns "economy" to its etymological origin, household management (52). The figure supplies the conceptual distance from nature necessary for us to reflect on the consequences of our actions and the need for change.

Only from this position of conceptual distance does Marsh's moral discourse make sense, as when he exhorts us to "make full atonement for our spendthrift waste of the bounties of nature" (44). If such waste were fully natural, there would be no need for—indeed no possibility of—"atonement," for there would be nothing, from nature's perspective, for which to atone. Here both moral and instrumental discourses point to the same end. For example, in noting the destruction wrought by logging on forest ecosystems, Marsh first rehearses what we will recognize as a familiar instrumental argument against the destruction of the South American rainforest today: some of the woodland plants "are known to possess valuable medicinal properties, and experiment may show that the number of these is greater than we now suppose"; therefore, they must be preserved for the health of future generations (248). Yet beyond this, Marsh continues,

He whose sympathies with nature have taught him to feel that there is a fellowship between all God's creatures; to love the brilliant ore better than the dull ingot, iodic silver and crystallized red copper better than the shillings and pennies forged from them by the coiner's cunning; a venerable oak tree better than the brandy cask whose staves are split out from its heart wood; a bed of anemones, hepaticas, or wood violets than the leeks or onions which he may grow on the soil they have enriched and in the air they made fragrant—he who has enjoyed that special training of the heart and intellect which can be acquired only in the unviolated sanctuaries of nature, "where man is distant, but God is near"—will not rashly assert his right to extirpate a tribe of harmless vegetables, barely because their products neither tickle his palate nor fill his pocket; and his regret at the dwindling area of the forest solitude will be augmented by the reflection that the nurselings of the woodland perish with the pines, the oaks, and the beeches that sheltered them. (248–49)

Preservation thus manifests desirable human qualities such as humility, forebearance, nurturance, and a love of beauty.[33] In turn, preservation provides opportunities to foster our self-reflective development of such qualities, to cultivate "sympathies." This cultivation is often manifested in our habit of projecting these qualities back again onto nature, and some of these very qualities (the understory plants are said to be the trees' "nurselings") have instrumental implications for the continuance of future generations. Moral and instrumental perspectives thus resonate with each other, their harmony indicating humankind's proper relation to the material environment in practice: we ought to "become . . . co-worker[s] with nature in the reconstruction of the damaged fabric which the negligence or the wantonness of former lodgers has rendered untenantable," and in the maintenance of that fabric once repaired (35).

Our Woods and Our Destiny

In this respect at least, Marsh's position is not so very different from that of his now more famous New England contemporary, Thoreau. In "The Dispersion of Seeds," a manuscript unfinished at his death in 1862, Thoreau addresses at a local level the sort of cooperative action that Marsh envisions on a global scale. This essay, which begins as an investigation into the natural propagation of plants, ends with a discussion of land management.[34] The turn to management occurs at the point in the text where Thoreau announces his discovery of forest succession, a phenomenon that came to Marsh's attention via the European literature that began to be published in the 1840s.[35] Thoreau, evidently the first American to identify the phenomenon, concludes that if we "attended more closely to the history of our woodlots," working in concert with the predictable regularity of succession, "we should manage them more wisely."[36] In one of many instances, he notes how "eight or ten years at least had been gained" by the judicious cutting of a particular pitch-pine woods to favor the succeeding white pines, which resulted in "a valuable woodland"; yet he finds that this technique was practiced in only "three out of the thirteen cases" he has observed in Concord (153). Instead, too often "the history of a woodlot is . . . a history of cross-purposes" (170). For example, he visits a "dense white-pine wood" that had been logged the previous winter, expecting to find the oak seedlings he knew must succeed the pines, given the recent fertility of oaks in the vicinity. He discovers instead that the landowner "has burned it all over and sowed winter rye there!" (172). The owner "no doubt means to let it grow up again in a year or two" to oaks, "but he thought it would be clear gain if he could extract a little rye from it in the meanwhile" (172–73). But in so doing, the landowner prevented nature from "pursu[ing] the way she had entered upon." Thus the oak seedlings have been wasted and the land no longer has large pines to attract the squirrels that bury the acorns that enable the oak succession. If the owner continues even a year or two in extirpating oak seedlings and planting rye, "oaks cannot spring up here, for they must be preceded by pines. Pines and birches may, however, if there are seeds ready to be blown hither; but it may take a long while, and moreover the land is 'pine-sick.'" Such "greediness that defeats its own ends," Thoreau argues, ought to be prohibited: "So he trifles with Nature. I am chagrined for him. That he should call himself an agriculturalist! He needs to have a guardian placed over him. . . . Forest wardens should be appointed by the town—overseers of poor husbandmen" (173). So ends "The Dispersion of Seeds" with a call for regulation that Cooper's Judge Temple might well have approved, had he Thoreau's understanding of environmental history. Such regulation would enforce the principle of cooperation with natural processes that Thoreau and Marsh both urged.

Thoreau, of course, was interested in wild as well as managed woodlands, for "in Wildness is the preservation of the World."[37] Yet it is interesting to note that following this often-quoted passage from the late essay "Walking," Thoreau remarks particularly on our economic dependence on the wild, a point that is fundamental to Marsh's study. Moving from a description of nature's processes to a meditation on our cultural engagement with its products, Thoreau observes that "every tree sends its fibres forth in search of the Wild. The cities import it at any price. Men plow and sail for it. From the forest and wilderness come the tonics and barks which brace mankind" (224). The wild he finds embodied in the West: "the future lies that way to me, and the earth seems more unexhausted and richer on that side" (217). He needs to imagine the West as limitless, the perpetual "home of the younger sons," a continual source of moral as well as economic value (223). Appealing to the stadialist theory of settlement that was used to legitimate the removal of the Cherokees and other indigenous peoples, he claims that "the farmer displaces the Indian even because he redeems the meadow, and so makes himself stronger and in some respects more natural," as well as producing his material livelihood from it (230). As we have seen, Marsh in effect closed off this idea of the West as infinite environmental capacity.

Thus I do not want to suggest that Thoreau and Marsh held identical positions. Marsh reacted more strongly than did Thoreau to the global history of environmental degradation, partly because Thoreau was often reluctant to imagine the vulnerability of the pastoral spaces he valued.[38] Marsh's observations led him to argue strenuously for the efficacy and necessity of human action to repair degradation and develop sustainable economic-environmental engagements. He did not, however, go so far in the direction of managerialism as did another New Englander similarly alarmed at deforestation, George B. Emerson.[39] In his *Report on the Trees and Shrubs Growing Naturally in the Forests of Massachusetts* (1846), Emerson insisted that no land whatever, "except the ocean beach, should be considered unimprovable"; thus "almost every acre of the surface [of Massachusetts] might be made productive" in some way.[40] Addressing "utilitarian readers," he even apologized for including some brief passages on "the beauty of our native trees," arguing that such passages may induce the more aesthetically minded to plant trees (vii). Primarily, however, he viewed trees as "crops," which ought to be rotated as "in cultivated fields" (19).[41]

For Marsh, management did not necessarily mean intervention. Sometimes it meant letting things alone. For example, he criticized the draining of wetlands along rivers, which often results in increased flooding and other detrimental effects (310). Marsh objected to irrigation, finding nonirrigated crops "superior in flavor and in nutritive power" and noting a number of evils including salinification of the soil and "prejudicial climatic effects" (321, 323). He went so far as to suggest that the discontinuation of irrigation in Egypt would eventually lead to the reforestation of the Nile region (317). In the case of forests, considerations of "immense collateral advantages" such as effects on climate and soil were sufficient evidence of value beyond any more immediate economic input that might be derived from them (279). He believed that in some cases, particularly in Europe where population density is great and woodland acreage comparatively small, "the sooner a natural wood is brought into the state of an artificially regulated one, the better it is for all the multiplied interests which depend on the wise administration of this branch of public economy" (260). In America, however, where great tracts of "primitive woodland" abound, he argued as well for preservation:

It is desirable that some large and easily accessible region of American soil should remain, as far as possible, in its primitive condition, at once a museum for the instruction of the student, a garden for the recreation of the nature lover, and an asylum where the indigenous tree, and humble plant that loves the shade, and fish and fowl and four-footed beast, may dwell and perpetuate their kind, in the enjoyment of such imperfect protection as the laws of a people jealous of restraint can afford them. (203–4)

Thoreau's argument for forest preservation in *The Maine Woods* addresses many of the same issues, invoking a perhaps deeper sense of "re-creation" but similarly imagining large tracts as a sort of historical repository:

The kings of England formerly had their forests "to hold the king's game," for sport or food, sometimes destroying villages to create or extend them; and I think that they were impelled by a true instinct. Why should not we, who have renounced the king's authority, have our national preserves, where no villages need be destroyed, in which the bear and the panther, and some even of the hunter race, may still exist, and not be "civilized off the face of the earth,"—our forests, not to hold the king's game merely, but to hold and preserve the king himself also, the lord of creation,—not for idle sport or food, but for inspiration and our own true re-creation? or shall we, like villains, grub them all up, poaching on our own national domains? [42]

But who is this "we" who might destroy or preserve such woodlands? Thoreau's evocation of contrasting modes of political authority—tyranny versus its renunciation—indicates that this is the key question. How could that "true instinct" of the English monarchs become embodied in American practices, especially since, as Marsh noted, Americans are "a people jealous of restraint" (few more so than Thoreau himself)? [43]

Most important, then, Marsh and Thoreau share common ground in asking the question of agency. This question, we have seen, was asked in one form or another by most of the georgics we have examined, from John Smith's concern over the dispersal of settlement at Jamestown and the consequent evacuation of the colony's moral authority through the Cherokees' national concern to retain their homeland and continue their particular mode of agricultural practice free from the intervention of the United States. As Thoreau asked the question, who would have the authority to compel the untutored farmer to manage his woodlot in cooperation with nature, or to compel the American people to set aside large tracts for preservation? The local economy of Concord might conceivably admit the appointment of forest wardens, but in the social ecology of the world at large, the necessity of foresight runs up against considerations of practice, property, and agency. If we ought to become co-workers with nature, how can we make sure that our labor is properly directed and genuinely cooperative?

Although Marsh does not develop a consistent answer to these questions, he addresses them more extensively than anyone had to this point. Consistency would elude him so long as he held to fundamental capitalist assumptions regarding property rights. These assumptions finally prevent him from imagining a structure of policy-making that could enact the programs of restoration, conservation, and preservation that were the logical end of his study of social ecology. Even so, we can see him struggling against the institutional fact of property at times, as for example in his vehement critique of the railroads, "joint-stock companies" that "have no souls" and "their managers, in general, no consciences." All such "private associations" have the legal capacity of agency but not of responsibility to the public good, being endowed with no "higher obligations than those of a pecuniary nature" (51). Marsh thought that governments, which were capable of "look[ing] to more distant as well as nobler ends" than were "private enterprises," thus ought to take responsibility for any large developmental or restorational project (436). "In countries where there exist municipalities endowed with an intelligent public spirit," municipal ownership of forests "would often prove advantageous"; yet while "forest communes" have succeeded, as for example in Lombardy, they have also failed, as in Switzerland where pasturage has so degraded the forest lands that there is "nothing left that is worth protecting" (202, 203). Regarding America, Marsh suggests that "the State should declare the remaining forest the inalienable property of the commonwealth," set some aside for preservation as wilderness, and manage the rest for productive uses (203).[44]

Despite his qualified hopes for government regulation, Marsh admits that "no legislation can secure the permanence of the forest in private hands" (250). American liberal individualism, manifested in land ownership, runs too deep. Thus Marsh counts finally on owners themselves to have "a strong interest in the protection of their domain against deterioration" (46). He concludes that "for prevention of the evils upon which I have so long dwelt, the American people must look to the diffusion of general intelligence on this subject, and to the enlightened self interest, for which they are remarkable, not to the action of their local or general legislatures" (259). Marsh hoped that his book would contribute to this program of enlightenment, especially since he wrote not for scientists but rather for a general readership of "educated, observing, and thinking men" (5). Such self-interest, however, even if enlightened, is not necessarily coextensive with the sense of moral obligation to the human future that Marsh attempts elsewhere to inculcate, as for example in his assertion that "the planter of a wood must be actuated by *higher motives* than those of an investment the profits of which consist in direct pecuniary gain to himself or even to his posterity" (278, emphasis added). Marsh saw that the fundamental categories of economy can be organized in various ways and do not depend theoretically on the category of individual property in land (as for example the Cherokees' land system did not), but he hoped that in practice the conventional American structure of individual property might act as a check on the actions of corporations, agents that routinely ignore all "higher obligations" (51). Any such obligations or motives by which labor might be reconceptualized for environmental good supplement but do not supplant the basic structure of individual self-interest that Marsh assumes.[45]

Man and Nature significantly influenced government policy, but as reviews of the first two editions indicate, it did less to enlighten the individual property owners whom Marsh considered his primary audience. The book led Congress to establish a national forestry commission and national forest reserves in 1873.[46] Citing these congressional actions, *Scribner's* characterized Marsh's "point of view" as "that of a law-maker or advocate of internal improvements," but said little of private citizens except in the roles of "teacher" and "voter."[47] Reviewers heeded Marsh's warnings of impending environmental apocalypse to a greater or lesser degree, but only rarely did they point his conclusions toward individual action. The *Christian Examiner*, to which Marsh sometimes contributed, took its review of the first edition as an opportunity to criticize contemporary assumptions of an "unlimited future of progress," noting that Marsh "hint[s] that the race has very nearly reached the meridian of its terrestrial day . . . that, unless something can be done to stay the waste or restore the loss, the material conditions of our civilization, of social progress, perhaps even of human life and society itself upon our planet, are already slipping from our hands." The means by which something might be done, however, remain vague to this reviewer, encompassed only in the general observation that "our personal and political economies should conform" to the "grand economies of nature."[48] The *Edinburgh Review*, in contrast, saw no reason to address the question of agency at all, but rather criticized Marsh for excessive "zeal," discounting his claims about climate and erosion as overgeneralized. This reviewer regarded woodlands primarily as sources of fuel, which might be replaced by coal; coal deposits in turn might eventually be exhausted, but at such a distant point in the future that it was "useless to speculate . . . on the general condition of mankind at [that] time."[49] The scientific journal *Nature* was similarly reserved, suggesting that, "viewed broadly," humankind's "interferences with the ordinary economy of nature . . . cannot do more than alter the balance of [natural] forces, giving to some a greater and to others a less share of work than in a natural state would be accomplished by them."[50] James Russell Lowell most nearly approached the spirit of Marsh's moral discourse, arguing that the book leads us "to reflect upon the rights and duties of government, as preventive and advisory, and to feel that there is a common interest which vastly transcends the claims of individual freedom of action" in our engagements with nature.[51] Only one review of the six I have located, however, took up any specific recommendation regarding land management practices. The *Nation* concluded that "the agriculturalist, as being in closest contact with nature, will perhaps derive the most profit from these pages." The farmers "on our Western plains" in "Minnesota or Kansas" ought to plant trees, not so much to alter the climate as to attract birds that would control grain-destroying insects.[52] Such a practice would, if carried out on a large enough scale, have the long-term effect of increasing the overall global ratio of woodland to tillage as Marsh recommended. The *Nation* did not, however, address the sense of moral obligation particularly noted by Lowell, which Marsh believed ought to ground any consideration of land practices. The gap between the systems-theory perspective that governs the analysis and the realm of individual behavior (think globally, act locally) finally proved too large for Marsh's moral discourse to bridge.

*   *   *

Like earlier writers in the American georgic tradition, Marsh develops a critical history of environmental engagement to urge us to action or restraint, as the situation requires. Like them, he employs rhetorics of excoriation, exhortation, and promise. Yet the promise of the environment seems more distant in *Man and Nature* than it did in the texts of the Hakluyts, John Smith, Edward Johnson, Robert Beverley, the Federal-era agrarians, the pre-Removal Cherokees, or in Thoreau's remarks on our westering spirit. Unlike these writers, Marsh saw the economy's systemic dependence on environmental capacities running up against its ultimate, global limits. The solutions he proposes to environmental crisis—government regulation, individual self-regulation, and recognition of our obligation to future generations—have at best been regarded as good ideas but not practiced. Perhaps it has been easier to imagine ourselves with Natty Bumppo, escaping to a frontier space, than to confront the fact of limits. When Marsh dispels this illusion of escape, we are left facing the historical contradiction registered in one of the earliest texts we have examined, Smith's *Generall Historie*. Describing the "benefit of libertie in the planters" arising from the first modest allotment of private holdings at

Jamestown, Smith hoped that now "for the industrious, there is reward sufficient," more than mere "bread," in working the land.[53] Yet he soon came to recognize the difficulties of proper management in an emergent capitalist system, in which too often "the desire of present gaine (in many) is so violent, and the endevours of many undertakers so negligent, every one so regarding their private gaine, that it is hard to effect any publike good."[54]

Dismal as this assessment was, in some ways our present situation is worse, for our ability to understand our relation to the environment has diminished in certain respects since Smith wrote, even as science has given us the possibility of greater understanding. Our "private gaine" has become increasingly detached from the source of that "gaine," the nature from which we ultimately derive all life and culture. For one thing, the critical mass of individual property owners whom Marsh hoped to enlighten can hardly be said to exist today. The soulless "joint-stock companies" that Marsh excoriated possess a vast amount of resources, but even individual owners of productive land are bound up in corporate networks that have no "higher obligations" than profits to stockholders (51). The management of government lands for private profit (mining, timbering, grazing, and so on) further complicates the question. Exacerbating this general structure of environmental alienation is the fact that most Americans today experience nature primarily in the pastoral mode, regarding nature (if it is regarded at all) as a site of leisure, not of labor. Renewed attention to the American georgic tradition can illustrate the economics of even our pastoral experiences. It can also inspire us to think through the implications of our production and our consumption, no matter how alienated from their ultimate environmental basis.[55]

In this sense, we are all potentially co-workers with nature. To begin working in concert, we might, for example, use the georgic tradition's insights to evaluate recent attempts to redirect our environmental engagements. One notable attempt, Paul Hawken's *Ecology of Commerce* (1993), assumes the Hakluyts' systemic perspective while appealing to the sense of moral obligation and the threat of environmental apocalypse deployed by Marsh. Hawken is more willing than Marsh to propose governmental intervention; for example, he recommends Pigovian taxes to encourage the development of a sustainable infrastructure.[56] But where we can see Marsh, at some moments, struggling against the constraints of property, Hawken's program still assumes, indeed depends on, capitalist relations of production. Even so, how his program might fare among "a people jealous of restraint" is open to question.

Further complicating the goal of economic cooperation with environmental processes is recent ecological research that criticizes the fundamental assumption of stability held by all the georgic writers examined here.[57] We are beginning to realize that nature does not exist in a state of equilibrium, even in the absence of human activity, nor does it tend to return to such a hypothetical state if disturbed. This new understanding of eternal dynamism may be disconcerting to environmentalists, for nature no longer seems to hold out a constant point of reference or ground for argument. Any formulation of programs directing our environmental engagements for the public good thus becomes increasingly problematic. These complications for a new georgic notwithstanding, one thing remains constant, and that is the necessity of labor itself. No matter how we understand nature, we produce our very being from it. As Marsh reminds us, labor is life.

Notes

Introduction

1. Thoreau, *Walden*, 162, hereafter cited parenthetically.
2. Gross's contextual studies of Thoreau's agriculture are suggestive in this regard. On the one hand Gross finds that, in contrast to the "interdependence and mutual cooperation" typical of eighteenth-century farming practices, Thoreau's individualism and rational systematization of life were "close in spirit to the advice of [nineteenth-century] agricultural reformers" ("Culture and Cultivation," 55). Yet Gross also argues that in his refusal to follow contemporarily recognized best practices—not manuring the field, hoeing the beans when they are wet thus enabling the spread of disease, and so on—Thoreau was spoofing those very reformers ("Great Bean Field Hoax"). See also Bromell, who argues that Thoreau reduced his labor to a theoretical minimum then amplified it again by suggesting that we love labor "for its own sake" (*By the Sweat of the Brow*, 218).
3. Emerson, *Complete Works*, 1:65.
4. Donahue, *Reclaiming the Commons*, 8.
5. An important exception to this emphasis on the pastoral tradition is Tichi, *New World, New Earth*, which traces the "ideological imperative" of "environmental reform" evident in a millennialist strain of American literature from the Puritans through Walt Whitman (viii). Here Biblical rather than classical texts form the originary locus of an American landscape ideal. While my debt to Tichi is readily apparent in Chapter 3, I see millennialism (and its subsequent secularization) as but one interpretive matrix for understanding Americans' engagements with the environment.
6. Poggioli, *Oaten Flute*, 4.
7. Marx, *Machine in the Garden*, 21, hereafter cited parenthetically.
8. We should note that history provides a very real counterforce to the rural scene of Virgil's *Georgics* as well. Book I ends on a plea for peace among images of armies on the march, fields abandoned, sickles beaten into swords—the destruction of agricultural productivity.
9. Alpers, *What Is Pastoral?* 13, 22, 50.
10. Buell, *Environmental Imagination*, 439, hereafter cited parenthetically.
11. Jehlen, *American Incarnation*.
12. See, e.g., Krech, *Ecological Indian*.
13. Cronon, "Trouble with Wilderness," provides a useful overview of these issues.

14. Williams, *The Country and the City*, 116.

15. Worster, *Nature's Economy*, 2. Eisenberg, *Ecology of Eden*, posits a similar distinction between "Planet Fetishers" and "Planet Managers."

16. See Smith, *Virgin Land.*

17. Spengemann, *New World of Words*, 43.

18. Smith, *Complete Works*, 2:464.

19. Marsh, *Man and Nature*, 465, hereafter cited parenthetically.

Chapter 1. Economy and Environment in Sixteenth-Century Promotional Literature

1. Parmenius was a Hungarian scholar, educated at Oxford, whose connection to colonial ventures came by way of the younger Richard Hakluyt, with whom he shared rooms in Christ Church. Parmenius intended to write a full chronicle of the expedition, but, like Gilbert, was killed in a shipwreck on the voyage home. See Quinn and Cheshire, *New Found Land.* On Gilbert's ventures, see Andrews, *Trade, Plunder, and Settlement*, 183–99.

2. Quinn and Cheshire, 175. The translation is Hakluyt's and was first printed in the 1589 *Principall Navigations.*

3. Quinn and Cheshire, 175–76. Transcribing Parmenius's letter in the "Discourse of Western Planting," Hakluyt added a marginal note claiming that "afterwardes they sett the woodds on fire wch burnte three weekes together" (Taylor, ed., *Original Writings*, 2:231, hereafter cited parenthetically as *O*). As far as I am aware, there is no other record of this decision to burn the woods. Edward Hayes's account of Gilbert's voyage does not mention it; see Hakluyt, *Principall Navigations*, 6:1–38. Nor is it mentioned by Sir George Peckham, who interviewed Hayes on his return to England; see Peckham, *True reporte on the late discoveries . . . by . . . Sir Humphrey Gilbert*, in Quinn, ed., *New American World*, 3:35–60.

4. Quinn and Cheshire, 183–84.

5. Hakluyt's translation expands Parmenius's noun, *terebynthina* (of the terebinth tree, *Pistacia terebinthus*, not a conifer but a member of the sumac family native to the Mediterranean region) into these two commodities.

6. On sustainable economics, see Daly, *Steady-State Economics*; Daly, "Steady-State Economics: A New Paradigm"; Daly and Cobb, *For the Common Good*; Neumayer, *Weak Versus Strong Sustainability.*

7. Daly, "Steady-State," 811. The flow of solar energy into the ecosystem ultimately limits the flow of energy from the ecosystem into the economy. The ecosystem can absorb only a limited outflow of matter and energy—that is, waste—from the economy while sustaining human life; this limit is ultimately determined by the planet's capacity to transfer heat energy to space.

8. Both the promotional genre and the closely related voyage genre developed a fundamentally economic conception of nationhood, which competed with other conceptions projected by other cultural formations, such as the Crown, the gentry, the law, and the church. See Helgerson, *Forms of Nationhood*, especially 151–91. On the systematization of European economic thought from the mid-sixteenth century on, particularly in terms of the central principle of the balance of trade, see Rich and Wilson, eds., *Cambridge Economic History*, 4:498–500.

9. Generic conventions of the promotional tract include a utilitarian tone, an emphasis on labor, and a rhetorical structure characterized by figures of blockage or indirection when the text addresses Europe and figures of openness or

expansive vision as it turns toward the New World. See Franklin, *Discoverers, Explorers, Settlers*, 87–94; Quinn, *Explorers and Colonies*, 106–7; Greene, *Intellectual Construction of America*, 34–46. Such figures persisted in later American promotions of westward expansion. Thomas Jefferson, for example, would argue that where land in Europe is "locked up against the cultivator," "we have an immensity of land courting the industry of the husbandman" (*Notes on Virginia*, 170). As late as the 1910s, promoters would use this rhetoric, now largely detached from economic theorization, to lure prospective homesteaders to eastern Montana; see Raban, *Bad Land*. While the model of colonial economics offered by the merchant promoters would become dominant, it was not the only one available in the sixteenth century. Gilbert's first voyage intended to establish a colony mainly as a pretense for capturing Spanish, Portuguese, and French shipping; see Andrews, *Trade, Plunder, and Settlement*, 187. Where Sir Walter Ralegh's Roanoke project was primarily mercantile, his later report on Guiana disdains trade in favor of conquest in order to establish military bases against Spain and exact tribute from the natives, for "where there is store of gold, it is in effect needless to remember other commodities for trade" (Ralegh, *Selected Writings*, 119).

10. According to the *OED*, the use of *waste* to refer to by-products of manufacturing processes did not develop until the eighteenth century.

11. Early texts such as these are rarely discussed in ecocritical contexts. Slovic, "Ecocriticism: Trajectories," gives a critique of ecocriticism's tendency to focus rather narrowly on the works of Thoreau and his heirs and related texts.

12. Recent ecocriticism values texts that move us from an anthropocentric to an eco- or biocentric world view; see, for example, Evernden, "Beyond Ecology." Buell, however, demonstrates how difficult it is for even the most committed ecocentrist to decenter human subjectivity; see *Environmental Imagination*, 143–79.

13. As Horwitz succinctly puts it, where the Aristotelian tradition viewed economics as a matter of "manag[ing] resources ready to hand," Locke's *Second Treatise* "redefined value as the product of human labor modifying nature" (*By the Law of Nature*, 7).

14. Daly, "Steady-State," 814.

15. More, *Utopia*, 66–67 (emphasis added), hereafter cited parenthetically as *U*. I quote from Ralph Robinson's 1551 translation (ed. Collins), in which More, of course, had no part, to present the topic in contemporary language.

16. Although the first official pronouncement on England's balance of trade came in 1381, the concept did not really catch on until the sixteenth century. Mercantilism was not fully recognized as an economic theory until it became an object of critique for the Physiocrats and Adam Smith; see Magnusson, *Mercantilism*, 9. Here I use "mercantilism" in the very general sense of the promotion of a favorable balance of trade.

17. See More, *Complete Works*, 4:428.

18. Halpern, *Poetics of Primitive Accumulation*, 45.

19. More would have concluded from Vespucci that iron was not abundant in the New World. He probably also knew that the increasing demand for iron in England had to be met with imports. See More, *Complete Works*, 427.

20. See Quinn, *Explorers and Colonies*, 108–9. In translating More's "*continente proximo*" as "nexte lande," rather than nearby mainland or a similar phrase, Robinson seems to point mid-sixteenth century English colonial thought directly toward Ireland (More, *U*, 66).

21. Dewar, ed., *Discourse of the Commonweal*, 126.

22. Ibid.

23. Crosby, *Ecological Imperialism*, 108; Kupperman, "Puzzle of the American Climate," 1265–68.

24. Smith, *Complete Works*, 3:271.

25. Kupperman, "Puzzle of the American Climate," 1267.

26. Hariot, *A Briefe and True Report of the New Found Land of Virginia*, 68, 72, hereafter cited parenthetically.

27. See Jehlen and Warner's note to Hariot, *Briefe and True Report*, 68. Shields, however, suggests that it was "nothing more than marsh grass" ("England's Staple Colonies," 130).

28. Subsequent promotional texts, from Robert Johnson's *Nova Britannia* (1609) through John Smith's *Generall Historie* (1624) and beyond, reiterated a particular desire for Mediterranean commodity environments. Even Thomas Jefferson tried, unsuccessfully, to introduce olive cultivation to America; see Miller, *Jefferson and Nature*, 222.

29. See McRae, *God Speed the Plough*, 135–68.

30. Nash, *Pierce Penilesse*, 85–86.

31. McRae, *God Speed*, 168.

32. See Appleby, *Economic Thought and Ideology*, 129–57.

33. Peckham had bought land rights in Newfoundland from Gilbert, the original patentee, and wrote the *True report of the late discoveries . . . by . . . Sir Humphrey Gilbert* in 1583 to attract investors and settlers; see Quinn, *New American*, 3:34.

34. Ibid., 3:36.

35. Christopher Carleill, *A breef and sommarie discourse upon the entended voyage to the hethermoste partes of America*, in Quinn, *New American*, 3:31.

36. See Peckham, *True reporte*, in Quinn, *New American*, 3:35–60. Edward Hayes's account of Gilbert's second voyage notes that the Newfoundland fishing fleet "have caried sheepe thither for fresh victuall and had them raised exceeding fat in lesse then three weekes," but Hayes does not mention their potential for wool production (Hakluyt, *Principall Navigations*, 6:22).

37. See Supple, *Commercial Crisis and Change*, 23; Andrews, *Trade, Plunder, and Settlement*, 6–9.

38. Peckham, *True reporte*, in Quinn, *New American*, 3:49–50.

39. See McRae, *God Speed*, 9–10, 23–24, 43–44.

40. See Jacob, *Fifteenth Century*, 346–85.

41. Carroll, "Nursery of Beggary," 35.

42. See Supple, *Commercial Crisis*, 135–62, 197–224.

43. Appleby, *Economic Thought and Ideology*, 41.

44. See Appleby, *Economic Thought and Ideology*.

45. Christensen, "Historical Roots for Ecological Economics," argues that in their attention to resource inputs, classical models provide an unrecognized starting point for a biophysical perspective on economics, but that these models must be extended to include both a recognition of solar energy as the primary input and a consideration of waste output.

46. Sustainable economics holds that natural capital is fundamentally nonsubstitutable for manufactured capital; it does not require that nonrenewable natural resources never be used, but it does require that receipts from nonrenewable resources be invested in the development of renewable resources (e.g., solar energy) so as to keep the total stock of natural capital constant. See Neumayer, *Weak Versus Strong Sustainability*, 26–27.

47. Daly and Cobb argue that the neglect of the category of land or resources

has been symptomatic of this ever increasing assumption of systemic closure. As concern for the productive capacity of physical nature has become more peripheral within the economic subdiscipline of land economics, land economics itself has become more peripheral to general economic analysis. Neoclassical models assume that "capital is a near perfect substitute for land and other natural resources" (*Common Good*, 97–117, 196). The disciplines of literary and cultural studies have reflected the preoccupations of mainstream economic theory in this regard. Symptomatic is Woodmansee and Osteen, eds., *New Economic Criticism*, which has substantial entries in the index for "labor" and "capital" but none for "land" or "resources."

48. See, for example, Goux, *Symbolic Economies*.

49. Worster, *Nature's Economy*, 291–311.

50. Note that this observation is distinct from any metaphorical or heuristic claim that economies behave like ecological systems—for example, that economic development, in which differentiation emerges from generality, can be thought of as imitating biological evolution. On such claims, see Jacobs, *Nature of Economies*.

51. Worster, *Nature's Economy*, 388–420; Botkin, *Discordant Harmonies*.

Chapter 2. "God Sells Us All Things for Our Labour"

1. Hariot, *A Briefe and True Reporte of the New Found Land of Virginia*, 68, hereafter cited parenthetically.

2. Asking after gold, pearls, spices, and so on, Columbus would be informed that great quantities of such goods were available in another land some days distant, if he would only go there as soon as he could—and wherever he went, he got the same story. See Columbus, *Journal of the First Voyage to America*.

3. On attempts to develop sericulture in Virginia, see Hatch, "Mulberry Trees and Silkworms." The *True Declaration of Virginia* mentions "innumerable White Mulberry trees," perhaps observing immature berries (22, hereafter cited parenthetically).

4. This project thus complements Smith's endeavors to argue for the primacy of "experience" in colonial management. As Egan argues, Smith was a key figure in developing a rhetoric of "experience" to supplant classical knowledge and aristocratic authority as a means of ordering the colonization process, casting the "man of experience" as "integral to the exploitation of colonial commodities" (*Authorizing Experience*, 9).

5. In compiling the *Generall Historie*, Smith used both his own previous writings, drawn from his experiences in Virginia and New England, as well as numerous other published reports. Barbour documents Smith's sources in his notes to the *Complete Works*. Franklin argues that Smith's use of sources prevents him from "tell[ing] the story he might like to, a tale of Virginian growth and promise" (*Discoverers, Explorers, Settlers*, 187). Even so, I believe that Smith's position on economic and environmental development remains fairly consistent throughout the *Generall Historie*. Thus, while many of the passages I quote have sources in these other texts, I take the *Generall Historie* to represent the synthesis of Smith's views on America up to 1624, organized into a developmental narrative culminating in his promotion of New England.

6. Smith, *Complete Works of Captain John Smith*, 2:411, hereafter cited parenthetically.

7. Kolodny, *Lay of the Land*, 4. Kolodny cites this passage particularly in her analysis of the implications of the feminized landscape (11). However, she finds, not in Smith but in other early promotional texts "a doctrine of use and labor that conflicts" with the feminized landscape's promise of gratification (25).

8. Lemay characterizes Smith as "the first American environmentalist, urging the planters to create their plantations with an eye toward the resulting landscape" (*American Dream of Captain John Smith*, 15).

9. In fact the *Lawes Divine, Morall, and Martiall* instituted by the Virginia Company and brought over by Lord De La Warr prescribed a workday of five to eight hours in summer and three to six in winter. See Morgan, *American Slavery, American Freedom*, 62, 89.

10. Morgan, 86–87.

11. Cf. Smith, *Works*, 2:154.

12. Morgan, 89.

13. As Silver demonstrates, the colonists failed to recognize the Indians' land management practices as such; *A New Face on the Countryside*, 64–65.

14. See my discussion of the land requirements of tobacco culture in Chapter 4. On soil exhaustion during the colonial era, see Craven, *Soil Exhaustion*, 25–71.

15. Donne, "Sermon Preached to the Honourable Company of the Virginian Plantation," *Sermons*, 4:269 (emphasis in original), hereafter cited parenthetically.

16. Kingsbury, *Records of the Virginia Company*, 4:556–57.

17. Barbour concludes that the fortifications on the peninsula would run "more or less along a line from modern Charles City to West Point" (Smith, *Works*, 2:303). The calculations are mine.

18. Virginians came to assume that a plantation required at least fifty acres per working hand, land enough for tobacco, corn, pasture, and fallow. See Morgan, *American Slavery*, 173; Kulikoff, *Tobacco and Slaves*, 47–48.

19. Franklin argues that he uses this occasion, recording his answers to questions put to him by the Crown's investigation, to position himself as "*the* Virginia voice, in England" (*Discoverers*, 188, emphasis in original). On the investigation of 1623 and its results, see Craven, *Dissolution of the Virginia Company*, 251–336.

20. On the establishment of modern parity pricing, see Atack and Passell, *A New Economic View of American History*, 668–71.

21. Craven, *Dissolution*, 332.

22. On Edmund Waller's and Andrew Marvell's indebtedness to the opening passages of Book V of the *Generall Historie*, see Barbour's note; Smith, *Works*, 2:340.

23. Waller, *Poetical Works*, 97, hereafter cited parenthetically.

24. Qtd. in Waller, 96.

25. Marvell, *Complete Poetry*, 10, 11.

26. Brockbank, "The Politics of Paradise," 185–86.

27. He relied particularly on *Mourt's Relation* (1622), Edward Winslow's *Good Newes from New England* (1624), and Richard Whitbourne's *A Discourse Containing a Loving Invitation to Adventurers in the New-found-land* (1622). See Smith, *Works*, 2:397.

28. Wood, *New England's Prospect*, 53.

Chapter 3. "Wonder-Working Providence" of the Market

1. Wood, *New England's Prospect,* 31, hereafter cited parenthetically.

2. See Egan's discussion of body and climate, *Authorizing Experience,* 47–57. Wood claims that people are healthier in New England and that the birth rate is higher (32–33).

3. Kupperman, "Puzzle of the American Climate," 1264.

4. We know that ocean winds moderate England's temperatures, but such an understanding of climatology was not available to Wood. Indeed, many seventeenth-century colonists noted New England's climatic extremes but none could explain the cause. See Kupperman, "Puzzle," 1281–82, 1272–74. Nor could such a view account for climatic change over time in England or greater extremes in New England of both heat and cold.

5. See McRae, *God Speed the Plough,* 135–68.

6. Egan understands Wood as desiring "pure English life as it originally was, rather than what it has become under Charles I" (*Authorizing,* 59). The political implications of this desire remain unclear, however, in the absence of information about Wood's beliefs. Vaughan (Introduction to Wood, *New England's Prospect,* 4–6) concludes that he was probably not a Puritan. However, Wood's stated intention, "God willing, to return [to New England] shortly again" may suggest Puritan leanings (20).

7. Bozeman, *To Live Ancient Lives,* demonstrates the importance of religious primitivism, the desire to recover the purity of the Biblical era, for American Puritan culture.

8. Johnson, *Wonder-Working Providence,* 21–22, hereafter cited parenthetically.

9. Tichi, *New World, New Earth,* 54.

10. Johnson, however, attributes this change as much to an "admirable Act of Christ" as to the actions of the colonists themselves (84).

11. Bradford, *Of Plymouth Plantation,* 254, hereafter cited parenthetically.

12. We generally take Bradford to exemplify the nostalgic, and Johnson the progressive modes of historiography in first-generation New England. The prevailing view is that Bradford wanted to continue to think of Plymouth as the exemplum or embodiment of the Reformation in the face of doubts issuing from the planting of the Bay colony and the success of the Puritan cause in England, but that he failed to achieve his purpose by means of historical narration. See Delbanco, *Puritan Ideal,* 193–95; Rosenmeier, "With My Owne Eyes"; Sargent, "William Bradford's 'Dialogue.'" In the case of Johnson, Arch sorts the prevailing interpretations into two categories, according to whether they view his tone as "triumphant" or "enervated" (*Authorizing the Past,* 80). On the former, see Gura, *Glimpse of Sion's Glory,* 229–34; Tichi, *New World,* 37–66. On the latter, see Delbanco, 189–92. Arch himself discerns an "ambiguity" of purpose, suggesting that Johnson was "hedging his bets" (80).

13. John Cotton, qtd. in Miller, *From Colony to Province,* 41. Followers of Max Weber, such as Innes, *Creating the Commonwealth,* emphasize the relation between free-market economics and Puritan culture's emphases on labor and on the authority granted to individual conscience. This authority, however, was tempered by practical as well as moral considerations of the common good. John Winthrop, for example, argued that "the care of the publique must oversway all private respects . . . for it is a true rule that particuler estates cannott subsist in the ruine of the publique" ("Modell of Christian Charity," 232). John Eliot especially wanted

to subordinate the interests of trade to the good of community and the goals of religion; see Bozeman, *Ancient Lives*, 264–86.

14. Burnham, "Anne Hutchinson and the Economics of Antinomian Selfhood," reads the Antinomian controversy in light of a conflict in economic theory between production-oriented gentry, such as Winthrop, and mercantilists such as the Hutchinson family. On Johnson's interest in defining the colony's boundaries, in relation to the contemporary mercantile language of "vent," see Burnham, 353–54.

15. Bozeman, *Ancient Lives*, 116.

16. Fishing and fur trading were economically important to both Plymouth and the Bay colony, as Bradford particularly recognized. However, agriculture especially defined the colonies' geographical as well as political-economic identities. See Rutman, *Husbandmen of Plymouth*, 2–27; Rutman, "Governor Winthrop's Garden Crop."

17. Innes, *Creating*, 286.

18. Winthrop, "Reasons to Be Considered," 135.

19. Ibid., 136–37. Others gave similar justifications. See Carroll, *Puritanism and the Wilderness*, 181–83; Vaughan, *New England Frontier*, 109–15. On the colonists' distinction between "natural" and "civil" rights to land as property, see Jennings, *Invasion of America*, 82, 135.

20. Winthrop, "Reasons," 136–37.

21. Cronon, *Changes in the Land*, 142.

22. Ibid., 162.

23. The battle, of course, was always in some way over land; see Jennings, *Invasion*. Anderson, "King Philip's Herds," argues that livestock production in particular was a major factor in the contentions that led to King Philip's War.

24. See Bradford, 85, 90, 100, 112, 120, 131, 132, 145, 178, 181.

25. Rutman, *Husbandmen*, 12.

26. This shift brought the structure of everyday life in the colony in line with its larger economic structure, that of a joint-stock company. However complicated the financial arrangements were among the colonists, the London partners, and (eventually) Massachusetts financiers, Plymouth from the beginning resembled a "modern corporation," with features such as limited liability, perpetual stock, dividend payments, and corporate managers (Innes, *Creating*, 206).

27. In this, the structure of *Wonder-Working Providence* might be thought of as fleshing out the filler material in contemporary almanacs. Samuel Danforth's almanacs, for example, include both a chronological list of the foundings of towns and a chronology of memorable occurrences.

28. See Arch, *Authorizing*, 57.

29. Carroll, *Puritanism*, 3.

30. Winthrop, "Reasons," 135.

31. Winthrop, "Modell of Christian Charity," 233.

32. Jennings, *Invasion*, 139.

33. Jameson concludes that the Rev. Blackstone was "presumably a Puritan" (see his note to Johnson, 46); this is unlikely. Blackstone evidently found life under religious authority uncongenial. He moved from Salem and farmed in relative isolation near Beacon Hill until the arrival of Winthrop and company. After this, Johnson loses track of him. Although not a church member, Blackstone was wealthy enough to be admitted to the freehold in Boston in 1631 but did not stay long. He sold up in 1634 to move to new land in Rhode Island. See Rutman, *Winthrop's Boston*, 28, 137, 213, 141.

34. Eggleston, "Land System of the New England Colonies," 587–89; Innes, *Creating*, 165, 215; Martin, *Profits in the Wilderness*, 149–61.

35. Dedham town covenant (1636), qtd. in Martin, *Profits*, 295.

36. Rutman, *Winthrop's Boston*, 137.

37. Innes, *Labor in a New Land*, 44.

38. Lockridge, *New England Town*, 69, 76.

39. Innes, *Labor*, 128, 122. Martin (295–302) finds a higher degree of commercialism in Dedham than does either Lockridge or Innes, but agrees with Lockridge that the economy was not a significant source of social conflict in that town.

40. Innes, *Labor*, 30.

41. Jameson suggests that this last may refer to Pynchon's "heretical book, *The Meritorious Price of Our Redemption*" (Johnson, 237). Pynchon and Moxon returned to England in 1652 and Pynchon's son John took over, "expand[ing] both his marketing network and his domain"; Springfield had trouble keeping a minster until the 1660s and even after that the position was "fragile and problematical" (Innes, *Labor*, 16, 147).

42. Innes, *Labor*, 9–16, 43.

43. Jameson has evidently added the words in parentheses. "Land" makes syntactical sense but "Lord" also makes sense, thematically, since Johnson notes the Cambridge men's lack of "Faith" and later emphasizes the Hartford minister's special effort in combating gross sins of worldliness.

44. Johnson seems to be accurate in his assessment that tillage comparatively "went but little on" in 1635, since wheat production did not increase significantly until the 1640s, when the colonists switched from winter to spring wheat. See McMahon, "A Comfortable Subsistence," 32.

45. See Innes, *Creating*, 282.

46. Winthrop, *History of New England*, 1:140.

47. Winthrop's rhetoric in reporting the objections advanced in the debate—for example, "that, in point of conscience, they ought not depart from us, being knit to us in one body"—indicates his disapproval. Governor Dudley's support of the migration would hardly have persuaded him, given their rivalry. Winthrop also realized that the new settlement would be exposed to "evident peril . . . from the Indians" (*History*, 1:140).

48. Jennings, *Invasion*, 135–36.

49. See Schramer and Sweet, "Violence and the Body Politic," 8–9. Egan identifies a similar logic in John Underhill's narrative of the Pequot War, *Newes from America* (1638), with which Johnson was no doubt familiar; *Authorizing Experience*, 28.

50. Winthrop, *History*, 2:31.

51. See Rutman, "Governor Winthrop's Garden"; Innes, *Creating*, 291, 295–96.

52. Vickers, *Farmers and Fishermen*, 51.

53. According to the *OED*, "staple" was in the earliest sense a place designated for the trade of a certain good or a group of merchants authorized to trade in such a good. Its use to designate the trade good itself developed during the seventeenth century in the context of colonialism, but the original sense persisted.

54. The colonists would soon learn to brew beer with maize; see Mood, "John Winthrop, Jr., on Indian Corn," 131–33. However, in early Concord, there is no barley and presumably not enough corn, so the colonists are compelled to drink water, a considerable hardship for "stomacks" accustomed to beer.

55. Bozeman characterizes Dunster as a "primitivist zealot" (*Ancient Lives*, 149).

56. A surculus is a young shoot or a scion for grafting.

57. Martin, *Profits*, 207.

58. On Keayne, see Innes, *Creating*, 160–91.

59. Danforth, *Almanack for 1648*; *Almanack for 1649*.

60. Historians continue to debate these motivations. Innes, *Creating*, finds a prevalent desire for increasing market embeddedness. Others identify a subsistence orientation, arguing that the primary goal was the perpetuation of accustomed practices and beliefs; see Merchant, *Ecological Revolutions*, 232; Wood, "Inventing American Capitalism," 45. For overviews of the transition-to-capitalism debate, see also Clark, "Rural America and the Transition to Capitalism"; Kulikoff, *Agrarian Origins of American Capitalism*, 13–33; Martin, *Profits in the Wilderness*, 1–5.

61. Elster provides this useful definition of "class"; *Making Sense of Marx*, 319–44.

62. *Wonder-Working Providence* was not published in America for over 200 years. Sales of the 1653 London edition were poor, although the text did see more circulation in 1658 when the remaining copies were bound into Ferdinando Gorges's *America Painted to the Life*. See Jameson, Introduction to *Johnson's Wonder-Working Providence*, 3–4. Bradford's history circulated only in a single manuscript and a partial copy in the Plymouth church records; later historians such as Nathaniel Morton, the Mathers, and William Hubbard used the manuscript as a source. See Morison, Introduction to Bradford's *Of Plymouth Plantation*, xxviii–xxix.

63. Qtd. in Miller, *From Colony to Province*, 4.

64. Hubbard, *Happiness of a People*, 59, hereafter cited parenthetically.

65. Bercovitch, *American Jeremiad*, 141.

66. Bercovitch, *Rites of Assent*, 79.

67. Williams, *Marxism and Literature*, 126.

Chapter 4. "Admirable Oeconomy"

1. Beverley, *History and Present State of Virginia*, 311, hereafter cited parenthetically.

2. See Sayre, *Les Sauvages Américains*, 218–47.

3. Banister lived in Virginia from 1678 until his death in 1692, collecting and cataloging specimens and drafting pieces of what he intended to be an exhaustive natural history of Virginia. On Beverley's probable meeting with Banister some time after 1689 and use of his manuscripts, see Ewan and Ewan, *John Banister*, 61.

4. Ewan and Ewan, 386. Banister may have taken his account of the beavers in turn from John Clayton, a cleric who spent two years in Virginia and was much interested in natural history; cf. Clayton's description of beavers, qtd. in Silver, *A New Face*, 98. A similar passage appears in Nicolas Denys's *Histoire Naturelle* (1672); see Sayre, *Les Sauvages*, 233. It is possible that Banister used Denys as a source, although there is no documentation of his familiarity with this text. William Wood's *New England's Prospect* (1635), which Banister knew well, describes beavers' use of "servants" but does not attribute any violence to the arrangement (Ewan and Ewan, 392, 401; Sayre, 235). Since the Old World beaver (possibly extinct in England by the time Banister and Beverley wrote) does not build large dams or work cooperatively to any great extent, this aspect of the American beaver's behavior was new to European writers and subject to misinterpretation. While American beavers do work cooperatively, they are unable to carry heavy logs; instead they build canals to float the logs to their destination. Beavers do not manage their

group labor by means violence; probably, the violence noted in Denys's and Banister's descriptions derive from observations of either territoriality or mating behaviors.

5. Jefferson's critique of tobacco culture, "a culture productive of infinite wretchedness," for man, beast, and land, is well known (*Notes on Virginia*, 173). Notable early nineteenth-century participants in this tradition included John Taylor and Edmund Ruffin. See Craven, *Soil Exhaustion*, 99–103, 134–44.

6. On Beverley's engagement with Edenic imagery, see Marx, *Machine in the Garden*, 73–88.

7. *True Declaration of Virginia*, 14.

8. If he did not set about writing the *History* expressly with the design of proposing economic diversification, nevertheless that was the result. The original impetus, as Wright notes in his introduction the *History*, was his review of the Virginia section of John Oldmixon's *British Empire in America* (which would be published in 1708). Beverley found the manuscript so garbled and inaccurate that he set about writing his own account, hoping, as he remarked in the preface to the second edition (1722), to correct English misperceptions. Much of Book IV, in any case, is explicitly directed toward the colonists themselves.

9. See Low, *Georgic Revolution*, 117–54; McRae, *God Speed the Plough*, 198–228.

10. Indeed, a recent analysis by Mancall and Weiss estimates the rate of real economic growth in the colonies as "close to zero" ("Was Economic Growth Likely?" 17).

11. See Rainbolt, *From Prescription to Persuasion*, 43–54.

12. Berkeley, *Discourse and View of Virginia*, 12, hereafter cited parenthetically.

13. Rainbolt, 37.

14. For histories of Bacon's Rebellion, see Morgan, *American Slavery, American Freedom*, 250–70; Webb, *1676*, 3–163.

15. Bacon, "Manifesto Concerning the Present Troubles," 227.

16. In his 1688 account of tobacco cultivation, John Clayton noted that the land could not be fertilized with dung because it imparted a foul taste to the smoke. See Clayton, *Letter to the Royal Society*, 21.

17. On this estimate, see Morgan, *American Slavery*, 173; Kulikoff, *Tobacco and Slaves*, 47–48.

18. Complaints about this method of taxation were important among the grievances discovered by the Crown's commission to investigate the causes of the rebellion. See Webb, *1676*, 160.

19. Eighty of the last hundred of Bacon's holdouts were Africans, most slaves but some free. See Webb, 6.

20. Webb, 3–163.

21. For a history of these issues, see Rainbolt.

22. The following account of the colonial tobacco economy draws on McCusker and Menard, *Economy of British America*, 117–43; Kulikoff, *Tobacco and Slaves*, 23–117.

23. Bailyn, *Peopling of British North America*, 28.

24. McCusker and Menard, 123.

25. See Beverley, *History of Virginia in Four Parts*, 84. While Beverley's cuts and revisions for the 1722 edition indicate a generally "more toleran[t]" tone (Wright, Introduction to Beverley, *History and Present State*, xxix), his economic criticisms remain in full force.

26. Linnaeus, qtd. in Foucault, *Order of Things*, 135, emphasis added.

27. See Ewan and Ewan, *John Banister*, 349–61.

28. Ewan and Ewan, 202. Under modern taxonomy, poison ivy, poison sumac, and poison oak are now classified under the genus *Toxicodendron* (formerly under the genus *Rhus*), but Banister and his contemporaries considered them to be *Hederas*, ivies.

29. Ibid., 253.

30. Ibid., 346–49.

31. Banister in contrast had evidently given up on this favorite project of the early promoters, remarking that flax for linen offered better prospects than silk. See Ewan and Ewan, 40.

32. In his later years particularly, Beverley believed that Virginia could become an important wine-making country. He took a one hundred guinea bet, at odds of ten to one, that he could produce seven hundred gallons of wine after seven years. The outcome remains unknown. See Wright, *First Gentlemen of Virginia*, 301.

33. Cf. Ewan and Ewan, 356.

34. Ewan and Ewan, 360.

35. See Alsop, *Character of Maryland*, 363–64.

36. See Clayton, *Letter*, 16, 22.

37. Winthrop, "Reasons to Be Considered," 137.

38. Dryden, *Works*, 5:161.

39. Ibid., 203.

40. Breen gives a detailed description of the colonists' method, which took fifteen months from seed to market; *Tobacco Culture*, 46–53. See also Ewan and Ewan, 630–61.

41. Craven, *Soil Exhaustion*, 16.

42. One such episode was the plant-cutting riots of 1682, a quasi-populist attempt to impose a tobacco stint instigated by Beverley's father. On the riots, see Morgan, 285–87. Jacobs, "Robert Beverley," goes so far as to argue that Beverley's primary motivation for the composition of the *History* was a desire to avenge his father's political humiliation stemming from his arrest for the riots. However, Beverley, Sr., was in fact treated rather gently after his arrest since the Virginia gentry agreed with the principle behind the plant-cutting. See Rutman and Rutman, *A Place in Time*, 160–61.

43. Beverley's concern for self-sufficiency by all accounts extended to the management of his own plantation. As one visitor remarked, "though rich, he has nothing about his house, but what is necessary. . . . He lives upon the product of his land" (qtd. in Wright, *First Gentlemen*, 301).

44. Jefferson, *Notes on Virginia*, 171.

45. Dryden, 207.

46. Ibid., 206.

47. See Williams, *The Country and the City*, 13–34, 120–41.

48. See Dash, *Tulipomania*, 208–12.

49. See Stiverson, *Poverty in a Land of Plenty*, 10. On tenancy in the Tidewater and Chesapeake regions, in addition to Stiverson, see Bliss, "Rise of Tenancy in Virginia"; Main, *Social Structure of Revolutionary America*, 45–54. Bailyn provides additional sources on tenancy in other colonies, *Peopling*, 157–58.

50. See McCusker and Menard's chart plotting prices and British import volumes of tobacco from 1620 to 1775, *Economy*, 121.

51. McCusker and Menard, 125–26.

52. Alsop, *Character of Maryland*, 364.

53. Ewan and Ewan, 373–74.

54. Breen, *Tobacco Culture*, 56.

55. See Breen 204–10; Appleby, *Liberalism and Republicanism*, 253–76; Kulikoff, *Tobacco and Slaves*, 120–22.

56. See Craven, *Soil Exhaustion*, 25–71.

57. On the development of Southern pastoral, see Simpson, *Dispossessed Garden*; Grammer, *Pastoral and Politics*. Chaplin, however, shows that in the lower South, the planter elite directed a discourse of cultural self-criticism against fears of the debilitating effects of climate, disease, and inherited wealth. They developed a race- and class-differentiated ethic of industriousness that valued education, self-discipline, and managerialism for the elite, while identifying climate and disease as constraints on white labor. See *Anxious Pursuit*, 92–130.

58. On the staple-colony georgic, see Shields, *Oracles of Empire*, 56–92; Shields, "England's Staple Colonies." Shields points out that tobacco culture failed to inspire an imitation of Virgil, *Oracles*, 57.

59. Woodmason's lines appeared in the *Gentleman's Magazine* as promotional copy for a book-length poem. They failed to attract enough subscribers and the book was never published. See Shields, *Oracles*, 69.

60. Ogilvie, *Carolina*, lines 691–702, hereafter cited parenthetically.

Chapter 5. Ideologies of Farming

1. Crèvecoeur, *Letters from an American Farmer*, 41, hereafter cited parenthetically as *L*.

2. Jefferson, *Notes on the State of Virginia*, 170–71, hereafter cited parenthetically as *N*.

3. Stiles, *United States Elevated*, 8.

4. Stiles, however, disagreed with Jefferson on the role of manufactures, arguing that they ought to be encouraged insofar as they promoted "subsistence and elegance among ourselves" (31).

5. Smith, *Virgin Land*, 122–32. See also Eisinger, "Land and Loyalty."

6. Chaplin demonstrates that this conflict was especially complicated in the deep South during the eighteenth century when the lowcountry elite, uneasy about their own dependence on slavery and wanting to maintain their political and economic dominance, attempted to limit the spread of slavery in the agricultural development of the upcountry. See *Anxious Pursuit*, 131–84.

7. Rush, *Essays Literary, Moral, and Philosophical*, 221, emphasis in original, hereafter cited parenthetically as *E*.

8. See Harper, *Transformation of Western Pennsylvania*, 109, 123; Shammas, "Rise of the Colonial Tenant," 490.

9. In *American Backwoods Frontier*, Jordan and Kaups argue that the backwoods method originated in the Savo-Karelian culture of eastern Finland, spread to Sweden, and moved out to the American frontier from its seventeenth-century base in the New Sweden colony on the Delaware River, strongly influencing other ethnic groups such as the Scotch-Irish. The shift from girdling trees to felling and burning them, which produced a quick and easy method of fertilization, was enabled by the adoption of the Scandinavian ax over the English broadax.

10. This division into two methods is necessarily schematic. The colonial New England method described by Merchant has some aspects of each, being primarily subsistence oriented but involving extensive manuring and a short-fallow system; see *Ecological Revolutions*, 155–56, 163–67.

11. On the development of print culture, see Warner, *Letters of the Republic*.

12. For a review of the historical literature on the agrarian crisis of the 1790s, see Sellers, *Market Revolution*, 17–18.

13. Merchant, *Ecological*, 187–231.

14. Agricola, "The Planter," 489, hereafter cited parenthetically.

15. See, for example, Marx, *Machine in the Garden*, 127.

16. Appleby, *Liberalism and Republicanism*, 253–56. Appleby disagrees on this point with Marx who, in distinguishing Jefferson from "fully-committed agrarians," argues that Jefferson "admits that an agricultural economy may be economically disadvantageous"; however, the passage from Query XIX of the *Notes* on which Marx grounds this claim is not so much an appeal to the security promised by the "contained self-sufficiency of the pastoral community" as it is an admission of the necessity of America's participation in the world market (Marx, *Machine*, 127). Self-sufficiency would, in fact, require the extensive development of manufactures in America, which Jefferson explicitly argues against in the *Notes*, although he would later revise his position.

17. Bliss puts the proportion of tenants at one-third for Loudon County in 1782 and finds that, in general, tenancy "spread over wide portions of Virginia, becoming intimately linked with the most prominent planting families" ("Rise of Tenancy," 429). According to Main, in pre-Revolutionary Northern Neck Virginia (south of the Potomac and north of the Rappahannock), over 70 percent of whites owned no land, in Tidewater, 30 percent, in the backcountry, 25 percent (*Social Structure of Revolutionary America*, 45, 53–54). Mitchell's study of settlement patterns in the Shenandoah Valley indicates that by 1800, landless rural laborers comprised one-third of the total population. In the lower Valley, at least 20 percent of land occupants were tenants at the end of the century, while in the upper Valley the large proportion of landless settlers suggests the probability of a great many unrecorded leases. See Mitchell, *Commercialism and Frontier*, 87, 128, 239.

18. Slaves, of course, also constituted "wealth." In Tidewater, only 6 percent owned more than twenty slaves, in Piedmont, only 3 percent. See Main, *Social Structure*, 55.

19. Even so, tobacco remained Jefferson's primary cash crop. See Miller, *Jefferson and Nature*, 221–22.

20. See Appleby, *Liberalism*, 261–64.

21. Eliot, *Essays upon Field Husbandry*, 16, hereafter cited parenthetically as *F*.

22. *American Husbandry*, 536, hereafter cited parenthetically as *A*.

23. Marx, *Machine*, 127.

24. The first poem, Franklin's editors tell us, was lifted from the *Gentleman's Magazine*, 1753. Franklin, *Papers*, 5:469, hereafter cited parenthetically as *P*.

25. Also missing is Horace's characterization of the poem's speaker as a money-lender.

26. He complicates this picture somewhat in the later letters. Although in Letter IX he does not recognize any class distinction among tenants, small holders, and planters in Carolina, he does worry that lawyers threaten to engross all property. In Letter XI, as Rigal notes (*American Manufactory*, 3–6), he leaves unanswered the question of how Mr. Bertram could afford to hire a plowman after deciding to take up the study of botany.

27. On the terms of leases and the development of tenancy as a response to the rural labor market, see Simler, "Tenancy in Colonial Pennsylvania," 558, 562–63.

28. Ibid., 560, 569.

29. Harper, *Transformation*, 117.

30. Ibid., 119–20.

31. The letter was first published in the *Columbian Magazine*, November 1786. See Rush, *Letters*, 1:406.

32. Qtd. in Richter, "Onas, the Long Knife," 148.

33. In the lower South, critiques of backwoodsmen tended to identify them not so much as migratory farmers but as hunters who had wholly adopted Native American ways (failing to recognize that Native Americans were farmers). See Chaplin, *Anxious Pursuit*, 283–84.

34. Spurrier, *Practical Farmer*, 124–25.

35. The book was published posthumously in 1825, but Lorain's references in *Hints to Emigrants* to his previous writings on farming suggest that parts of the book may have circulated in some form in his lifetime. Jehlen dates the composition at the turn of the century; see *American Incarnation*, 66.

36. Lorain, *Nature and Reason*, 502.

37. Lorain, *Hints*, 13–14.

38. Jordan and Kaups, *American Backwoods*, 78.

39. Lorain, *Hints*, 6.

40. Ibid., 12.

41. Cochrane, *Development of American Agriculture*, 55–56.

42. See Cochrane, 54–55; Mitchell, *Commercialism*, 79–80.

43. Harper, *Transformation*, 80.

44. See Harper, 72; Fletcher, *Pennsylvania Agriculture*, 28–31.

45. Filson, *Discovery, Settlement, and Present State of Kentucke*, 107, hereafter cited parenthetically as *D*.

46. By 1800, 6.5 million acres, more than a quarter of the total land of Kentucky, were patented by fewer than fifty individuals; see Friedenberg, *Life, Liberty, and the Pursuit of Land*, 220. Speculation was rampant as well in western Pennsylvania, as heavily capitalized investors purchased lands designated for bounties for Revolutionary War veterans; see Richter, "Onas," 135. It may be worthwhile to clarify that both Pennsylvania and Virginia lands were administered by state governments. However, federally administered lands such as the Northwest Territory, Tennessee, etc., were also subject to massive speculation, with similar effects on ownership patterns and farming practices; see Cochrane, 41–56.

47. Kentucky's great market did not yet exist, since the Pinckney Treaty would not formally open the lower Mississippi to downriver trade until 1796. In 1794, Alexander Addison, a prominent western Pennsylvanian, stated that "a very respectable trade is carried on to the Spanish settlements" on the Mississippi, noting that only three years earlier (in 1791), there had been "hardly any" trade (qtd. in Harper, *Transformation*, xi). Kentuckians, also served by the Ohio River system, would have found the situation to be the same. Writing in 1784, Filson mistrusts the existing treaty with Spain but nevertheless puts faith in an unhindered future downriver trade, eased perhaps by a canal "through the gut of Iberville" (southwest of what is now Baton Rouge) (Filson, 48). This is speculation on Filson's part, related to the speculation in land that he participated in and encouraged.

48. Landlords were often dissatisfied with tenants because they failed to make the stipulated improvements, neglected upkeep, or abandoned the farm altogether. See Lorain, *Nature*, 499–503; Harper, 65; Bliss, 436–37.

49. Both before and after the Revolution, Pennsylvania allowed only twelve months' credit and required full payment before a patent would be issued on a maximum of four hundred acres; see Harper, 9. Prior to 1792, the state-mandated purchase price was high and relatively few patents were issued. In the Land Act

of 1792 the price was drastically reduced and a provision was added that an individual could make any number of applications for four hundred-acre lots, which encouraged speculation even as it made small freeholding possible. See Fletcher, *Pennsylvania*, 25, 27, 29–31.

50. In his memorial "In Honour of American Beer and Cyder," published in the *American Museum* to commemorate the July 4, 1788, Philadelphia procession celebrating the ratification of the Constitution, Rush urged readers to "Learn . . . to despise Spiritous Liquors, as Anti-Federal." The memorial is reprinted in Rigal, *American Manufactory*, 39.

51. Slaughter, *Whiskey Rebellion*, 73, 71.

52. Ibid., 246.

53. Jehlen, *American Incarnation*, 27. Jehlen's project is "to abstract" rather than "to particularize and contextualize" as I am doing here (21).

54. See Pearce, *Savages of America*, 67–73; Cronon, *Changes in the Land*, 54–81.

55. Fletcher, 23.

56. Relatively few individuals found themselves in this situation, since no whites permanently settled in Kentucky before 1775 and the ones that later did had only one year in which to make their preemption claim; preemption rights ceased to be valid in 1780. See Filson, 37; Friedenberg, 213.

57. See Cochrane, *Development*, 58; Opie, *Law of the Land*, 43–56.

58. See Lawson-Peebles, *Landscape and Written Expression*, 243–62; Looby, *Voicing America*, 193–202.

59. Brown, *Edgar Huntly*, 176, 200, hereafter cited parenthetically as *H.*

60. These fragments were part of Brown's ongoing and unfinished "History of the Carrils." See Lawson-Peebles, 256–57. Brown founded and edited the *Literary Magazine*, which ran from 1803 to 1807.

61. Brown, "Agricultural Improvement," 88, hereafter cited parenthetically as "A."

62. Brown, "Political Improvement," 121, hereafter cited parenthetically as "P."

63. Lorain, *Nature*, 502.

64. In this sense, we can think of market agrarianism as a precursor of other nineteenth-century "visionary compacts," its "terms of agreement" being the supposed opportunity of full participation in a market economy and the naturalization of that economy; see Pease, *Visionary Compacts*, x.

65. For Jefferson, this may in part be because he came to disapprove of land speculation (after a frustrated foray into speculation in 1769) and to hope for its eventual disappearance. His draft of the Ordinance of 1785 regarding the Northwest Territory favored a general distribution of land. But he acceded to Alexander Hamilton's view that the land ought to be sold in large blocks because he recognized that this would generate needed federal revenue. See Friedenberg, 163, 275, 381. The terms of the Ordinance of 1785 and the Land Act of 1796 put the minimum outlay for land beyond the resources of the typical pioneer and encouraged speculation; most men who acquired small farms outright on federal lands during this period did so on military service warrants. See Cochrane, 42–47.

66. An analysis of these recent trends is beyond the scope of this book. For one suggestive account, which outlines some potential grounds for cooperation among environmentalists and farmers, see Greider, "Last Farm Crisis."

Chapter 6. Cherokee "Improvements" and the Removal Debate

1. Emerson, *Works*, 1:94. For other instances, see Maddox, *Removals*, 15–19.

2. Removal "could finally be written into law and enforced in the 1830s," Krupat argues, "because by that time, a certain *story* about America and about 'civilization' had become sufficiently acceptable that it could be used as ideological justification" (*Ethnocriticism*, 133, emphasis in original). This story of Indian savagism emplotted as tragedy gained legitimacy by means of white culture's modal assumptions about the justice of tragic fate; see Krupat, 134–36. Pastoral or georgic representations were thus attempts to cast the discourse in a more promising literary mode. On the "middle landscape" topos, see Marx, *Machine in the Garden*.

3. The narrative of civilization, "progressing from past to present, from east to west, from lower to higher," conceptualized "the Indian, not as one to be civilized and to be lived with, but rather as one whose nature and whose way of life was an obstacle to civilized progress westward" (Pearce, *Savages of America*, 49, 41). Krupat has been especially influential in reminding us of Pearce's importance in theorizing this narrative.

4. The Cherokee syllabary enabled print literacy, in white terms an "improvement." However, as Murray argues, Sequoyah himself saw the syllabary "as a way of preserving Cherokee values and traditions" (*Forked Tongues*, 26). His first known composition in the syllabary concerned national politics, a brief for a court case involving a boundary dispute between the Cherokees and the states of Georgia and Tennessee; see Murray, 28. The case for the syllabary's identity-conserving function becomes even stronger if we accept Traveler Bird's account of its preconquest provenance. This account positions Sequoyah not as an inventor but rather as a vessel of tradition, the last scribe of the Seven Clans Society, a secret society that originated with the syllabary's inventors, the Taliwa people of the southern plains. See Krupat, "America's Histories," 137.

5. On Apess's assertion of a primarily political definition of Indian identity in the face of contemporary white assumptions about racial and cultural differences, see Konkle, "Indian Literacy, U. S. Colonialism."

6. On the use of Mother Earth mythology by Native American spokesmen such as Charles Eastman and Russell Means, see Gill, *Mother Earth*.

7. Krupat, *Ethnocriticism*, 157.

8. McLoughlin, *Cherokee Renascence*, 280–84.

9. Perdue and Green, *Cherokee Removal*, 116–17, emphases added.

10. Jackson, qtd. in Krupat, *Ethnocriticism*, 141, emphasis added by Krupat.

11. Preemption Act of 1830, qtd. in Opie, *Law of the Land*, 55.

12. "Memorials of the Cherokee Indians," presented to Congress February 15, 1830, in Krupat, *Ethnocriticism*, 164, 165. Krupat reprints the entire text of the Memorials, 164–72.

13. Ibid., 167.

14. Ibid., 172.

15. Boudinot, *Cherokee Editor*, 72, hereafter cited parenthetically.

16. Goodwin, *Cherokees in Transition*, 125–26; Dunaway, *First American Frontier*, 31–32, 37.

17. Perdue, *Cherokee Women*, 13–15. Since these stories were recorded (primarily by anthropologist James Mooney) c. 1900, after the Cherokees had seen massive economic and cultural changes, it is difficult to reconstruct the nuances of precolonization history regarding gender roles, relative economic priority, and so on solely from them.

18. On the Choctaws, see White, *Roots of Dependency*, 1–33. Some colonists regarded the mixed mode as transitional, assuming that the Choctaws took up agriculture only as game was overhunted and became scarcer. White (16–19) criticizes anthropologists who maintain the early colonists' assumptions in this regard, pointing out that the hunting-horticulture balance among the Choctaws dates back at least to 1000 B.C.

19. White, 9–10, 32. A similar, game-producing buffer zone existed between the Chippewa and Sioux in what is now Minnesota; see Hickerson, *Chippewa and Their Neighbors*.

20. Hatley, *Dividing Paths*, 161–62; Silver, *New Face on the Countryside*, 88–103; Dunaway, *First American*, 32–33.

21. White, *Roots*, 21; Perdue, *Cherokee Women*, 17, 19; Dunaway, *First American*, 37–38.

22. McLoughlin, *Cherokee Renascence*, 6; Dunaway, *First American*, 38.

23. Corn Tassel, "Speech at Treaty Talks," 154, 155.

24. Qtd. in McLoughlin, *Cherokee Renascence*, 6.

25. On the decline of the deer population during the eighteenth century, see Silver, *New Face*, 92–97; Dunaway, *First American*, 46.

26. Hatley, *Dividing Paths*, 213–14.

27. Ibid., 216–18; Dunaway, *First American*, 47–48.

28. James McHenry (Secretary of War to John Adams), 1799, quoted in Prucha, *Great Father*, 1:142. On Jefferson's plan to use Louisiana Purchase lands as a haven for the Eastern tribes, see Sheehan, *Seeds of Extinction*, 245–50.

29. Timberlake, *Memoirs*, 96–99, hereafter cited parenthetically.

30. When Timberlake was visiting the Cherokees, the French possessed the Mississippi basin, but at the end of the Seven Years' War (1763), they ceded it to Spain. Timberlake's memoirs were published two years later.

31. Evidently there was some internal conflict at the time. Between 1808 and 1825, the National Council enacted several laws to promote male dominance, including eliminating matrilineal control over land. See Dunaway, "Rethinking Cherokee Acculturation," 170.

32. Sturtevant, "John Ridge on Cherokee Civilization," 81.

33. On the transformation and persistence of traditional gender roles from precontact through the removal era, see Perdue, *Cherokee Women*.

34. Dunaway, "Rethinking," 164.

35. Perdue, *Cherokee Women*, 126–27.

36. Dunaway, "Rethinking," 164–65.

37. Perdue and Green, *Cherokee Removal*, 124.

38. Dunaway, "Rethinking," 163.

39. Traditionally, an unmarried or widowed woman's possessions—not land, which was never construed as property, but rather portable items such as knives, blankets, kettles, horses—went to the nearest male relatives, usually her older brothers. Such possessions as cattle herds would, then, normally go to men (McLoughlin 294, 332).

40. Sturtevant, "John Ridge," 82.

41. Prucha, 1:186.

42. McLoughlin, 284.

43. Brown, "Cherokee Indians," 106, emphasis in original, hereafter cited parenthetically.

44. According to Creek law, any chief who signed a cession treaty without the

consent of the full national council would be put to death; McIntosh was executed and the Creeks refused to honor the treaty he had signed. See McLoughlin, 372.

45. The primary impetus for what is often construed as voluntary emigration to Arkansas was a concern for subsistence. Particularly in 1817, many of the residents whose lands were closest to the Georgia border had seen white squatters usurp so much land that they could not grow enough corn to get through the winter. The Cherokee National Council did not like to see the nation split, but could do nothing to prevent some people from moving to where they believed they could live unharassed. See McLoughlin, 222, 370–71.

46. See Boime, *Magisterial Gaze.*

47. On this four-stage theory of social evolution, see Dekker, *American Historical Romance*, 75, 81–82. Chaplin however points out that by the late eighteenth century, many Southerners did not hold this stadialist theory of social change, but rather assumed that the "savage" state was inevitably static and thus claimed that Native Americans could not become "civilized"; see *Anxious Pursuit*, 60–62. Many of the writers Chaplin cites on this point are Georgians, whose political interest in holding such a view is clearly evident in relation to the Cherokee case.

48. Boime, 79.

49. White, *Roots*, 22–23.

50. Dunaway, "Rethinking," 157.

51. Brown, "Cherokee," 105.

52. See, for example, Perdue, *Cherokee Women*, 104, 119, 136.

53. Bourne, *Narratives of the Career of Hernando de Soto*, 1:221.

54. See Bartram, *Travels*, 401; Perdue, *Cherokee Women*, 24, 27.

55. Perdue concludes that the Cherokees gave little thought to their adoption of slave labor but notes that only 8 percent of heads of households owned slaves by 1835; see *Cherokee Women*, 126, 223.

56. Ibid., 125–26.

57. McLoughlin, 292.

58. A full text of the Constitution is reprinted in Starr, *History of the Cherokee Indians*, 55–63.

59. As Perdue points out, these actions of the Council to codify land tenure according to the principle of national ownership "occurred in virtual contradiction to the goals of the civilization program" that whites were urging on the Cherokees, "which was intended to produce the private ownership of realty" (*Cherokee Women*, 193).

60. Editorial, *Cherokee Phoenix*, vol. 5, no. 1, Aug. 25, 1832. The *Phoenix* published this statement in both English and Cherokee in its first number after the resignation of Elias Boudinot as editor. The National Council had forced Boudinot to resign when he began to view removal as inevitable. His resignation thus provided the Council with an opportunity to reaffirm its position through the *Phoenix*, which the Council subsidized.

61. John Marshall, in Perdue and Green, *Cherokee Removal*, 73.

62. Brown, "Cherokee," 105.

63. Bartram, *Travels*, 284, emphasis added.

64. On the translation of Indian assumptions about land into the category of "property," see Cheyfitz, *Poetics of Imperialism*, 41–82.

65. Evarts, *"William Penn" Essays and Other Writings*, 54–55, hereafter cited parenthetically.

66. In 1832, in view of Jackson's refusal to enforce the Supreme Court's deci-

sion against Georgia's extension of its state laws over the Cherokee territories, Boudinot and other prominent Cherokees such as John Ridge began to rethink their own positions on Removal. At that point, Boudinot wanted to open a debate on the issue in the *Phoenix* but the Council refused and Boudinot resigned. See Boudinot, *Cherokee Editor*, 162–75.

67. For details of this case, see McLoughlin, 440–44; Perdue and Green, *Cherokee Removal*, 63–75.

68. See Ross, *Papers*, 1:283, 290, 297, 309.

69. Figures are taken from Wilms, "Cherokee Indian Land Use," 69, 80, 136.

70. Atack and Passell, *New Economic View*, 278.

71. Wilms, 70.

72. Wilms, 60; White, 22–23.

73. Qtd. in Usner, "Iroquois Livelihood and Jeffersonian Agrarianism," 225.

74. Tenancy and wage labor were quite common among whites. In southern Appalachia in 1860, between 30 and 50 percent of households did not own land. See Dunaway, *First American*, 75.

75. As Elias Boudinot noted in his letter resigning the editorship of the *Phoenix* in 1832, a major purpose of the paper was "the proper representation of our *grievances* to the people of the United States" (*Cherokee Phoenix*, vol. 4, no. 52, Aug. 11, 1832, emphasis added). Stories from the *Phoenix* were picked up by other papers, and sympathetic commentaries on the stories from those papers were in turn printed in the *Phoenix*. During two numbers in July 1831, for example, the *Phoenix* printed commentary from a dozen papers that had picked up its reportage of Georgia's abuses, such as the arrest of missionaries. See *Phoenix*, vol. 4, nos. 4 and 5, July 16 and 23, 1831.

76. *Phoenix*, vol. 4, no. 9, August 27, 1831.

77. *Phoenix*, vol. 4, no. 1, June 25, 1831.

78. *Phoenix*, vol. 4, no. 5, July 23, 1831.

79. Ross, 309. At this time the *Phoenix*, under the editorship of Elijah Hicks and in its last issues, suggested the inferiority of the land by reporting extensively on outbreaks of cholera among emigrants there; see, for example, vol. 5, no. 52, May 31, 1834.

80. McLoughlin, 112–13.

81. See Boudinot, 178.

82. While the General Allotment (Dawes) Act of 1887 abolished national ownership in common and required individuals to take separate allotments, the Cherokees lost less total land under the Act than did most nations. See Prucha, 2:754.

83. Perdue and Green, *Cherokee Removal*, 78.

84. Ibid., 80–81.

85. This "first deliberate attempt in prose fiction" was "singularly successful with the public," Simms later noted in reflecting on the beginnings of his career (*Guy Rivers*, 10, hereafter cited parenthetically).

86. Simms's premature removal of the Cherokees from his fictional landscape becomes especially emphatic if we recall that elsewhere Simms would argue that the treatment of Indian subject matter (even intermarriage with whites) gave American writers a unique opportunity to create a national literature and distinguish it from England's. See Maddox, 37–40.

87. On the Georgia resolution and the actions of the Guard, see McLoughlin, 432–33.

88. Jackson, Introduction to Ridge, *Life and Adventures of Joaquín Murieta*, xv–xvi.

89. Ridge, *Life and Adventures of Joaquín Murieta*, 10, hereafter cited parenthetically.

90. Walker points out that Ridge does not mention the force of California law in excluding Mexicans from the gold fields. They had to pay an oppressive tax from which Americans and European immigrants were exempt. See *Indian Nation*, 126.

91. Parins, *John Rollin Ridge*, 54, 72–74.

92. Ibid., 91.

93. On Ridge's careful efforts to document the spaces Joaquín occupies, see Lowe, "I Am Joaquín!"

94. Walker argues that Ridge "oppos[es] a concept of natural law to mere legalisms, at times making the law the opposite of justice, and generally insisting that honor requires individuals not protected by law to transgress its boundaries even to the extent of murder" (112).

95. Parins, 21, 29.

96. For example, in a letter of 1849 to his cousin, Stand Watie, he writes that "there is a deep-seated principle of revenge in me which will never be satisfied until it reaches its object. . . . Whenever you say the word, I am there," referring to a plot to capture John Ross (Parins, 56). Weaver reads the novel as "a thinly veiled revenge fantasy in which the Mexicans stand in for pro-Removal Cherokees and the Anglos represent, not themselves, but *other Cherokees*—the Ross party" (*That the People Might Live*, 78, emphasis in original).

97. McLoughlin, 44; Parins 4; Mooney, *Myths of the Cherokee*, 107.

98. Cherokees do appear at one point in the novel, assisting the whites in the pursuit of Joaquín by extorting information from two Mexicans who sympathize with the outlaw, then hanging them (124–28). The episode seems to recall the Ross party's execution of members of the Ridge party; see Lowe, 113–14.

99. Ridge himself was never free of that burden. The "Publishers' Preface" to the novel described him, with amazing inaccuracy, as "a 'Cherokee Indian' born in the woods—reared in the midst of the wildest scenery" (2).

100. Krupat, *Ethnocriticism*, 167.

101. A full review of the literature is beyond the scope of the present study. Worster gives a good account in *Wealth of Nature*, 45–111.

102. I should point out that the Cherokee tradition of households occupying and using but not owning agricultural land over generations has only a partial analogue in the white nostalgic ideal of the family farm, despite the pictures of middle landscapes that the Cherokees painted for white viewing. The farm crises of the 1980s and 1990s especially have shown the generational continuity of the family farm to be inconsistent in the long run with capitalist property relations.

Chapter 7. "Co-Workers with Nature"

1. I wish to stress that the terms "Indian" and "white" within quotation marks represent schematized positions, not the actualities whose complications are evident, for example, in the history of the Cherokees' engagement with their environment.

2. In the first study of Cooper's ideas regarding the environment, Robinson

categorizes the characters' positions according to this tripartite scheme; see "Conservation in Cooper's *The Pioneers*."

3. Cooper, *Pioneers*, 233, hereafter cited parenthetically.

4. On Cooper's general project of educating his readership, see Wallace, *Early Cooper and His Audience*.

5. Marsh, *Man and Nature*, 38, hereafter cited parenthetically.

6. *True Declaration*, 15.

7. Ibid., 12.

8. Buell credits *Man and Nature* with originating the discourse of environmental apocalypticism evident in such works as Rachel Carson's *Silent Spring*; see *Environmental Imagination*, 301–2.

9. Thoreau, *Faith in a Seed*, 170.

10. For a history of the perceptual approach, see Evernden, *Social Creation of Nature*. Evernden's own resolution to the dilemma is perceptual, moving from phenomenology to the reconstruction of an original or childlike sense of "wonder" or "astonishment" at the world.

11. A few years ago at the Modern Language Association's annual meeting, I attended a session on nature writing. To encourage audience participation, the presenters asked us to describe our current interests. When my turn came I said, "agriculture." Afterward, the man sitting next to me asked, "Agriculture? But farmers are the bad guys." I recall responding with something not very articulate about farmers being sensitive to the land in their own ways—my grandfather said he would never plow up his grove, because you had to leave some of the land for itself—and so on. Instead, I ought to have asked him what he'd eaten for breakfast and how it got to his table. We might not have agreed in the end, but such a response would, I imagine, have provided more common ground for conversation.

12. Emerson, *Works*, 1:65.

13. Cole's painting may have been inspired by Cooper's description. We know Cole was familiar with Cooper's works; for example, he painted a scene from Chapter 29 of *Last of the Mohicans* in 1827. Cole's *Falls* restores a human presence to the Kaaterskill, a lone Indian looking over the precipice, perhaps to register a concern that the wilderness depicted here is, like the Indian, threatened by the progress of civilization. For evidence that Cole's contemporaries saw the figure of the Indian in this scene as "a natural growth," see Horwitz, *By the Law of Nature*, 45.

14. Ringe, Introduction to *Pioneers*, xxi. Smith sets this agenda by observing that Cooper was working through "the antithesis between nature and civilization, between freedom and law, that has governed most American interpretations of the westward movement" (*Virgin Land*, 60). Franklin further argues that Natty's "symbolic purpose" is "to speak for nature by speaking out for his own assaulted rights" (*New World of James Fenimore Cooper*, 105). As Thomas has demonstrated in his critique of this interpretive school, however, "Natty's forest freedom grows out of the same assumptions that justify Temple's legal system," for each defines freedom as independence from the wills of others (*Cross-Examinations of Law and Literature*, 41). Knowing that such freedom is a mere fiction under capitalist social relations, yet unable to imagine a reconfiguration of these relations, Cooper offers in Natty the compensatory fiction of escape.

15. Interference with spring sowing was so extensive as to lead to the invention of the seed drill, which buried the seeds to prevent the birds' access to the seeds. See Halliday, "Extinction of the Passenger Pigeon," 158.

16. On the passage of the law, see Swann, "Guns Mean Democracy," 104–6, 119.

17. Swann reprints the entire text of the law, passed March 31, 1798; see "Guns," 103–4.

18. I take this information on the lake whitefish (*Coregonus clupeaformis*) from Harman et al., *State of Otsego Lake*, 262.

19. Swann argues that this apparent contradiction indicates that Temple is interested in passing such laws primarily as a "symbol of power" (104). No doubt this is true, but as I will go on to discuss, that exercise of power is bound up with Temple's seemingly genuine, albeit misinformed, interest in resource conservation.

20. On railroads, logging, hunting, and the decline of the passenger pigeon in New York, see Steadman, "And Live on Pigeon Pie." Only thirty-six years after a colony of three million pigeons was observed in Petosky, Michigan, the species was extinct. The puzzling rapidity of the pigeon's decline indicated by such observations suggests that hunting, rather than habitat destruction, brought the population below a crucial threshold. Even when hunting became no longer economically feasible, the pigeon continued to decline because it was adapted to feeding and breeding in very large colonies; reproduction rates, a function of colony size, could no longer offset mortality. See Halliday, "Extinction."

21. Seining was finally banned on Otsego Lake in 1915 to protect not the whitefish but the lake trout. The whitefish and lake trout populations both remain steady today, but the whitefish have diminished of late—not because of overfishing, but because of the 1988 introduction of the alewife, which preys on whitefish hatchlings. See Harman et al., *Otsego Lake*, 3–4, 261–62, 275.

22. On William Cooper's failure in the sugar business, see Taylor, *Cooper's Town*, 119–34.

23. Ibid., 133–34.

24. Robinson, "Conservation in *The Pioneers*," 571.

25. Swann reprints the text of this law, which bans the killing of deer from January through July, 102–3.

26. Thomas cites this passage as evidence that Temple disagreed with the assumption that game ownership was vested in the state, but does not address passages in which Temple approves the New York legislature's passage of game laws; see *Cross-Examinations*, 33. Swann, linking game laws to the history of gun control in Europe, argues that they exercise class power and that Temple's approval of them indicates his aristocratic ambitions.

27. See Merchant, *Ecological Revolutions*, 185–90; Taylor, *Cooper's Town*, 89–93.

28. Merchant, 232, 231.

29. However, in a thoughtful analysis of the history of Western ideas about nature from the Renaissance through modern environmentalism, Evernden argues that the two most common positions in this history—one regarding nature as instrumental object and another regarding nature as "an extended self . . . entitled to the same concern as any other person"—both depend on a structure of apartness, a nature-culture dualism constructed by "the centrality of the perceiving human subject" (*Social Creation*, 101, 102).

30. This is roughly the idea of "classical static stability," which assumes "constancy [of an ecosystem] unless disturbed, and the ability and tendency to return to the state of constancy following a disturbance" (Botkin, *Discordant Harmonies*, 42). This view, predominant in the scientific community through the 1970s, is still the assumption on which much environmental policy is based. More recently, research such as extensive core-sample studies of pollen counts, which enable historical reconstructions of ecosystems over the past 70,000 years, suggests that

there is no determinate equilibrium state toward which any given region tends, but such research has only rarely impacted policy as yet. See Botkin, 51–71. Evidence of even such drastic climatic change as the ice ages was unavailable to Marsh.

31. On later, Enlightenment formulations of this idea (for example, Pope's "Essay on Man" or Buffon's *Natural History*) see Botkin, 85–86.

32. Qtd. in Lowenthal, Introduction to *Man and Nature*, xxiv.

33. I elaborate here on a formulation given by Proctor, "Whose Nature?" 294.

34. Merchant locates Thoreau's work on forest succession as a response to deforestation in New England; see *Ecological Revolutions*, 229–30.

35. Botkin observes that the first use of the term "succession" appears in Thomas Pownal's *Topographical Description of the Dominion of the United States* (1784), and therefore credits Thoreau only with the reintroduction of the term. However, Pownal does not describe one species succeeding another in a regular pattern, but only a general process of older trees succeeding younger trees. See Botkin, *Discordant*, 51, 52.

36. Thoreau, *Faith in a Seed*, 164, hereafter cited parenthetically.

37. Thoreau, *Writings*, 5:224, hereafter cited parenthetically.

38. On this point, see Buell, *Environmental Imagination*, 120, 306–7.

39. Merchant gives a brief survey of other such responses to deforestation, 227–28.

40. Emerson, *Report*, 21, 22, hereafter cited parenthetically.

41. That is, Emerson too at least partly recognized the phenomenon of forest succession, but thought it could be improved through analogy to agricultural techniques of planting and harvest, for he assumed that a particular species died off because it had "exhausted [the soil] of the nutriment essential to it" and so was succeeded by another species that required different nutriments (29).

42. Thoreau, *Maine Woods*, 712.

43. The historical answer to this question, of course, separated Thoreau's two aims. Native Americans were contained on reservations, although not ones large enough to permit even those tribes who did exist primarily as "a hunter race" to continue so. The National Park system, partly a result of Thoreau's influence on John Muir, cordoned of some land from all economic uses except tourism, our answer to Thoreau's call for a space of "true re-creation."

44. Whether the combined histories of the Bureau of Land Management, the National Forests, and the National Parks and National Monuments have subsequently lived up to Marsh's vision is another question, of course, one beyond the scope of the present study.

45. This concession of one's will to higher motives resembles the rhetoric of "transcendent or combinatory agency" that Horwitz finds characteristic of nineteenth-century American appeals to nature as ground of value, in which "individual identity and agency are perfected in their occulting, absorption, or sublation by wider forces, usually called natural or universal" (*Law of Nature*, 240). However, as Marsh conceives it, this mode of agency in its moment of perfection does not, as in the instances analyzed by Horwitz, give the subject greater access to the material benefits of property and the capitalist market. Rather it provides the ultimate moral persuasion for withholding from oneself such benefits.

46. See Lowenthal, Introduction to *Man and Nature*, xxii. No doubt it also helped promote the passage of the Timber Culture Act of 1873, which offered western lands to settlers who would plant woods on their parcels. This act was a

failure, since most of the specified lands were too arid to support trees, and was repealed in 1891. See Opie, *Law of the Land*, 101.

47. Review of *Man and Nature*, *Scribner's*, 120.

48. Review of *Man and Nature*, *Christian Examiner*, 66, 70.

49. Review of *Man and Nature*, *Edinburgh Review*, 247, 249.

50. Review of *Man and Nature*, *Nature*, 82.

51. Lowell, review of *Man and Nature*, *North American Review*, 319–20.

52. Review of *Man and Nature*, *Nation*, 224. On the latter point, cf. Marsh 249–50.

53. Smith, *Works*, 2:247. Lemay identifies this passage as the first expression of the "American dream"; see *American Dream*, 217.

54. Smith, 2:464.

55. One recent text especially worth considering along these lines is Richard Powers's *Gain*. The penetrating description of environmental inputs and outputs required in the production of a disposable camera, for example, encapsulates the novel's larger meditation: "The world sells to us at a loss, until we learn to afford it" (348).

56. Pigovian taxes, so called after the British economist A. C. Pigou, would measure all real costs of the production of a commodity, including environmental degradation and future generations' access to resources and a good environment, and make producers internalize those costs. The taxes would be reinvested in the development of sustainable modes of production, while the pricing structure would encourage changes in consumption and production patterns. For example, such a tax would price coal, which is currently the cheapest form of energy, as the most expensive, since it causes great environmental degradation in mining and is the most polluting of all nonrenewable energy sources. Solar energy, infinitely renewable and nonpolluting, would be the cheapest when all real costs are factored into its pricing. See Hawken, *Ecology of Commerce*, 82–90; Neumayer, *Weak Versus Strong Sustainability*, 26–27.

57. John Smith's uncertainty regarding Bermuda represents a possible exception. Marsh did call for further investigation in some cases, for example on forest succession, but would probably not have been prepared to understand any nonequilibrist findings. For a history of the equilibrium concept, its influence on environmental policy, and an outline of a new program for action based on an understanding of nature's dynamism, see Botkin, *Discordant Harmonies*. Botkin does not, however, address the question of agency, that is, the means by which such a program could be implemented.

Works Cited

Agricola. "The Planter. No. IX." *American Magazine and Chronicle for the British Colonies* 1 (July 1758): 486–92.

Alpers, Paul. *What Is Pastoral?* Chicago: University of Chicago Press, 1996.

Alsop, George. *A Character of the Province of Maryland.* In *Narratives of Early Maryland, 1633–1684,* ed. Clayton Holman Hall, 335–87. New York: Charles Scribner's Sons, 1910.

American Husbandry. 1775. Ed. Harry J. Carman. New York: Columbia University Press, 1939.

Anderson, Virginia DeJohn. "King Philip's Herds: Indians, Colonists, and the Problem of Livestock in Early New England." *William and Mary Quarterly,* 3rd ser., 51 (1994): 601–24.

Andrews, Kenneth R. *Trade, Plunder, and Settlement: Maritime Enterprise and the Genesis of the British Empire, 1480–1630.* Cambridge: Cambridge University Press, 1984.

Appleby, Joyce. *Economic Thought and Ideology in Seventeenth-Century England.* Princeton: Princeton University Press, 1978.

———. *Liberalism and Republicanism in the Historical Imagination.* Cambridge: Harvard University Press, 1992.

Arch, Stephen Carl. *Authorizing the Past: The Rhetoric of History in Seventeenth-Century New England.* DeKalb: Northern Illinois University Press, 1994.

Atack, Jeremy, and Peter Passell. *A New Economic View of American History from Colonial Times to 1940.* 2nd ed. New York: Norton, 1994.

Bacon, Nathaniel. "Manifesto Concerning the Present Troubles in Virginia." 1676. In *English Literatures of America, 1500–1800,* ed. Myra Jehlen and Michael Warner, 225–27. New York: Routledge, 1997.

Bailyn, Bernard. *The Peopling of British North America: An Introduction.* New York: Knopf, 1986.

Bartram, William. *Travels Through North and South Carolina, Georgia, East and West Florida, the Cherokee Country, the Extensive Territories of the Muscogulges, or Creek Confederacy, and the Country of the Chactaws.* 1791. Reprint, New York: Penguin, 1988.

Bercovitch, Sacvan. *The American Jeremiad.* Madison: University of Wisconsin Press, 1978.

———. *The Rites of Assent: Transformations in the Symbolic Construction of America.* New York: Routledge, 1993.

Berkeley, Sir William. *A Discourse and View of Virginia.* 1663. Norwalk, Conn.: William H. Smith, 1914.

Beverley, Robert. *The History and Present State of Virginia.* 1705. Ed. Louis B. Wright. Chapel Hill: University of North Carolina Press, 1947.

———. *The History of Virginia in Four Parts.* 1722. Richmond, Va.: J. W. Randolph, 1855.

Bliss, Willard F. "The Rise of Tenancy in Virginia." *Virginia Magazine of History and Biography* 58 (1950): 427–41.

Boime, Albert. *The Magisterial Gaze: Manifest Destiny and American Landscape Painting c. 1830–1865.* Washington, D.C.: Smithsonian Institution Press, 1991.

Botkin, Daniel. *Discordant Harmonies: A New Ecology for the Twenty-First Century.* New York: Oxford University Press, 1992.

Boudinot, Elias. *Cherokee Editor: The Writings of Elias Boudinot.* Ed. Theda Perdue. Knoxville: University of Tennessee Press, 1983.

Bourne, Edward Gaylord, ed. *Narratives of the Career of Hernando de Soto in the Conquest of Florida, As Told by a Knight of Elvas.* Trans. Buckingham Smith. 2 vols. New York: Allerton Book Company, 1922.

Bozeman, Theodore Dwight. *To Live Ancient Lives: The Primitivist Dimension in Puritanism.* Chapel Hill: University of North Carolina Press, 1988.

Bradford, William. *Of Plymouth Plantation, 1620–1647.* Ed. Samuel Eliot Morison. New York: Knopf, 1952.

Breen, Timothy. *Tobacco Culture: The Mentality of the Great Tidewater Planters on the Eve of Revolution.* Princeton: Princeton University Press, 1985.

Brockbank, Philip. "The Politics of Paradise: 'Bermudas'." In *Approaches to Andrew Marvell: The York Tercentenary Lectures,* ed. C. A. Patrides, 174–93. London: Routledge and Kegan Paul, 1978.

Bromell, Nicholas K. *By the Sweat of the Brow: Literature and Labor in Antebellum America.* Chicago: University of Chicago Press, 1993.

Brown, Charles Brockden. *Edgar Huntly, Or, Memoirs of a Sleep-Walker.* 1799. Ed. Norman S. Grabo. New York: Penguin, 1988.

———. "A Specimen of Agricultural Improvement." *Literary Magazine, and American Register* 3, no. 17 (February 1805): 86–93.

———. "A Specimen of Political Improvement." *Literary Magazine, and American Register* 3, no. 17 (February 1805): 120–28.

Brown, David. "The Cherokee Indians." *Niles' Weekly Register* 29, no. 735 (15 October 1825): 105–7.

Buell, Lawrence. *The Environmental Imagination: Thoreau, Nature Writing, and the Formation of American Culture.* Cambridge: Belknap—Harvard University Press, 1995.

Burnham, Michelle. "Anne Hutchinson and the Economics of Antinomian Selfhood in Colonial New England." *Criticism* 39 (1997): 337–58.

Carroll, Peter N. *Puritanism and the Wilderness: The Intellectual Significance of the New England Frontier, 1629–1700.* New York: Columbia University Press, 1969.

Carroll, William C. "'The Nursery of Beggary': Enclosure, Vagary, and Sedition in the Tudor-Stuart Period." In *Enclosure Acts: Sexuality, Property, and Culture in Early Modern England,* ed. Richard Burt and John Michael Archer, 34–47. Ithaca: Cornell University Press, 1994.

Chaplin, Joyce. *An Anxious Pursuit: Agricultural Innovation and Modernity in the Lower South, 1730–1815.* Chapel Hill: University of North Carolina Press, 1993.

Cheyfitz, Eric. *The Poetics of Imperialism: Translation and Colonization from* The Tempest *to* Tarzan. New York: Oxford University Press, 1991.

Christensen, Paul P. "Historical Roots for Ecological Economics—Biophysical Versus Allocative Approaches." *Ecological Economics* 1 (1989): 17–36.

Clark, Christopher. "Rural America and the Transition to Capitalism." *Journal of the Early Republic* 16 (1996): 223–36.

Clayton, John. *A Letter from Mr. John Clayton . . . to the Royal Society, May 12, 1688*. In *Tracts and Other Papers, Relating Principally to the Origin, Settlement, and Progress of the Colonies in North America*, ed. Peter Force, vol. 4, no. 12. 1844. Reprint, New York: Peter Smith, 1947.

Cochrane, Willard. *The Development of American Agriculture: A Historical Analysis*. Minneapolis: University of Minnesota Press, 1979.

Columbus, Christopher. "From *Journal of the First Voyage to America, 1492–1493*." In *The Heath Anthology of American Literature*, 3rd ed., ed. Paul Lauter, vol. 1, 117–25. Boston: Houghton Mifflin, 1998.

Cooper, James Fenimore. *The Pioneers, or the Sources of the Susquehanna; A Descriptive Tale*. 1823. Ed. James Franklin Beard, et al. Albany: State University of New York Press, 1980.

Corn Tassel. "Speech at Treaty Talks with Virginia and North Carolina, 1777." In *The World Turned Upside Down: Indian Voices from Early America*, ed. Colin G. Calloway, 154–55. Boston: Bedford-St. Martin's, 1994.

Craven, Wesley Frank. *Dissolution of the Virginia Company: The Failure of a Colonial Experiment*. New York: Oxford University Press, 1932.

———. *Soil Exhaustion As a Factor in the Agricultural History of Virginia and Maryland, 1606–1860*. University of Illinois Studies in the Social Sciences 13, no. 1 (March 1925): 9–179.

Crèvecoeur, J. Hector St. John de. *Letters from an American Farmer*. 1782. Ed. Susan Manning. Oxford: Oxford University Press, 1998.

Cronon, William. *Changes in the Land: Indians, Colonists, and the Ecology of Colonial New England*. New York: Hill and Wang, 1983.

———. "The Trouble with Wilderness; Or, Getting Back to the Wrong Nature." In *Uncommon Ground: Rethinking the Human Place in Nature*, ed. William Cronon, 69–90. New York: Norton, 1996.

Crosby, Alfred W. *Ecological Imperialism: The Biological Expansion of Europe, 900–1900*. Cambridge: Cambridge University Press, 1986.

Daly, Herman E. "Steady-State Economics: A New Paradigm." *New Literary History* 24 (1993): 811–16.

———. *Steady-State Economics: The Economics of Biophysical Equilibrium and Moral Growth*. San Francisco: W. H. Freeman, 1977.

Daly, Herman E., and John B. Cobb, Jr. *For the Common Good: Redirecting the Economy Toward Community, the Environment, and a Sustainable Future*. 2nd ed. Boston: Beacon, 1994.

Danforth, Samuel. *An Almanack for the Year of Our Lord 1648*. Cambridge, Mass., 1648. Reprint, *Early American Imprints, 1639–1800*, ed. Clifford K. Shipton. Worcester, Mass.: American Antiquarian Society-Readex, 1957. Microcard.

———. *An Almanack for the Year of Our Lord 1649*. Cambridge, Mass., 1649. Reprint, *Early American Imprints, 1639–1800*, ed. Clifford K. Shipton. Worcester, Mass.: American Antiquarian Society-Readex, 1957. Microcard.

Dash, Mike. *Tulipomania: The Story of the World's Most Coveted Flower and the Extraordinary Passions It Aroused*. New York: Crown, 1999.

Dekker, George. *American Historical Romance*. Cambridge: Cambridge University Press, 1987.

Delbanco, Andrew. *The Puritan Ideal*. Cambridge: Harvard University Press, 1989.

Dewar, Mary, ed. *A Discourse of the Commonweal of This Realm of England, Attributed to Thomas Smith.* 1581. Charlottesville: University Press of Virginia, 1969.

Donne, John. *The Sermons of John Donne.* Ed. George R. Potter and Evelyn M. Simpson. Vol. 4. Berkeley: University of California Press, 1959.

Donahue, Brian. *Reclaiming the Commons: Community Farms and Forests in a New England Town.* New Haven: Yale University Press, 1999.

Dryden, John. *The Works of John Dryden.* Ed. Alan Roper. Vol. 5. Berkeley: University of California Press, 1987.

Dunaway, Wilma. *The First American Frontier: Transition to Capitalism in Southern Appalachia, 1700–1860.* Chapel Hill: University of North Carolina Press, 1996.

———. "Rethinking Cherokee Acculturation: Agrarian Capitalism and Women's Resistance to the Cult of Domesticity, 1800–1838." *American Indian Culture and Research Journal* 21 (1997): 155–92.

Egan, Jim. *Authorizing Experience: Refigurations of the Body Politic in Seventeenth-Century New England Writing.* Princeton: Princeton University Press, 1999.

Eggleston, Melville. "The Land System of the New England Colonies." *Johns Hopkins University Studies in Historical and Political Science* 4 (1886): 549–600.

Eisenberg, Evan. *The Ecology of Eden: An Inquiry into the Dream of Paradise and a New Vision of Our Role in Nature.* New York: Vintage, 1999.

Eisinger, Chester E. "Land and Loyalty: Literary Expressions of Agrarian Nationalism in the Seventeenth and Eighteenth Centuries." *American Literature* 21 (1949): 160–78.

Eliot, Jared. *Essays upon Field Husbandry and Other Papers, 1748–1762.* Ed. Harry J. Carman, et al. New York: Columbia University Press, 1934.

Elster, Jon. *Making Sense of Marx.* Cambridge: Cambridge University Press, 1985.

Emerson, George B. *A Report on the Trees and Shrubs Growing Naturally in Massachusetts.* Boston: Dutton and Wentworth, 1846.

Emerson, Ralph Waldo. *The Complete Works of Ralph Waldo Emerson.* Ed. Edward Waldo Emerson. Vol. 1. Boston: Houghton, Mifflin, 1904.

Evarts, Jeremiah. *Cherokee Removal: The "William Penn" Essays and Other Writings.* Ed. Francis Paul Prucha. Knoxville: University of Tennessee Press, 1981.

Evernden, Neil. "Beyond Ecology: Self, Place, and the Pathetic Fallacy." In *The Ecocriticism Reader: Landmarks in Literary Ecology,* ed. Cheryll Glotfelty and Harold Fromm, 92–104. Athens: University of Georgia Press, 1996.

———. *The Social Creation of Nature.* Baltimore: Johns Hopkins University Press, 1992.

Ewan, Joseph, and Nesta Ewan. *John Banister and His Natural History of Virginia, 1678–1692.* Urbana: University of Illinois Press, 1970.

Filson, John. *The Discovery, Settlement, and Present State of Kentucke: And an Essay Toward the Topography, and Natural History of that Important Country.* 1784. Reprint, Ann Arbor: University Microfilms, 1966.

Fletcher, Stevenson Whitcomb. *Pennsylvania Agriculture and Country Life, 1640–1840.* Vol. 1. Harrisburg: Pennsylvania Historical Museum and Commission, 1950.

Foucault, Michel. *The Order of Things: An Archaeology of the Human Sciences.* New York: Vintage, 1973.

Franklin, Benjamin. *The Papers of Benjamin Franklin.* Vol. 5. New Haven: Yale University Press, 1962.

Franklin, Wayne. *Discoverers, Explorers, Settlers: The Diligent Writers of Early America.* Chicago: University of Chicago Press, 1979.

————. *The New World of James Fenimore Cooper.* Chicago: University of Chicago Press, 1982.

Friedenberg, Daniel M. *Life, Liberty, and the Pursuit of Land: The Plunder of Early America.* Buffalo: Prometheus, 1992.

Gill, Sam D. *Mother Earth: An American Story.* Chicago: University of Chicago Press, 1987.

Goodwin, Gary C. *Cherokees in Transition: A Study of Changing Culture and Environment Prior to 1775.* Chicago: University of Chicago Department of Geography, 1977.

Goux, Jean-Joseph. *Symbolic Economies: After Marx and Freud.* Trans. Jennifer Curtiss Gage. Ithaca: Cornell University Press, 1990.

Grammer, John M. *Pastoral and Politics in the Old South.* Baton Rouge: Louisiana State University Press, 1996.

Greene, Jack P. *The Intellectual Construction of America: Exceptionalism and Identity from 1492 to 1800.* Chapel Hill: University of North Carolina Press, 1993.

Greider, William. "The Last Farm Crisis." *Nation* 271, no. 16 (20 November 2000): 11–18.

Gross, Robert A. "Culture and Cultivation: Agriculture and Society in Thoreau's Concord." *Journal of American History* 69 (1982): 42–61.

————. "The Great Bean Field Hoax: Thoreau and the Agricultural Reformers." *Virginia Quarterly Review* 61 (1985): 483–97.

Gura, Philip F. *A Glimpse of Sion's Glory: Puritan Radicalism in New England, 1620–1660.* Middletown, Conn.: Wesleyan University Press, 1984.

Hakluyt, Richard. *The Principall Navigations, Voyages, Traffiques, & Discoveries of the English Nation.* Vol 6. London: J. M. Dent; New York: E. P. Dutton, 1927.

Halliday, T. R. "The Extinction of the Passenger Pigeon *Ectopistes migratorius* and Its Relevance to Contemporary Conservation." *Biological Conservation* 17 (1980): 157–62.

Halpern, Richard. *The Poetics of Primitive Accumulation: English Renaissance Culture and the Genealogy of Capital.* Ithaca: Cornell University Press, 1991.

Hariot, Thomas. *A Briefe and True Reporte of the New Found Land of Virginia.* 1588. In *The English Literatures of America, 1500–1800*, ed. Myra Jehlen and Michael Warner, 64–89. New York: Routledge, 1997.

Harman, Willard N., Leonard P. Sohacki, Matthew F. Albright, and Daniel L. Rosen. *The State of Otsego Lake, 1936–1996.* Oneonta Biological Field Station Occasional Papers, no. 30. Cooperstown: State University of New York, College at Oneonta, 1997.

Harper, R. Eugene. *The Transformation of Western Pennsylvania, 1770–1800.* Pittsburgh: University of Pittsburgh Press, 1991.

Hatch, Charles. "Mulberry Trees and Silkworms: Sericulture in Early Virginia." *Virginia Magazine of History and Biography* 65 (1957): 3–61.

Hatley, Tom. *The Dividing Paths: Cherokees and South Carolinians Through the Era of Revolution.* New York: Oxford University Press, 1993.

Hawken, Paul. *The Ecology of Commerce: A Declaration of Sustainability.* New York: HarperCollins, 1993.

Helgerson, Richard. *Forms of Nationhood: The Elizabethan Writings of England.* Chicago: University of Chicago Press, 1992.

Hickerson, Harold. *The Chippewa and Their Neighbors: A Study in Ethnohistory.* New York: Holt, Rinehart and Winston, 1970.

Horwitz, Howard. *By the Law of Nature: Form and Value in Nineteenth-Century America.* New York: Oxford University Press, 1991.

Hubbard, William. *The Happiness of a People in the Wisdome of Their Rulers Directing and in the Obedience of Their Brethren Attending unto What Israel Ought to Do.*
Boston: John Fisher, 1676. Reprint, *Early American Imprints, 1639–1800,* ed.
Clifford K. Shipton. Worcester, Mass.: American Antiquarian Society-Readex,
1960. Microcard.

Innes, Stephen. *Creating the Commonwealth: The Economic Culture of Puritan New England.* New York: Norton, 1995.

————. *Labor in a New Land: Economy and Society in Seventeenth-Century Springfield.*
Princeton: Princeton University Press, 1983.

Jackson, Joseph Henry. Introduction to *The Life and Adventures of Joaquín Murieta,
the Celebrated California Bandit,* by John Rollin Ridge. Norman: University of
Oklahoma Press, 1955.

Jacob, E. F. *The Fifteenth Century, 1399–1485.* Oxford: Clarendon, 1961.

Jacobs, Jane. *The Nature of Economies.* New York: Modern Library, 2000.

Jacobs, Wilbur R. "Robert Beverley: Colonial Ecologist and Indian Lover." In
Essays in Early Virginia Literature Honoring Richard Beale Davis, ed. J. A. Leo
Lemay, 91–99. New York: Burt Franklin, 1977.

Jameson, J. Franklin. Introduction to *Johnson's Wonder-Working Providence, 1628–
1651.* New York: Charles Scribner's Sons, 1910.

Jehlen, Myra. *American Incarnation: The Individual, the Nation, and the Continent.*
Cambridge: Harvard University Press, 1986.

Jehlen, Myra, and Michael Warner, eds. *The English Literatures of America, 1500–
1800.* New York: Routledge, 1997.

Jefferson, Thomas. *Notes on the State of Virginia.* 1785. Ed. Frank Shuffleton. New
York: Penguin, 1999.

Jennings, Francis. *The Invasion of America: Indians, Colonialism, and the Cant of Conquest.* New York: Norton, 1976.

Johnson, Edward. *Johnson's Wonder-Working Providence, 1628–1651.* Ed. J. Franklin
Jameson. New York: Charles Scribner's Sons, 1910.

Jordan, Terry G., and Matti Kaups. *The American Backwoods Frontier: An Ethnic and
Ecological Interpretation.* Baltimore: Johns Hopkins University Press, 1992.

Kingsbury, Susan M., ed. *The Records of the Virginia Company of London.* Vol. 4. Washington, D.C.: U.S. Government Printing Office, 1933.

Kolodny, Annette. *The Lay of the Land: Metaphor as Experience and History in American
Life and Letters.* Chapel Hill: University of North Carolina Press, 1975.

Konkle, Maureen. "Indian Literacy, U. S. Colonialism, and Literary Criticism."
American Literature 69 (1997): 457–86.

Krech, Shepard, III. *The Ecological Indian: Myth and History.* New York: Norton,
1999.

Krupat, Arnold. "America's Histories." *American Literary History* 10 (1998): 124–
46.

————. *Ethnocriticism: Ethnography, History, Literature.* Berkeley: University of California Press, 1992.

Kulikoff, Allan. *The Agrarian Origins of American Capitalism.* Charlottesville: University Press of Virginia, 1992.

————. *Tobacco and Slaves: The Development of Southern Cultures in the Chesapeake,
1680–1800.* Chapel Hill: University of North Carolina Press, 1986.

Kupperman, Karen Ordahl. "The Puzzle of the American Climate in the Early
Colonial Period." *American Historical Review* 87 (1982): 1262–89.

Lawson-Peebles, Robert. *Landscape and Written Expression in Revolutionary America:
The World Turned Upside Down.* Cambridge: Cambridge University Press, 1988.

Lemay, J. A. Leo. *The American Dream of Captain John Smith*. Charlottesville: University Press of Virginia, 1991.

Lockridge, Kenneth A. *A New England Town, The First Hundred Years: Dedham, Massachusetts, 1636–1736*. New York: Norton, 1970.

Looby, Christopher. *Voicing America: Language, Literary Form, and the Origins of the United States*. Chicago: University of Chicago Press, 1996.

Lorain, John. *Hints to Emigrants, or a Comparative Estimate of the Advantages of Pennsylvania, and of the Western Territories, &c.* Philadelphia: Littell and Henry, 1819.

———. *Nature and Reason Harmonized in the Practice of Husbandry*. Philadelphia: H. C. Carey and I. Lea, 1825.

Low, Anthony. *The Georgic Revolution*. Princeton: Princeton University Press, 1985.

Lowe, John. "'I Am Joaquín!': Space and Freedom in Yellow Bird's *The Life and Adventures of Joaquín Murieta, the Celebrated California Bandit*." In *Early Native American Writing: New Critical Essays*, ed. Helen Jaskoski, 104–21. Cambridge: Cambridge University Press, 1996.

Lowell, James Russell. Review of *Man and Nature*, by George Perkins Marsh. *North American Review* 99, no. 204 (July 1864): 318–20.

Lowenthal, David. Introduction to *Man and Nature*, by George Perkins Marsh. Cambridge: Belknap—Harvard University Press, 1998.

Maddox, Lucy. *Removals: Nineteenth-Century American Literature and the Politics of Indian Affairs*. New York: Oxford University Press, 1991.

Magnusson, Lars. *Mercantilism: The Shaping of an Economic Language*. London: Routledge, 1994.

Main, Jackson Turner. *The Social Structure of Revolutionary America*. Princeton: Princeton University Press, 1965.

Review of *Man and Nature*, by George Perkins Marsh. *Christian Examiner* 77 (5th ser., vol. 15, no. 1) (July 1864): 65–73.

Review of *Man and Nature*, by George Perkins Marsh. *Edinburgh Review*, American Edition 120, no. 246 (October 1864): 239–59.

Review of *Man and Nature*, by George Perkins Marsh. *Nation* 19, no. 483 (1 October 1874): 223–24.

Review of *Man and Nature*, by George Perkins Marsh. *Nature* 11 (3 December 1874): 82–83.

Review of *Man and Nature*, by George Perkins Marsh. *Scribner's Monthly* 9, no. 1 (November 1874): 119–21.

Mancall, Peter C., and Thomas Weiss. "Was Economic Growth Likely in British North America?" *Journal of Economic History* 59 (March 1999): 17–40.

Marsh, George Perkins. *Man and Nature*. 1864. Ed. David Lowenthal. Reprint, Cambridge: Belknap—Harvard University Press, 1998.

Martin, John Frederick. *Profits in the Wilderness: Entrepreneurship and the Founding of New England Towns in the Seventeenth Century*. Chapel Hill: University of North Carolina Press, 1991.

Marvell, Andrew. *Andrew Marvell: Complete Poetry*. Ed. George DeF. Lord. New York: Modern Library, 1968.

Marx, Leo. *The Machine in the Garden: Technology and the Pastoral Ideal in America*. Oxford: Oxford University Press, 1964.

McCusker, John, and Russell Menard. *The Economy of British America, 1607–1789*. Chapel Hill: University of North Carolina Press, 1985.

McLoughlin, William G. *Cherokee Renascence in the New Republic*. Princeton: Princeton University Press, 1986.

McMahon, Sarah F. "A Comfortable Subsistence: The Changing Composition of

Diet in Rural New England, 1620–1840." *William and Mary Quarterly* 42 (1985): 26–65.

McRae, Andrew. *God Speed the Plough: The Representation of Agrarian England, 1500–1660*. Cambridge: Cambridge University Press, 1996.

Merchant, Carolyn. *Ecological Revolutions: Nature, Gender, and Science in New England*. Chapel Hill: University of North Carolina Press, 1989.

Miller, Charles A. *Jefferson and Nature: An Interpretation*. Baltimore: Johns Hopkins University Press, 1988.

Miller, Perry. *The New England Mind: From Colony to Province*. Cambridge: Harvard University Press, 1953.

Mitchell, Robert D. *Commercialism and Frontier: Perspectives on the Early Shenandoah Valley*. Charlottesville: University Press of Virginia, 1977.

Mood, Fulmer. "John Winthrop, Jr., on Indian Corn." *New England Quarterly* 10 (1937): 121–33.

Mooney, James. *Myths of the Cherokee*. 1900. Reprint, New York: Johnson Reprint, 1970.

More, Thomas. *Sir Thomas More's Utopia*. Ed. J. Churton Collins. Oxford: Clarendon, 1949.

———. *The Complete Works of St. Thomas More*. Ed. Edward Surtz and J. H. Hexter. Vol. 4. New Haven: Yale University Press, 1963.

Morgan, Edmund S. *American Slavery, American Freedom: The Ordeal of Colonial Virginia*. New York: Norton, 1975.

Morison, Samuel Eliot. Introduction to *Of Plymouth Plantation, 1620–1647*, by William Bradford. New York: Knopf, 1952.

Murray, David. *Forked Tongues: Speech, Writing, and Representation in North American Indian Texts*. Bloomington: Indiana University Press, 1991.

Nash, Thomas. *Pierce Penilesse, His Supplication to the Divell*. Ed. G. B. Harrison. London: Bodley Head; New York: E. P. Dutton, 1924.

Neumayer, Eric. *Weak Versus Strong Sustainability: Exploring the Limits of Two Opposing Paradigms*. Cheltenham, U.K.: Edward Elgar, 1999.

Ogilvie, George. *Carolina; Or, the Planter. Southern Literary Journal*, special issue, ed. David Shields (1986): 21–101.

Opie, John. *The Law of the Land: Two Hundred Years of American Farmland Policy*. Lincoln: University of Nebraska Press, 1994.

Parins, James W. *John Rollin Ridge: His Life and Works*. Lincoln: University of Nebraska Press, 1991.

Pearce, Roy Harvey. *The Savages of America: A Study of the Indian and the Idea of Civilization*. Baltimore: Johns Hopkins University Press, 1965.

Pease, Donald. *Visionary Compacts: American Renaissance Writings in Cultural Context*. Madison: University of Wisconsin Press, 1987.

Perdue, Theda. *Cherokee Women: Gender and Cultural Change, 1700–1835*. Lincoln: University of Nebraska Press, 1998.

Perdue, Theda, and Michael P. Green, eds. *The Cherokee Removal: A Brief History with Documents*. Boston: Bedford-St. Martin's, 1995.

Poggioli, Renato. *The Oaten Flute: Essays on Pastoral Poetry and the Pastoral Ideal*. Cambridge: Harvard University Press, 1975.

Powers, Richard. *Gain*. New York: Picador USA, 1999.

Proctor, James D. "Whose Nature? The Contested Moral Terrain of Ancient Forests." In *Uncommon Ground: Rethinking the Human Place in Nature*, ed. William Cronon, 269–97. New York: Norton, 1996.

Prucha, Francis Paul. *The Great Father: The United States Government and the American Indians*. Vol. 1. Lincoln: University of Nebraska Press, 1984.

Quinn, David B. *Explorers and Colonies: America, 1500–1625*. London: Hambledon Press, 1990.

———., ed. *New American World: A Documentary History of North America to 1612*. Vol. 3. New York: Arno, 1979.

Quinn, David B., and Neil M. Cheshire. *The New Found Land of Stephen Parmenius: The Life and Writings of a Hungarian Poet, Drowned on a Voyage from Newfoundland, 1583*. Toronto: University of Toronto Press, 1972.

Raban, Jonathan. *Bad Land: An American Romance*. New York: Vintage, 1997.

Rainbolt, John C. *From Prescription to Persuasion: Manipulation of the Eighteenth-Century Virginia Economy*. Port Washington, N.Y.: Kenikat Press, 1974.

Ralegh, Walter. *Selected Writings*. Ed. Gerald Hammond. Manchester, U.K.: Carcanet-Fyfield, 1984.

Rich, E. E., and C. H. Wilson, eds. *The Cambridge Economic History of Europe*. Vol. 4. Cambridge: Cambridge University Press, 1967.

Richter, Daniel K. "Onas, the Long Knife: Pennsylvanians and Indians, 1783–1794." In *Native Americans and the Early Republic*, ed. Frederick E. Hoxie, Ronald Hoffman, and Peter J. Albert, 125–61. Charlottesville: University Press of Virginia, 1999.

Ridge, John Rollin. *The Life and Adventures of Joaquín Murieta, the Celebrated California Bandit*. 1854. Reprint, Norman: University of Oklahoma Press, 1955.

Rigal, Laura. *The American Manufactory: Art, Labor, and the World of Things in the Early Republic*. Princeton: Princeton University Press, 1998.

Ringe, Donald A. Introduction to *The Pioneers*, by James Fenimore Cooper. New York: Penguin, 1988.

Robinson, E. Arthur. "Conservation in Cooper's *The Pioneers*." *PMLA* 82 (1967): 564–78.

Rosenmeier, Jesper. "'With My Owne Eyes': William Bradford's *Of Plymouth Plantation*." In *Typology and Early American Literature*, ed. Sacvan Bercovitch, 69–105. Amherst: University of Massachusetts Press, 1972.

Ross, John. *The Papers of Chief John Ross*. Ed. Gary E. Moulton. Vol. 1. Norman: University of Oklahoma Press, 1985.

Rush, Benjamin. *Essays Literary, Moral, and Philosophical*. Philadelphia: Thomas and Samuel F. Bradford, 1798. Reprint, *Early American Imprints, 1639–1800*, ed. Clifford K. Shipton. Worcester, Mass.: American Antiquarian Society-Readex, 1962. Microcard.

———. *Letters of Benjamin Rush*. Ed. L. H. Butterfield. Vol. 1. Princeton: Princeton University Press, 1951.

Rutman, Darrett B. "Governor Winthrop's Garden Crop." In Rutman, *Small Worlds, Large Questions: Explorations in Early American Social History, 1600–1850*, 93–112. Charlottesville: University Press of Virginia, 1994.

———. *Husbandmen of Plymouth: Farms and Villages in the Old Colony, 1620–1692*. Boston: Beacon, 1967.

———. *Winthrop's Boston: Portrait of a Puritan Town, 1630–1649*. Chapel Hill: University of North Carolina Press, 1965.

Rutman, Darrett B., and Anita Rutman. *A Place in Time: Middlesex County, Virginia, 1650–1750*. New York: Norton, 1984.

Sayre, Gordon M. *Les Sauvages Américains: Representations of Native Americans in French and English Colonial Literature*. Chapel Hill: University of North Carolina Press, 1997.

Sargent, Mark. "William Bradford's 'Dialogue' with History." *New England Quarterly* 63 (1992): 389–421.

Schramer, James, and Timothy Sweet. "Violence and the Body Politic in Seventeenth-Century New England." *Arizona Quarterly* 48, no. 2 (Summer 1992): 1–32.

Sellers, Charles. *The Market Revolution: Jacksonian America, 1815–1846.* New York: Oxford University Press, 1991.

Shammas, Carole. "The Rise of the Colonial Tenant." *Reviews in American History* 6 (1978): 490–95.

Sheehan, Bernard W. *Seeds of Extinction: Jeffersonian Philanthropy and the American Indian.* Chapel Hill: University of North Carolina Press, 1973.

Shields, David. "England's Staple Colonies." In *Teaching the Literatures of Early America,* ed. Carla Mulford, 129–42. New York: Modern Language Association, 1999.

———. *Oracles of Empire: Poetry, Politics, and Commerce in British America, 1690–1750.* Chicago: University of Chicago Press, 1990.

Silver, Timothy. *A New Face on the Countryside: Indians, Colonists, and Slaves in South Atlantic Forests, 1500–1800.* Cambridge: Cambridge University Press, 1990.

Simler, Lucy. "Tenancy in Colonial Pennsylvania: The Case of Chester County." *William and Mary Quarterly,* 3rd ser., 43 (1986): 542–69.

Simms, William Gilmore. *Guy Rivers: A Tale of Georgia.* 1834, 1885. Reprint, New York: AMS Press, 1970.

Simpson, Lewis P. *The Dispossessed Garden: Pastoral and History in Southern Literature.* Athens: University of Georgia Press, 1975.

Slaughter, Thomas P. *The Whiskey Rebellion: Frontier Epilogue to the American Revolution.* New York: Oxford University Press, 1986.

Slovic, Scott. "Ecocriticism: Trajectories in Theory and Practice." Paper presented at the annual meeting of the Modern Language Association, San Francisco, 29 December 1998.

Smith, Henry Nash. *Virgin Land: The American West as Symbol and Myth.* Cambridge: Harvard University Press, 1970.

Smith, John. *The Complete Works of Captain John Smith.* Ed. Philip L. Barbour. 3 vols. Chapel Hill: University of North Carolina Press, 1986.

Spengemann, William. *A New World of Words: Redefining Early American Literature.* New Haven: Yale University Press, 1994.

Spurrier, John. *The Practical Farmer: Being a New and Compendious System of Husbandry Adapted to the Different Soils and Climates of America.* 1793. Reprint, Wilmington, Del.: Scholarly Resources, 1974.

Starr, Emmet. *History of the Cherokee Indians and Their Legends and Folk Lore.* 1921. Reprint, Millwood, N.Y.: Krause Reprint, 1977.

Steadman, David W. ". . . And Live on Pigeon Pie." *New York State Conservationist* 50 (April 1996): 20–23.

Stiles, Ezra. *The United States Elevated to Glory and Honor.* New Haven: Thomas and Samuel Green, 1783. Reprint, *Early American Imprints, 1639–1800,* ed. Clifford K. Shipton. Worcester, Mass.: American Antiquarian Society-Readex, 1958. Microcard.

Stiverson, Gregory A. *Poverty in a Land of Plenty: Tenancy in Eighteenth-Century Maryland.* Baltimore: Johns Hopkins University Press, 1977.

Sturtevant, William C., ed. "John Ridge on Cherokee Civilization in 1826." *Journal of Cherokee Studies* 6 (1981): 79–91.

Supple, B. E. *Commercial Crisis and Change in England, 1600–1642: A Study in the Instability of a Mercantile Economy.* Cambridge: Cambridge University Press, 1959.

Swann, Charles. "Guns Mean Democracy: *The Pioneers* and the Game Laws." In *James Fenimore Cooper: New Critical Essays,* ed. Robert Clark, 96–120. New York: Barnes & Noble, 1985.

Taylor, Alan. *William Cooper's Town: Power and Persuasion on the Frontier of the Early American Republic.* New York: Knopf, 1995.

Taylor, E. G. R., ed. *Original Writings and Correspondence of the Two Richard Hakluyts.* 2 vols. London: Hakluyt Society, 1935.

Thomas, Brook. *Cross-Examinations of Law and Literature: Cooper, Hawthorne, Melville, and Stowe.* Cambridge: Cambridge University Press, 1987.

Thoreau, Henry David. *Faith in a Seed: "The Dispersion of Seeds" and Other Late Natural History Writings.* Washington, D.C.: Island Books, 1993.

———. *The Maine Woods.* In *A Week on the Concord and Merrimack Rivers. Walden; Or, Life in the Woods. The Maine Woods. Cape Cod,* ed. Robert Sayre, 589–845. New York: Library of America, 1985.

———. *Walden.* Ed. J. Lyndon Shanley. Princeton: Princeton University Press, 1989.

———. *The Writings of Henry David Thoreau.* Vol. 5. Boston: Houghton Mifflin, 1906.

Tichi, Cecelia. *New World, New Earth: Environmental Reform in American Literature from the Puritans Through Whitman.* New Haven: Yale University Press, 1979.

Timberlake, Henry. *The Memoirs of Lieut. Henry Timberlake.* 1765. Reprint, Marietta, Ga.: Continental Book, 1948.

A True Declaration of the Estate of the Colonie in Virginia. 1610. In *Tracts and Other Papers, Relating Principally to the Origin, Settlement, and Progress of the Colonies in North America,* ed. Peter Force, vol. 3, no. 1. 1844. Reprint, New York: Peter Smith, 1947.

Usner, Daniel H., Jr. "Iroquois Livelihood and Jeffersonian Agrarianism: Reaching Behind the Models and Metaphors." In *Native Americans and the Early Republic,* ed. Frederick E. Hoxie, Ronald Hoffman, and Peter J. Albert, 200–225. Charlottesville: University Press of Virginia, 1999.

Vaughan, Alden T. Introduction to *New England's Prospect,* by William Wood. Amherst: University of Massachusetts Press, 1977.

———. *New England Frontier: Puritans and Indians, 1620–1675.* 3rd ed. Norman: University of Oklahoma Press, 1995.

Vickers, Daniel. *Farmers and Fishermen: Two Centuries of Work in Essex County, Massachusetts, 1630–1850.* Chapel Hill: University of North Carolina Press, 1994.

Walker, Cheryl. *Indian Nation: Native American Literature and Nineteenth-Century Nationalisms.* Durham: Duke University Press, 1997.

Wallace, James D. *Early Cooper and His Audience.* New York: Columbia University Press, 1986.

Waller, Edmund. *The Poetical Works of Edmund Waller.* Ed. Robert Bell. London: John W. Parker and Son, 1854.

Warner, Michael. *The Letters of the Republic: Publication and the Public Sphere in Eighteenth-Century America.* Cambridge: Harvard University Press, 1990.

Weaver, Jace. *That the People Might Live: Native American Literatures and Native American Community.* New York: Oxford University Press, 1997.

Webb, Stephen Saunders. *1676: The End of American Independence.* New York: Knopf, 1984.

White, Richard. *The Roots of Dependency: Subsistence, Environment, and Social Change Among the Choctaws, Pawnees, and Navajos.* Lincoln: University of Nebraska Press, 1983.

Williams, Raymond. *The Country and the City.* New York: Oxford University Press, 1975.

———. *Marxism and Literature.* Oxford: Oxford University Press, 1977.

Wilms, Douglas C. "Cherokee Indian Land Use in Georgia, 1800–1838." Ph.D. dissertation, University of Georgia, 1974.

Winthrop, John. "From *A Modell of Christian Charity.*" In *The Heath Anthology of American Literature,* 3rd ed., ed. Paul Lauter, vol. 1, 226–34. Boston: Houghton Mifflin, 1998.

———. *The History of New England from 1630 to 1649.* Ed. James Savage. 2 vols. Boston: Phelps and Farnham, 1825. Reprint, Salem, N.H.: Ayer, 1992.

———. "Reasons to Be Considered for Justifying the Undertakers of the Intended Plantation in New England." In *Envisioning America: English Plans for the Colonization of North America, 1580–1640,* ed. Peter Mancall, 133–39. Boston: Bedford-St. Martin's, 1995.

Wood, Gordon S. "Inventing American Capitalism." *New York Review of Books* 41, no. 11 (9 June 1994): 44–49.

Wood, William. *New England's Prospect.* Ed. Alden T. Vaughan. Amherst: University of Massachusetts Press, 1977.

Woodmansee, Martha, and Mark Osteen, eds. *The New Economic Criticism: Studies at the Interface of Literature and Economics.* New York: Routledge, 1999.

Worster, Donald. *Nature's Economy: A History of Ecological Ideas.* 2nd ed. Cambridge: Cambridge University Press, 1994.

———. *The Wealth of Nature: Environmental History and the Environmental Imagination.* New York: Oxford University Press, 1993.

Wright, Louis B. *The First Gentlemen of Virginia: Intellectual Qualities of the Early Colonial Ruling Class.* San Marino, Calif.: Huntington Library, 1940.

———. Introduction to *The History and Present State of Virginia,* by Robert Beverley. Chapel Hill: University of North Carolina Press, 1947.

Index

Acknowledgments

I am grateful to those who offered valuable advice on various portions of the manuscript: Dennis Allen (who was kind enough to read it all), Laura Brady, Michelle Burnham, Kathleen Diffley, Jim Egan, Carla Mulford, Dana Nelson. Lawrence Buell deserves particular thanks for reading the manuscript for the University of Pennsylvania Press. I have drawn additional insight from conversations or correspondence with colleagues at West Virginia University and elsewhere, including Ralph Bauer, Jonathan Burton, Amy Howard Green, Mark Kamrath, Tom Kinnahan, Robert Markley, Donald Ross, Jr., Gordon Sayre, Laura Sayre, James Schramer, Andy Vann, and the students in my 1999 American Studies seminar. My editor, Eric Halpern, has been a pleasure to work with. Most of all I am grateful for Laura's loving and patient support throughout what has been a long project.

*   *   *

A summer research grant sponsored by the Radiological Consultants Association of West Virginia gave me a start on this project. A sabbatical leave funded by West Virginia University enabled me to complete a good portion of the manuscript.

Two chapters have appeared elsewhere in somewhat different form. An earlier version of Chapter 1 was published as "Economy, Ecology, and *Utopia* in Early Colonial Promotional Literature," *American Literature* 71, no. 3 (1999): 399–427. Copyright © 1999 by Duke University Press. Used by permission. An earlier version of Chapter 5 appeared as "American Pastoralism and the Marketplace: Eighteenth-Century Ideologies of Farming," *Early American Literature* 29, no. 1 (1994): 59–80. Copyright © 1994 by the Department of English, University of North Carolina at Chapel Hill. Used by permission.